CHRISTIAN DOCTRINE IN GLOBAL PERSPECTIVE

Series Editor: David Smith

Consulting Editor: John Stott

CHRISTIAN
DOCTRINE
IN GLOBAL
PERSPECTIVE

The Bible and Other Faiths

CHRISTIAN RESPONSIBILITY
IN A WORLD OF
RELIGIONS

Ida Glaser

Series Editor: David Smith
Consulting Editor: John Stott

IVP Academic

An imprint of InterVarsity Press
Downers Grove, Illinois

InterVarsity Press
P.O. Box 1400, Downers Grove, IL 60515-1426
Internet: www.ivpress.com
E-mail: mail@ivpress.com

InterVarsity Press® is the book-publishing division of InterVarsity Christian Fellowship/USA®, a student movement active on campus at hundreds of universities, colleges and schools of nursing in the United States of America, and a member movement of the International Fellowship of Evangelical Students. For information about local and regional activities, write Public Relations Dept., InterVarsity Christian Fellowship/USA, 6400 Schroeder Rd., P.O. Box 7895, Madison, WI 53707-7895, or visit the IVCF website at <www.intervarsity.org>.

All Scripture quotations, unless otherwise indicated, are taken from the Holy Bible, New International Version®. NIV®. Copyright ©1973, 1978, 1984 by International Bible Society. Used by permission of Hodder and Stoughton Ltd. All rights reserved. "NIV" is a registered trademark of International Bible Society. UK trademark number 1448790. Distributed in North America by permission of Zondervan Publishing House.

Cover design: Cindy Kiple

Cover image: Images.com/Corbis

ISBN-10: 0-8308-3311-0
ISBN-13: 978-0-8308-3311-5

Printed in the United States of America ∞

Library of Congress Cataloging-in-Publication Data

Glaser, Ida.
  The Bible and other faiths: Christian responsibility in a world of
  religions / Ida Glaser.
      p. cm.—(Christian doctrine in global perspective)
  Includes bibliographical references and index.
  ISBN 0-8308-3304-8 (pbk.: alk. paper)
  1. Christianity and other religions. I. Title. II. Series.
  BR127.G54 2005
  261.2—dc22

                                                                    2005012136

P   18   17   16   15   14   13   12   11   10   9   8   7   6   5   4   3   2   1

Y   19   18   17   16   15   14   13   12   11   10   09   08   07   06

CONTENTS

SERIES PREFACE

THIS BOOK IS ONE OF A SERIES TITLED Christian Doctrine in Global Perspective being published by a partnership between Langham Literature (incorporating the Evangelical Literature Trust) and InterVarsity Press. Langham Literature is a program of the Langham Partnership International.

The vision for the series has arisen from the knowledge that during the twentieth century a dramatic shift in the Christian center of gravity took place. There are now many more Christians in Africa, Asia and Latin America than there are in Europe and North America. Two major issues have resulted, both of which Christian Doctrine in Global Perspective seeks to address.

First, the basic theological texts available to pastors, students and lay readers in the southern hemisphere have for too long been written by Western authors from a Western perspective. What is needed now are more books by non-Western writers that reflect their own cultures. In consequence, this series has an international authorship, and we thank God that he has raised up so many gifted writers from the developing world whose resolve is to be both biblically faithful and contextually relevant.

Second, what is needed is that non-Western authors will write not only for non-Western readers, but for Western readers as well. Indeed, the adjective *global* is intended to express our desire that biblical understanding will flow freely in all directions. Certainly we in the West need to listen to and learn from our sisters and brothers in other parts of the world. And the decay of many Western churches urgently needs an injection of non-Western Christian vitality. We pray that this series will open up channels of communication in fulfillment of the apostle Paul's conviction that it is only *together with all the saints* that we will be able to grasp the dimensions of Christ's love (Eph 3:18).

Never before in the church's long and checkered history has this possibility been so close to realization. We hope and pray that Christian Doctrine in Global Perspective may, in God's good providence, play a part in making it a reality in the twenty-first century.

John R. W. Stott
David W. Smith

ACKNOWLEDGMENTS

The book has been a team effort. It has my name on the cover, but it would not have been written without many other people, and without insights from many parts of the world.

Dan Beeby (UK and Taiwan), Margaret Chen (Malaysia), Derek D'Souza (India and UK), Kevin Ellis (UK), Falak Sher Falak (Pakistan), Najeeb Awaz (Syria), John Moxon (UK), Philip Seddon (UK) and Dick Seed (South Africa and Germany) formed the group that helped with the initial research. This was a course that I organized, 'Reading the Bible in its own Interfaith Context', in the Centre for Mission Education and Training at Selly Oak, Birmingham, UK, during the summer term, 2000. Most of the group contributed papers, and all joined the discussion.

I taught much of the material in this book to the students of the 'Missionary Encounter with the World's Religions' MA class at the Theological College of Northern Nigeria, and some to the students of St Francis of Assisi College, Wusasa. They greatly helped me by their responses. Some of this book was first written in Nigeria, and so owes much to their influence.

The final shaping of the book, using the 'dangerous triangle' of people, land and power (see ch. 7), is in response to visits to Kenya and India in the summer of 2003. In Kenya I was part of a study group on 'Conflict, Suffering and Mission' chaired by Bishop Ben Kwashi of Jos, Nigeria, at the Evangelical Fellowship in the Anglican Communion's International Conference, 'Anglican Life in Mission'. In India I was lecturing at Union Biblical Seminary, Pune, and particularly benefited from interactions with Drs P. S. Jacob and Jacob Thomas, and from T. Mangthianlal's sharing of his journey towards a biblical understanding of the plight of his Zo people, whose territory is divided between India, Bangladesh and Myanmar.

I am indebted to Dan Beeby and Chris Wright for the hermeneutical model underlying the book's structure (see ch. 3). Their approaches to the Old Testament have greatly influenced my thinking. Kevin Ellis has helped with the New Testament material. He has cast his scholarly eye over it, and offered many suggestions. Pradip Sudra was a great help in discussing the concept and shape of the book, and read and commented on the Old Testament chapters. David Smith has been an encouraging and long-suffering editor, and Barbara Colebrook-Peace's careful reading of the whole manuscript has been invaluable.

During the writing, I have been involved in setting up the Edinburgh Centre for Muslim–Christian Studies, and have been a postdoctoral fellow at the department of Islamic and Middle Eastern Studies in the University of Edinburgh. This has given me access to valuable library resources, as well as being a stimulating context in which to develop ideas.

Finally, I wish to thank the Anglican mission agency Crosslinks, who have been my employers throughout, and the Sir Halley Stewart Trust, who made a considerable grant towards my employment costs in the year 2003–4.

IDA GLASER
Edinburgh, September 2004

PART I

SETTING THE SCENE

I

PEOPLE AND PLACES

Every sentence of this book is written in acute awareness of blood and tears being shed as human beings, made in the image of God, show the effects of their 'fall' in the contexts of their religions. It is also written in the belief that Jesus Christ is God's gift to his fallen world.

As I started writing, people were looking for survivors under the rubble of the New York World Trade Center that was destroyed on 11 September 2001. People in Jos, Nigeria, were rebuilding their lives after mosques and churches were burnt down and many Christians and Muslims were killed and injured. The radio was carrying programmes about clashes between nationalistic Hindus and people of other faiths in India. Buddhists and Hindus continued the civil war in Sri Lanka, and Catholics and Protestants seemed unable to settle their political differences in Northern Ireland. No wonder the British atheist scientist Richard Dawkins sees religion as destructive! He calls his article about the attack on the World Trade Center 'Religion's misguided missiles' and comments, 'To fill a world with religion, or religions of the Abrahamic kind, is like littering the streets with loaded guns.'[1]

What should Christians think about all this? And what should they do? What difference can Jesus Christ make to these results of the 'fall'? I was asked to write a book on theology: a biblical theology of Christianity and other religions. I thought of all the questions Christian students ask about religions: Is Christ the only way? Is there any truth in religions? Where does it come from? Can people of other religions get to heaven? Are they worshipping God or the devil? Should we try to convert them? How can we convert them? Now, I am not sure that these are the right questions.

As I have studied the Bible, lived among people of different religions and talked with many Christians, I have realized that there are more urgent questions. How can we understand religions and the way they affect human beings? What has God done for people of different religions? What is he doing among them? And what does he require of us? How should we respond to their gods? How do the great commandments (Matt. 22:34–40) and the great commission (Matt. 28:16–20) relate to people of other religions? And to places of interreligious conflict?

Of course, the two sets of questions are related. What we believe about Christ and about the religions will change our ideas of how God relates to people and of what we should do. The difference is that the second set of questions focuses on other people's welfare and our own responsibility. The first set is more about how we should judge other people. It is the second set that I find most urgent for actual relationships with people.

In August 2001 I led a seminar for teachers from theological colleges in Uganda. We were thinking about how and why they taught Islam. The key question, I suggested to them, is, 'How should we, as Christians, live in relation to Muslims? What does God want of us?' We looked at the Sermon on the Mount, at the Great Commandment of Matthew 22:39 and at the Great Commission of Matthew 28:18–20. Then we read Micah 6:8 (my translation):

He has showed you, O human being, what is good.
And what does the LORD require of you?

> To act justly and to love mercy
> and to walk humbly with your God.

Then I asked, 'How are we getting along? Are we living like that in relation to Muslims? What stops us?'

The answers came immediately: 'Muslims say that Jesus is not the Son of God. They criticize the Bible. They won't let us preach. They are setting up lots of new mosques. They want to "take over" our town. They are persecuting Christians in Sudan. They won't eat our food. They are trying to marry our daughters . . .'

I repeated what they had said, and they got the point. Even if all those things were true, is there anything in Muslims that Christians can blame for their own lack of obedience to God? Nothing in Muslims, Hindus, Sikhs, Buddhists, atheists, or even other Christians, can stop us from doing what God requires: only what is in us can do that.

In January 2002 I went to Jos, Nigeria. People told me how, during the conflict the previous September, Christian and Muslim youths set up roadblocks and stopped cars. Only if people were from the 'right' religion were they allowed through. To find out their religion, Muslims asked them to recite the *shahada*.[2] Those who failed were killed. Christians asked them to recite John 3:16. Those who failed were killed.

The title for this book comes from the Ugandan experience. The urgency comes from the Nigerian story. As we read the Bible we may not find answers to all our questions about other people. But, if the Bible is God's word to human beings, we can expect the answer to 'What does the Lord require of us?' Perhaps the world will then be able to appreciate that it was in love that God sent his only Son, and find the life instead of death promised in John 3:16.

About me

My own first experience of interfaith relationships was, I suppose, when my Christian mother bore me and my Jewish father held me in his arms and gave me the name of his mother, Ida, who died in

Auschwitz.³ My father, my brothers and I were all baptized together when I was 6 years old, and I committed my life to Jesus Christ at 14. Not much later came my most difficult experience of interfaith relationships: my parents died in a car accident, and I was cared for by a Jewish aunt who wept over me and asked, 'How can you be a Christian when the Christians put your grandmother in the gas chamber?' Neither my parents nor my aunt were obviously 'religious'. Yet the effects of religion were there, in the identity questions produced by a mixed marriage, and in the far-reaching effects of prejudice and violence.

It was at university in London that I first got to know people from Hindu and Muslim families. I remember asking one Muslim postgraduate engineering student why he believed in Islam. 'Because that is what my mother taught me,' he replied. 'She would never tell me anything wrong.' On another occasion I was trying to explain to a Muslim student why I believed that Jesus had to die. 'Do you mean that God couldn't forgive sin without Jesus dying?' he asked. 'That means that your God is not merciful.' I was beginning to learn that people of other faiths might think very differently from me. Yet I later learnt that they could be more like me than I thought. I asked one Muslim friend, 'Doesn't your religion teach that God is very different from you and very far away?' She thought carefully before responding: 'Well, I suppose that is what they teach us, but I know different because I pray.'

Another influence from university days is a friend who was brought up in a Hindu family in a village in Sri Lanka. As a small child she was fascinated by the gods. One day, she asked herself, 'Is there nothing more than this?' and she asked the gods to show her. Many years later, in a most surprising way, she came to England to study. There she met Christians who told her about Jesus. She fell in love with him and decided to follow him. Over many years I have learnt from her something of the family tensions and cultural challenges that can face someone who turns to Christ, and have seen how important it is that churches understand.

I could continue the stories, of welcoming international students to London, of learning to teach physics to Muslim girls in Malaysia and The Maldives, of living alongside Muslims and Hindus and Sikhs in a deprived inner-city area in England, and of trying to help Christian people to reach out to their neighbours of other faiths. I could add all the study I have done, especially on Islam, and on relationships between the Qur'an and the Bible, and between Muslims and Christians. This would take up too much space. All I want to do here is to give you some idea of who I am, and to say that the most important lessons I have learnt about people of other faiths have not been from books but from experiences.

Why do I tell you all this? First, I believe it is important to know something about the author of a book. However 'academic' and 'objective' a piece of writing seems to be, it is sure to be affected by the beliefs and the experiences of the person who wrote it.[4] In my case, I am a Christian convinced that the Bible is God's book for human beings, and happy to identify with the Lausanne tradition represented by the Global Christian Library. I therefore believe that what I write is dealing with 'objective' issues, and that my ideas can be right or wrong. But readers will be able to judge for themselves much more easily if they know something about me.

Second, I believe that theology is more than a theoretical exercise. The question of how Christians relate to people of other faiths in today's world is not just a matter of stating sound doctrine, or even of finding ways of communicating the gospel. It is literally a matter of life and death and eternity for millions of people. I study the Bible because I want to live to please God, and I write this book because I want others to find resources for living for him. My theology is part of my life and my life is part of my theology.

About words: 'religion' or 'faith'?

I have used the word 'religion' several times, but I have also used the word 'faith'. This is because not many religious people use the word 'religion' to describe themselves. Christians may say, 'Ours is not a religion. It is a relationship with God.' Muslims may say,

'Islam is not a religion. It is a *din*, a way of life.' Hindus may say that 'religion' as defined by others is far too narrow. For them, religion or *dharma* is their duty to God and the rest of humanity, which encompasses all aspects of life. I find that most people prefer the word 'faith' to the word 'religion', so I shall try to use 'faith' when I refer to how people describe themselves.

However, there are also places where I shall continue to use the word 'religion'. First, the word 'religion' is a term used by Western academics to describe people's beliefs, practices and ways of life: I shall usually use the word in this sense. Second, I think that the theologian Karl Barth made a helpful distinction when he argued that all religion, including Christianity, is unbelief.[5] He defined all religions as human efforts. If we start with any kind of religion, he says, we are not starting with God's revelation of himself. Religion is, therefore, a substitute for revelation, and leads us away from God. The only true 'religion' is a response to revelation: that response is faith, which is a humble acceptance of God's gift to us. I shall sometimes use the word 'religion' to describe human efforts to reach God.

Readers who want to know more about academic ideas of religion and religious studies will find chapter 2 of this book interesting. Chapter 2 also introduces some common theological discussions about religions and faiths. Readers who want to go straight to the biblical material might prefer to read chapter 2 last.

From time to time, you will find passages that look like this. They invite you to read a Bible passage or to think about your own situation. I do hope that you will stop at these passages, because they are an important part of the book, and you will usually find that the next part makes more sense if you heed them. I think of this as your contribution to the book, just like the contributions of all the people I have mentioned in the acknowledgments. Here, I invite you to read chapter 1 again, and to write down the questions and challenges that it raises for you. Which of your questions do you think the Bible might answer?

2

THE ACADEMIC SCENE

- Why do all that study? You should just share the gospel with them!
- How can you say that non-Christians worship the same God as Christians?
- How can you say that all other faiths are wrong?

Some Christians are puzzled by the discussions and academic studies in which other Christians are involved – they seem like an unnecessary complication. Some are angry at the theological stances of others – they seem like disloyalty to Christ. Sometimes this turns into a 'West/rest' division: for example, Western Christians may be accused of being too tolerant towards other faiths, and non-Western Christians may be accused of being too hostile towards them.

This chapter will help us to understand the tensions. Some have to do with the history of how different Christian peoples have come into contact with people of different faiths; some have to do with the particular faiths they have met; and some are due to theological differences. In the academic world, faiths are mainly studied in two disciplines: theology and religious studies. Both disciplines grew up in the West, and both have therefore been influenced by the development of Western thought.

Religious studies

'Religion' is not a biblical word. Even in English the word has changed its meaning over the past two centuries. It came from a Latin word meaning 'rendering service to the gods'. In European languages it took on a Christian meaning, and meant honouring God through the Christian faith. 'Religious' people were pious Christians or members of religious orders – monks and nuns. Non-Christians were classified only as Jews, Muslims and 'heathen' or 'pagans'.

As Westerners developed their contacts with people who were not Christians, largely through the colonial movements of the eighteenth and nineteenth centuries, they realized that other people were not simply 'pagans': they had their own highly developed ways of thinking, believing and living. Some tried to describe and understand the varied worship and beliefs they found; and, of course, they wrote in terms of what they knew already. They used the word 'religion', and then tried to discover what it meant. Their writings are still influential.

Looking back, we can see that they were observing something that human beings worldwide seem to share, and were trying to define and explain it. In all cultures, and at all times, human beings have believed in something beyond themselves that shapes the way they live and produces traditions that can be called 'religious'. Even the so-called atheists of the twentieth century have started to talk about the 'spiritual' side of life; and an atheist philosophy like communism could not kill religious instincts. Religion, it seems, is something deep within human beings. But that 'something' takes such different forms that definition is difficult; and, because it is not only a human 'something', it is impossible to explain it in purely human terms.

Much of the study of religion was motivated by the need to

understand. Colonial administrators needed to understand the people with whom they were dealing, especially where, as often among Muslims and Hindus, there was a deliberate policy of not interfering with local traditions. There were also people who travelled and were fascinated by the new languages and ideas they encountered; and, of course, there were the missionaries. Whilst most missionaries started by seeing people of other faiths simply as heathen in need of Christ, many became involved in translation work, and studied the faiths of the people to whom they went. Some made great contributions to Western understandings of other faiths.[1]

The climate of Western thought in the nineteenth century made it inevitable that people would start analysing all this information, and looking for theories to account for it. Dewi Hughes's helpful introduction to religious studies from a Christian perspective explores this.[2] He discusses two particularly influential strands of thought: both are in the tradition of 'enlightenment' thinking that supposed that human beings were at last growing up. Previously, it was thought, people had been bound by irrational doctrines and superstitions. Now they were learning to use their own reason and experience.

1. *Idealism* recognized that the material world was not all that existed, and that reason alone could not reach complete knowledge of the world. In fact, the mind and the spirit were more important than material things – some even said that they were the only true reality. This did not necessarily require belief in God: 'mind' and 'spirit' can be understood as aspects of humanity.

   Immanuel Kant was one of the greatest philosophers in this tradition. He distinguished between what he called 'historical religion' and 'natural religion'. 'Historical religion' is the actual religion we see, with all its doctrines, traditions and institutions. It often has bad effects, producing superstition, war and exploitation. 'Natural religion' is the

true religion of mind and spirit – the ideal behind all the
irrational 'historical religion'. Kant thought that all faiths
must have some aspects of this 'natural religion': 'There is
only *one* (true) religion but there can be *faiths* of several
kinds. We can say further that even in the various churches,
severed from one another by reason of the diversity of their
modes of belief, one and the same religion yet can be found.'[3]

2. *Positivism* rejected all ideas of the supernatural, and tried
   to understand everything in terms of science. Some
   philosophers, such as A. J. Ayer, went so far as to say that
   nothing could be a fact if it could not be tested by
   observation. These were called 'logical positivists'.

   The word 'positivism' comes from the French philosopher
   Auguste Comte. He believed that human thinking had
   developed through three stages: theological, metaphysical
   and positive. That is, human beings had started thinking in
   terms of God – that, said Comte, was fiction. The next stage
   was looking for abstract ideas and forces to explain life. The
   final stage, which he thought he had reached, realized that
   all these ideas were unnecessary superstitions. The final,
   'positive', stage was scientific. Religions had useful functions
   in society, but were to be understood in purely human
   terms.[4] The study of religion was a 'science' like the study of
   any other aspect of humanity.

These two approaches seem to be opposites, since one sees the
basis of the world as outside the material realm, and the other
rejects everything non-material. However, they were both part of
the same stream of history. Both shared some ideas that have
affected religious studies ever since:

- *Objectivity.* Both wanted to explain the world in a way that
  would include all peoples, cultures, places and histories. They
  thought their ideas were 'objective', and not dependent on
  any particular person, place, time or religion.

- *Science*. Both saw religion as open to investigation by human
  means. They saw reason and experience as the main ways of
  gaining knowledge, and this applied to religion as well as to
  the material world and other aspects of humanity.
- *Essentialism*. Both looked for big ideas that would include
  everything. Their question about religion was, 'What is it
  really?' They did not only want to know the meaning of the
  word, and what all religions had in common. They wanted
  to know what underlay all the religions – to find a general
  'theory of religion'.[5] This is sometimes called the search for
  the essence of religion.
- *Evolution*. This was the time of Darwin's theory of biological
  evolution, and many people also believed that human beings
  were evolving socially and morally. Religion was part of this.
  Some thought that people would evolve away from belief in
  God; but others saw religion as evolving from more primitive
  expressions through to monotheism, with Christianity as its
  highest expression.

Present-day religious studies builds on all this. It continues to
study religion in human terms, and has developed specialisms
based on the human sciences. There is anthropology of religion,
sociology of religion, psychology of religion, and philosophy of
religion. In addition, the influence of the 'Romantic movement' of
the late nineteenth century has left an interest in the feelings and
the beauty that surround religion, so that some scholars make a
particular study of religious experience. There is also 'phenom-
enology of religion', which studies observable aspects of religion,
such as religious objects, places of worship, rituals, authority
figures and rites of passage.

Such studies have given rise to many theories that try to explain
all 'religion'. Anthropologists can see it as an aspect of human
culture. Sociologists can see it in terms of its function in society.
Psychologists can see it as an expression of something deep in the
human mind. Philosophers may point to the mystical experience

that appears in all religions. Phenomenologists might say that we need to focus on studying the aspects of religion we can actually see before we can make any progress in the theories.

In all this, scholars are aware of difficulties and inconsistencies, and have challenged much of the original agenda of religious studies.[6]

- *There are difficulties in defining religion.* This is not only because it is difficult to say what religions have in common, but also because there are some things that we might want to exclude. For example, do we want to include Satanism? And what should we do with Buddhism, which does not believe in a god, and with communism, which rejects religion but displays many of the functions of a religion? Anyway, most people dislike their faith being called 'religion'.
- *There are difficulties in finding the 'essence' of religion*, not least because no-one who actually believes in any one religion will accept most definitions. Few will accept that their faith is 'really' something happening in their mind, or needed to organize their society. Even the idea that what is 'real' is the actual religious experience, quite independently of what people believe, will not be accepted by many. Who is to say that Muslims, Hindus, Buddhists, Jews, Christians and others all experience the same thing?
- Most seriously, *scientific approaches to religions are not necessarily 'objective'.* Everyone has some starting point to their thinking: everyone has some assumptions. If we assume that there is no God, or if we try to be 'neutral' and stand outside all religions, we are choosing a starting point just as much as if we study from a Christian or a Muslim or a Hindu point of view.

Today's religious studies have also been influenced by the increasing interaction between people of different religions across the world. In every Western country there are now many people from different faiths. This has resulted in emphasis on the study of particular religions not only through books but also through contact with believers. All this has contributed to what is known as 'postmodern' thinking. No longer is reason the main judge; and no longer do people expect there to be one 'truth'. They are ready to accept that different ideas can be true for different people, and very often follow feelings rather than reason. Many feel that life is not to be understood only within the material or human realm, and believe that all religions are equally valid – or invalid. They see the need for moral values, and look to 'faith' to provide them.

What might a Christian think about all this?

First, I suggest that a Christian can thank God for religious studies. It has broken down many barriers between human beings and dispelled much ignorance. It means that Christians as well as others can easily obtain information about the beliefs and practices of their fellow human beings, and see how much we have in common.

Second, it helps us to understand the human aspects of religion. We have said that it is impossible to understand religion in purely human terms; yet it is clear that all religion has human aspects. This is true of Christianity as well as of other religions. Religious studies can help us to understand why Christians act in the way that they do. It can bring us face to face with history – bad as well as good. It can help us to see how faith affects society.

However, it is helpful to be aware of religious studies rooting in Western thinking. This means that it may look only at the human aspects of religions. An academic discipline does not have the tools to look at any supernatural aspects. It can therefore be *reductionist*. That is, because religion can be studied as something human, it can be thought of as *only* human. This is, of course, not a necessary conclusion, but it is an easy one to make.

It is also helpful to be aware of assumptions made about knowledge and authority.[7] Academic thinking is generally based on reason and observation, and this determines what it can know.

It sees religious authorities such as scriptures, teachers and spiritual experience as objects to be studied rather than authorities to be submitted to. In practice, this can mean that people studying a religion seem to think that they have authority above the people who actually practise it. We may want to question the idea that it is possible to have a grand theory of all religion and, even more basically, to ask whether the category of 'religion' is a useful one.

In summary, Christians can learn much from and contribute much to religious studies, but they need to be aware of its basis. Further, they will want to understand both their own religion and others in the light of what they know about God, and of the authorities that they recognize: that is, to think about them – and about religious studies – theologically.

Theology

Theology is always done in a context. Western theology is no exception: it has been affected by the whole religious studies movement described above. This is not only in its attitudes towards other faiths. The ancient religions surrounding Israel were the subject of much research, and this contributed to critical and historical understandings of the Bible. We shall look at some of this research in Part 2. It will help us to think about how the biblical authors interacted with the faiths that surrounded them.

For the Western theologians of the last two centuries, the research had a different effect. It led them to seeing the development of Israel's religion as one human development alongside other human developments. As they looked at the Bible as a human book, some felt unable to continue thinking of it as a revealed book.

However, they still wanted to be Christian. They recognized Christian worship and morality as central to their lives, and they loved Jesus and the ideas of the cross and the resurrection. What resulted was reinterpretation of the Christian faith; and, of course, much controversy with those Christians who continued to believe in the traditional doctrines. This is not the place to explore the reinterpretations or the controversy: we shall only consider the implications for Christian thinking about other faiths.

The legacy of 'evolution'

Traditionally, European Christians had seen all non-Christian peoples as living in darkness and needing the light of Christ. Missionaries saw themselves as taking the gospel to the lost. As some Christians began to understand religions as human phenomena, they still saw Christianity as the best way. The problem was that this was often understood in terms of evolution. As the idea of physical evolution was extended to the idea of the evolution of society and of ideas, Christianity was seen as the peak of religious development. Hughes quotes one of the most influential students of religion, James Frazer:

> As savage races are not all on the same plane, but have stopped or tarried at different points of the upward path, we can to a certain extent, by comparing them with each other, construct a scale of social progression and mark out roughly some of the stages on the long road that leads from savagery to civilization. In the kingdom of the mind such a scale of mental evolution answers to the scale of morphological evolution in the animal kingdom.[8]

The implication is clear. Just as we can look at animals and work out which came first, we can study different religions and work out which came first. The early ones are 'savage', and the later ones are 'civilized'. Human beings are developing on an upward path, but some have got stuck at the early stages. The earliest stages were, it was thought, magical practices, which then evolved through beliefs in spirits and many gods to monotheism. Frazer himself thought that the next stage would replace all religious explanations by scientific ones. Others saw the highest development of monotheism as Christianity.

Most scholars now reject such evolutionary ideas. Some even argue that religions started with an original monotheism, which degenerated into polytheism. Yet there are some ideas that still affect Western thinking.

- The link between 'Christianity' and 'civilization'. The 'Christianity' that was spread by the missionaries came in a Western package, with the assumption that Western culture was Christian and therefore more civilized than other cultures.
- The idea that Christianity is the peak of human development. This implies not only that Christianity is superior to other religions, but also that Christians are superior to other people because they have reached a higher stage.

Most thinking people now reject these ideas. They know that there are many different cultural expressions of the Christian faith, that humanity is not evolving towards a superior state, and that Christians are not superior to other people. They see that such ideas have led to arrogance, abuse of power, and exploitation of people considered as 'inferior'. They therefore want to oppose these ideas, wherever they find them, which means that they want to affirm non-Western cultures and non-Christian faiths.

Christians who believe that their faith is a response to something God has really done in Christ will know that they are not superior to anyone else. They know that they have only responded to God's grace, and that they are sinners like everyone else. They know that salvation is a gift from God, and has nothing to do with so-called advanced culture. But those who see Christianity mainly as a human response to what all peoples can know of God may not understand this. If we say, 'Jesus is the only way of salvation,' some people will think we mean, 'Christians are superior to other people.' If we say, 'We want Buddhists and Hindus and Muslims to come to faith in Jesus Christ,' some people will think we mean, 'They should change their culture and become like us.' If we say, 'There is no salvation in other faiths,' they will think we mean, 'Everyone except ourselves is bad.'

Theologies of other faiths

We are now ready to consider how Christian theologians have tried to understand other faiths. We shall not try to look at all the theologians and their ideas, but to outline some of the main ways of thinking. These are often classified as 'exclusivist', 'inclusivist' and 'pluralist'. Not all Christians fit neatly into one of these categories, and even when they do fit, they probably describe their beliefs in different ways. However, this classification provides a helpful framework for discussion.

1. *Exclusivists* believe that salvation is only available through faith in Jesus Christ. All peoples can know something about God through general revelation; that is, by looking at his creation and at themselves. This is because the creation shows something of the Creator, and because they themselves are made in his image. However, God has chosen to reveal himself very specially through Israel and supremely in Jesus Christ, and we can only learn about this reliably through the Bible. The Holy Spirit can work in anyone anywhere, but he comes through Jesus Christ and leads to Jesus Christ. Therefore we need to preach the gospel of Jesus Christ to all peoples.

2. *Inclusivists* agree that salvation is through Christ, but ask whether perhaps people who belong to other faiths might still be saved through him. Perhaps there are some who, like the 'sheep' of Matthew 25:37, do not realize that they are serving Christ. Perhaps there are others who, like the tax collector of Luke 18:13, recognize their sin and call to God for mercy. Surely Christ's death would save them?

   Some inclusivists would go on to suggest that there might be special revelation outside that recorded in the Bible. Perhaps the histories of other peoples, or their holy books, can function for them like the history of Israel and the Old Testament do for Christians, pointing them to Christ. Some would say that theology should be 'theocentric' rather than

'Christocentric'; that is, that we need to think more about God, the Father of all peoples, than about Jesus Christ who came to a particular people at a particular time. Although Christ came in the historical person of Jesus of Nazareth, we can see him at work in many places and at many times; and we cannot limit the Holy Spirit to his link with Jesus.

3. *Pluralists* say that Christ is *not* the only way to salvation: salvation is available through all faiths. Some even believe that all people will be saved, whether they follow a faith or not. They usually believe that God can be seen in his creation, but tend to think of the different faiths as different human responses to what different people see of him rather than as results of any special revelation. Some pluralists would go on say that we should not speak of God but of 'the transcendent' or of 'reality', since not all faiths have a place for God but all have a sense of something absolute. 'Christ' is then a universal being called 'the cosmic Christ', and the Holy Spirit is better understood as a universal spirit affecting all peoples.

A key question here is what is meant by 'salvation'. Discussions are often about the basic question of who will go to heaven, but 'salvation' can also mean coming into relationship with God, being released from the power of sin, or being spiritually, mentally or physically healed. It is important to understand how a writer uses this word, and other words, before trying to assess his or her ideas. It is also helpful to ask where the ideas come from.

Exclusivism is a way of describing some of the traditional Christian thinking that focuses on Jesus as the revelation of God, the cross as the way of salvation, and biblical condemnation of worship of anything other than God. *Inclusivism* keeps much of this traditional understanding, but asks whether we can have more positive views of people of other faiths. It reacts against colonial attitudes, and fears that exclusivist ideas make Christians superior to other people. 'Surely God will not judge people simply because they have not heard the gospel?' say inclusivists. 'Surely we have no right to say that all those millions of people of different faiths are lost? Yes, we want to be faithful to Christ, but how can we love our neighbours if we think they are damned?'

Both exclusivist and inclusivist thinkers see Jesus Christ as the ultimate revelation of God. Both go to the Bible with their questions, although they may read it differently. Pluralists no longer accept Christ or the Bible as higher than other religious authorities; and this leads them to ideas about God that sometimes seem no longer Christian. How, we wonder, can people who still call themselves 'Christian' think like this?

Chapter 3 will help us to understand this by looking at the way Wesley Ariarajah interprets the Bible. In general, however, pluralism rises out of a combination of people's experience and some of the modern ideas we have just explored. This can be seen from the papers in an influential book edited by the British Presbyterian philosopher of religion John Hick and the American Catholic theologian Paul Knitter, *The Myth of Christian Uniqueness*.[9] In the preface, Knitter explains why the idea of 'Christian uniqueness' is a problem: 'It has come to signify the unique definitiveness, absoluteness, normativeness, superiority of Christianity in comparison with other religions of the world.'[10]

This is just the problem of 'superiority' we have already discussed. (The other ideas can be found in the rest of the book: the idea that all religions are basically human, the reaction against colonialism and ideas of superiority; and the suggestion that, despite their differences, all religious people are somehow aiming at the same thing.) Knitter goes on to point out that Christians are now becoming more aware of 'the vitality [of other faiths], their influence in our modern world, their depths, beauty and attractiveness'. They therefore want more interaction and cooperation with people of other faiths, and see that this needs changed attitudes. This is the experience that has led to pluralism.

We can see that much of what underlies pluralism is the same as what underlies other Western liberal thought. However, this is not only a Western issue. Four of the contributors to *The Myth of Christian Uniqueness* are Asian – Raimundo Panikkar and Stanley Samartha from India, Seiichi Yagi from Japan and Aloysius Pieris from Sri Lanka. It is not unusual to find Christians who live in Buddhist or Hindu contexts expressing pluralist ideas, and others arguing against them from inclusivist or exclusivist perspectives.[11] Those who live in Muslim contexts tend to think differently. This is, perhaps, because Hindus and Buddhists themselves believe that there are many ways to God, but Muslims believe that the revelation to Muhammad is absolute. There is also far more history of hostility between Muslims and Christians than between Hindus or Buddhists and Christians. It is not only Western theologians who are influenced by their experiences and by the people around them!

Thinking about the theologies

Who is right? How do we decide between 'exclusivism', 'inclusivism' and 'pluralism'? Should our decision depend on our experience and our context?

I hope that by the end of this book readers will be able to come back to this chapter to make some assessment of these theological issues. Here, I want to point out that even these classifications reflect the Western academic background. In some ways, this can be helpful; but it can also mean that they do not even ask the right questions.

One of the reasons for the debates is the realization that all faiths, including Christianity, are human. This, as we have said, is positive: the most important thing about all people of all faiths is that we are all human beings. The problem is that some people suppose that, if something is human, it cannot be from God. The more 'liberal' Christians, who are inclusivist or pluralist, may see the human aspects of the Bible and conclude that we cannot trust it as God's revelation. The more 'conservative' Christians, who are exclusivist or inclusivist, can react by rejecting historical and critical studies of the human aspects of the text. Exclusivists can be so busy saying that Christ is the one way of salvation that they are unable to treat people of other faiths as fellow human beings made in the image of God, and they may be unable to recognize the human shortcomings in Christians. Pluralists can be so busy looking for the common humanity in people of all faiths that they deny God's revelation of himself.

Further, the debates continue the academic concern to find a general theory of religion. They try to find a theology of 'other faiths' in general. This may be mistaken. We may never be able to say anything that is true of all people of other faiths. It may even be that the whole idea of 'religions' or 'faiths' is unhelpful. Perhaps God is not interested in what human beings call 'religions'.

How shall we find out? I have said that academic thinking tries to use reason and observation, and to be 'detached' from what it studies. Even in theology, the Bible can be treated as an object to be studied rather than an authority to be submitted to. But I agree with Karl Barth, quoted above,[12] that we have to make a choice here: either we start from our human understanding, or we start from God's revelation. We cannot be 'detached' from what we study. If we try to be, that means that we think we are somehow higher than it: we make ourselves the judges.

We know that we are not able to judge ourselves rightly, let alone to judge our fellow Christians or people of other faiths. We want to hear God's judgment. This book is in the Lausanne tradition of understanding the Bible as God's written Word. That is where we shall start our search for answers to our questions about people of other faiths.

Table 2.1. Exclusivism, Inclusivism, Pluralism: A Summary

Exclusivism	Inclusivism	Pluralism
Salvation through explicit faith in Christ alone.	Salvation through Christ but not needing explicit faith in Him. 'Anonymous Christians.'	Salvation available through all faiths.
General revelation God's special revelation through Israel, Christ, the Bible only.	*General revelation* There may be special revelation elsewhere. Other histories can have the function of the Old Testament.	*General revelation* Religions as different human responses to the transcendent (= no special revelation?).
Christocentric Christ is Jesus of Nazareth. Holy Spirit given through Him.	*Theocentric* Christ is seen in Jesus, but not confined to him. Holy Spirit at work everywhere.	*Reality-centred* Cosmic Christ. Universal spirit.

3

READING THE BIBLE

What does the Bible say about other faiths?
When asked this question, I often start with Psalm 148.

Please read Psalm 148 slowly and carefully now.

What does this say about other faiths? At first glance, not a lot! It declares that all creatures are under the Creator, it calls all to worship him, and it mentions his special relationship with Israel. This has some implications for different religions, but does not, apparently, address them directly.

But suppose we take a second glance, recalling that the worship of Israel, as expressed in this psalm, was the worship of a people surrounded by other peoples with a variety of other religions. There were stories of many beings in the spiritual realms, each with different interests and powers. There were gods associated with the sun and the moon and the stars. There were stories of primeval battles in which gods quelled the monsters of the chaotic waters and divided the waters into those above and those below. There was the Canaanite god Baal, the lord of the elements and the controller of fertility. The Egyptian gods included animals, such as frogs and cows. Many peoples regarded their kings as divine or divine favourites, and most saw their particular nations as being under their particular gods.

In the light of this, what does Psalm 148 say about different religions? It challenges them!

- Their gods, it says, are not gods at all. Sun, moon and stars; hills, animals and kings: all are created by and under the control of the one Creator God.
- All the aspects of existence that their gods are said to control – the waters, the weather and fertility – are in fact subject to the will of this one God.
- There are not different gods for different peoples – all peoples are called to worship this one God.
- Even the other 'gods themselves' are to worship the One.

In sum, there is only one God, who is over all other apparent gods, and who makes demands on all peoples. This is revolutionary if we apply it in today's world, but we have not finished. The psalm goes on to say that this God is to be worshipped under a particular name, revealed to a particular people who have received particular favour. The last verses of the previous psalm underline the point:

> He has revealed his word to Jacob,
>> his laws and decrees to Israel.
> He has done this for no other nation;
>> they do not know his laws.
>> (Psalm 147:19–20)

As we come to the Bible, we shall have to be careful how we read it. This chapter explains what I hope to do.

Getting started

I have said that I want to start with God's revelation and therefore with the Bible; but that is impossible.

First, we have to read the Bible being who we are. In fact, none of us *starts* by accepting God's revelation in Christ or in the Bible. If we believe in original sin, we know that we need God to lead us to this understanding; and he leads us all in different ways. As we continue to follow Jesus and to study the Bible, we bring our own questions and experiences with us. We *cannot* 'start from the Bible' because, whether we like it or not, we have already started before we open the Bible.

What we *can* do is to recognize the Bible as having priority over our own thinking. It is in that sense that I want it to come first. Whenever we recognize God's revelation, we can try to accept it rather than to argue with it. In this way, we can, little by little, increase our understanding of what God is saying, and come to know and serve him better. We shall then be able to speak of him in ways that are both faithful to his revelation and appropriate to the people we live among.

How did you reach your present ideas about the Bible? What ideas and experiences about other faiths do you bring to your study?

I have spelt this out because I do not want to pretend that what I write will be purely biblical, or that anyone who disagrees with me is *not* 'starting from the Bible'. But I also want to point out that all knowledge develops in this way. We always start from where we are, and respond to what we see and hear and experience. We always understand things in terms of what we know already. This means that we always need to hear in a language that we understand. This has important consequences for how God speaks. In our Bible study we shall see how he reveals himself in terms people can understand, and how their understanding grows as they respond to him. We shall not be looking at a static situation, in which there are Jews and people who follow other religious systems. It is a dynamic situation, in which communities change, circumstances change, ideas change, and even 'gods' change. It is into this changing world that God speaks: in thinking about our relationship with people from different religions, we need to see *how* he does this as well as *what* he says.

Second, it is not obvious where in the Bible we could 'start'. The Bible is a big book, and 'religion' is not a Bible word. It cannot be found in the Old Testament, and the few cases where English translations of the New Testament use the word have nothing to do with the variety of world religions of which it is used today.[1] If we ask what the Bible says about specific religions, we shall also be disappointed. It never mentions Hinduism, Buddhism or Islam – the first two were, as far as we know, unknown or unnamed in Bible times and places, and the last arose more than half a millennium after the New Testament was completed. Judaism is mentioned, of course, but present-day Judaism is different in many ways from that of either Old Testament or New Testament times. And what about 'Christianity'? That is another word that cannot be found in the Bible. We cannot simply turn to the Bible and expect it to set out the answers to our questions: it is not that kind of book.

So, then, how shall we get started? We are not the first people to come to the Bible with questions about religions. Others have used it in different ways, and we are going to find some help from their ideas.

Looking for themes
This is a common method. Two themes often considered as relating to other faiths are idolatry and the uniqueness of Christ.

• *The uniqueness of Christ.* Many writers point out that the New Testament is full of references to the greatness, the universality and the uniqueness of the Lord Jesus Christ. He is the only begotten Son from the Father (John 1:14, 18), the name above every name (Phil. 2:9–10), the one in whom all

things hold together (Col. 1:17), the radiance of God's glory,
the exact representation of his being (Heb. 1:3). Further, he
is the only one who has opened the way of salvation: two
much-quoted verses are John 14:6 and Acts 4:12.[2]

- *Idolatry.* The first two of the ten commandments forbid
  the worship of any god but Yahweh, and the making and
  worship of images. It is often noted that the religions
  surrounding Israel are described throughout the Old
  Testament as idol worship. Israel was frequently condemned
  for idolatry, and some of the prophets not only condemn it
  but mock it. The New Testament, too, forbids idol worship,
  and Acts records clashes between the early missionaries and
  people who worshipped other gods.

During the twentieth century, a number of books appeared
that asked, 'Are there other themes in the Bible that might let us
have a more positive view of other faiths?' Three themes expressing God's universal concern are often identified:

- *Positive attitudes towards the nations.* God is not only
  concerned with Israel. There are places in the Old Testament
  where it is said that God also leads other nations (e.g. Amos
  9:7). He sends Jonah to Israel's enemies in Nineveh, and uses
  Cyrus, the Persian king, to bring Israel home from exile (Isa.
  45:1). There are some records of non-Israelites coming to
  faith in the God of Israel (e.g. Rahab in Josh. 2, Naaman in 2
  Kgs 5 and Nebuchadnezzar in Dan. 2 – 4), and there is a
  future vision of all nations turning to him (e.g. Isa. 2:2–3;
  19:24–25; 61:1–3; 66:23; Zech. 2:11; 14:16–19).
- *Surprising salvation.* The Sermon on the Mount shows that
  God's blessing is not necessarily for those who follow the right
  religion, but for those whose hearts are right. The parable of
  the good Samaritan shocked the religious expert of Luke 10:25
  by showing someone from a different religion doing what
  would 'inherit eternal life'. In all four Gospels, Jesus surprised

people by saying that people who were not religious or not Jewish were saved. These included Roman centurions (Matt. 8:5–13; Luke 7:1–10), the Canaanite or Syro-Phoenician woman (Matt. 15:21–28; Mark 7:24–30), the thankful Samaritan leper (Luke 17:1–19) and the Samaritan woman (John 4). Jesus' announcement of his ministry in Nazareth is followed by a reminder of God's blessing on non-Israelites (Luke 4:24–27), and the parable of the sheep and the goats suggests that even the people who are saved will be surprised (Matt. 25:31–46)!

- *Righteous Gentiles.* Such Old Testament characters as Melchizedek (Gen. 14:17–24), Jethro (Exod. 18:8–12) and Job clearly worshipped the one true God, although they were outside the covenants and, as far as we know, knew nothing of God's revelation to Abraham and his descendants. Melchizedek and Jethro were both priests, who apparently worshipped Yahweh by different names. Even Balaam, who was a priest of a different god, was able to hear and respond to Yahweh.

  In the New Testament, there are the Gentiles mentioned above who responded to Jesus with more understanding than did many Jews. There are also the wise men, who discerned God's work before the religious leaders did (Matt. 2:1–6) and Cornelius, whose prayers and almsgiving pleased God (Acts 10:1–8).

It is interesting that we can find exclusivists, inclusivists and pluralists using these same passages. Exclusivists will argue that they point to the fact that salvation for all peoples is found in Jesus Christ. Inclusivists will emphasize the fact that some people had some knowledge of the true God before they knew about Christ. Pluralists tend to focus on one set of texts and reinterpret or even discount others.

This means that different people read particular verses in different ways. A Church of England report, which represents a wide range of theological opinions, comments on the interpretation of John 14:6:

Such passages are accepted by many exclusivists as expressing Jesus' definitive self-understanding; inclusivists tend to point out that they need to be interpreted in terms of the logos Christology of the Prologue that pervades the Gospel as a whole, while pluralists tend to assume that the logos Christology was a mistaken development.[3]

That is:

- *Exclusivists* take the verse to mean quite literally what it says: that Jesus saw himself as the only way to God.
- *Inclusivists* may say, 'Yes, but what is it about Jesus that is the only way? Does it have to be the particular historical individual Jesus of Nazareth? We need to read this verse in the context of the rest of John's Gospel. John sees Jesus of Nazareth as the *logos* – the eternal Word – made flesh. John 1:9 tells us that this *logos* gives light to everyone. We cannot limit it.'
- *Pluralists* may say that the New Testament statements about the uniqueness of Christ should be read as expressing faith rather than fact. They are meaningful for Christians, but not for others. The early Christians experienced Jesus as 'the way, the truth and the life' for them, but this does not mean that he is the only way for others.

The last idea is strange to many Christians. How can Jesus be the way and the truth and the life for one person and not for others? Wesley Ariarajah explains this position:

When my little girl tells me that I am the best daddy in the world, and there can be no father like me, she is speaking the truth. For this comes out of her experience. She is honest about it; she knows no other person in the role of her father . . . But of course it is not true in another sense . . . in the next house there is another little girl who also thinks that her daddy is the best father in the whole world. And she too is right . . . For here we are dealing not with absolute truths, but with the language of faith and love . . .

The language of the Bible is also the language of faith . . . [4]

Does this mean that we can prove whatever we want from the Bible? It certainly means that people do argue all sorts of different things from the Bible. But it also means that looking for themes may not be the best way of doing things. To begin with, we may choose the wrong themes! We tend to choose the themes according to our questions, and we may not know the best questions to ask. In this case, the apparent question is, 'Does God save people only through Jesus Christ?', but underneath this is the question 'Does He love all peoples, or only Christians?' Now, of course, these are two quite different questions. But they are linked because we tend to make some assumptions. One is that we know who the 'Christians' are. Another is that these are the people who are saved. Some people who ask these questions assume that God does not love the people he does not save, and that, if we think we are saved and others are not, we think we are somehow God's favourites. Looking for themes may not help us to untangle these assumptions.

But the biggest problem with the 'thematic' approach is that it is selective:

1. We choose the passages we think are relevant to our theme: there may be many other passages that are relevant, and that address questions we have never thought of asking.
2. If we find 'themes' that seem to go in different directions, we may emphasize one rather than the other. Thus exclusivists may stress the uniqueness of Christ and try to explain away 'surprising salvation'. Pluralists may stress God's universal love and say that biblical views of idolatry do not apply to, for example, today's Hindus.
3. Those who see the Bible as essentially a human book feel free to speak of different traditions within it. This can lead to their seeing the 'traditions' with which they disagree as adaptations of faith relevant to the time and place, but with no direct meaning for today.[5]
4. While the thematic approach may put too much emphasis on

the context of particular passages, it may also ignore the context. For example, in looking at 'idolatry', we may focus only on what is said and not notice to whom it is said and why.[6]

So, as we read the Bible, we can have these themes in mind; and we shall doubtless have in mind many other biblical themes with which we are familiar, but we need to find a more comprehensive way of reading.

A canonical approach

Dan Beeby, in his *Canon and Mission*,[7] argues for the importance of reading the whole Bible. He speaks of 'canonical interpretation', which does not set one part of the Bible over against another, or choose which parts to emphasize. He notes several ways of looking at the overall pattern of the Bible, which can help us to see God's mission to his world. Here are some:

1. *The 'U' pattern.* This pattern goes from the heights to the depths and back again. God creates the good world, but it goes wrong at the fall, continues in sin, reaches the depths when people crucify Christ, and then is little by little restored as the new creation. The pattern can be seen in many of the stories of the Bible, and especially in the life of Christ, who comes down from heaven right to death, and then is raised and returns to heaven.

2. *Promise and fulfilment.* This sees the New Testament as showing the fulfilment in Christ of all to which the Old Testament points, and then pointing on towards the fulfilment of all that Christ came to bring.

3. *From beginning to end.* The Bible moves from the perfect Garden of Eden to the perfect heavenly city of Revelation. It is the story of how God's world becomes full of people, and how God works to make his world what he wants it to be.

4. *Relationships.* The Bible tells of five basic relationships, which went wrong at the beginning, and which God restores through

Christ: the relationships of God to creation, of God to humanity, of human beings to other human beings, of human beings to creation, and of individual people to themselves.

5. *Promises, blessings and covenants.* These can be found in Genesis 1 – 11, where they are given to all God's creatures, with no conditions attached. Then, beginning with God's call to Abraham in Genesis 12, there are covenants made with Israel. The Bible can be seen as the story of how these covenants work out. It is important here that the covenant with Abraham is not only for the blessing of his descendants, but that through them all the nations should be blessed (Gen. 12:3).

All these patterns underline the same thing: the Bible portrays God working in the whole of his world during the whole of history. Although most of it is about Israel, its concern is for all peoples. *If we look at the overall shape of the Bible, we have to conclude that, whatever Israel was chosen for, God's purposes have always been for the whole of humanity and not only for one particular nation.* Jesus is at the centre of all the patterns, so it is clear that Jesus is sent for the whole of humanity, and not for any one particular group of people.

Where do the different religions fit into all this? Beeby suggests that the nations surrounding Israel are parallel to people of different faiths in our times.[8] Nations are not the same as religious groups but, during most of human history, there have been strong links between peoples and their religions. In Old Testament times there were no nations as we know them. Rather, there were groups of people, which we might call ethnic groups, with their rulers, their rituals, their territories and their gods. These aspects were so closely bound together that they could be difficult to separate.

Beeby notes that Israel *existed for the nations* – God did not call Abraham only for his own sake, but to bring *blessing to all nations*. Further, *Israel lived among the nations*, and was constantly interacting with them. Much of the Bible's story is about her *struggles with the nations*; but we can also see how she *depended on the nations*. For example, she survived famine by going to Egypt at the time of

Joseph, but then she had to be rescued from Egypt at the time of Moses. In all this, Israel was supposed to be a *witness to the nations* – she was supposed to show them what God was like – although she often failed. Similarly, when we move to the New Testament, the church does not exist for its own sake but for the sake of the nations. The early Christians lived among the nations, and both learnt from them and struggled with them; and they were certainly called to be witnesses to all the nations. This, Beeby suggests, can be a basis for our relationships with people of different faiths.

These are very helpful themes, and we shall consider them further in our biblical studies in part 2 of this book. But it is also important that *this link between nations and gods is one that continues today*. We have already seen how religious studies scholars describe religions as human systems, linked with culture, language and social organization. In fact, religion can be seen as part of the way that a particular group of people expresses and organizes itself.

This is not only how religious studies scholars see religion: people often see their faith as an intrinsic part of their ethnic, national, family or community identity. Thus it is assumed by most that Turks are Muslim, that Sikhs are Punjabi, that people who practise Judaism are Jews, and even that British people are generally Christian. Our study will show how revolutionary the Bible is in dealing with such thinking.

A hermeneutical approach

'Hermeneutics' is the art of interpretation.[9] We have already pointed out that everyone interprets what they read in terms of what they know already. That warns us that we may not always understand what the writers wanted to say. For example, when we read 'nations' in the Bible, we may think of something like the nation states that exist today. In fact, such 'nations' have only existed for a few hundred years. The 'nations' of Bible times were often more like what we would call tribal groups.

Scholars distinguish three levels of reading a text, all of which help us to see its meaning in different ways.

Author-centred reading: the text as a window

This focuses on the author and the world in which he or she was writing. It uses the text as a window through which we can see that world, and try to understand what it meant to the person who wrote it and to the people among whom he or she was writing.

In thinking about other faiths, this approach means that we recognize that the biblical authors were surrounded by people with different religions. We shall need to learn about those religions, and to see how they affected the biblical authors and how the writings would have spoken to people in that context. For example, there were many different accounts of the creation of the world and of human beings in the ancient Near East. Genesis 1 uses some of the ideas from these accounts, but in a very different context. We shall consider how this both communicated well with people and challenged their whole way of thinking.

Text-centred reading: the text as picture

This focuses on the text itself, not only on what it says but also on how it says it. It is like looking at a picture in detail, to see exactly how the paint was applied, as well as looking at the overall effect.

In thinking about other faiths, this approach means that we look at what the biblical writers say about the surrounding peoples and religions, but also that we see how they use language and images from those people and religions. For example, Hosea rebukes the people of Israel for worshipping Baal, but he does so by using ideas and images that come from the Baal cults.

Reader-centred focus: the text as mirror

This focuses on the reader's world: what does this mean for me, today? It is like looking in a mirror, to find out more about oneself and one's situation.

In thinking about other faiths, this approach means that we

look in the text for things that parallel our own situation, and ask what it means for us today. For example, where do we find parallels to the idolatry of Old Testament times? Christians often call Hindu ways of worship 'idolatory', but, in India, the Hindu 'idols' may have a very similar role to that of what Christians may call 'icons'. How can the Bible help us to think about Hinduism? And about how we, as Christians, should worship in Hindu contexts?

We may also ask how people of other faiths might understand the Bible. For example, the Qur'an includes references to many biblical characters, including Jesus, but it presents them in an Islamic framework. How, then, do Muslims react to the Bible when they read it? How can we help them to understand the gospel of Jesus Christ?

It is important to keep all these three approaches in mind when we read the Bible. To miss any one would give an unbalanced picture. In parts 2 and 3 of this book we shall explore the first two approaches. That is, we shall be looking at how the biblical writings relate to the religions of the time, and asking what the text actually says and how it says it. There will be questions to help the reader begin to think about how it applies today, but I shall not begin to answer them until part 4. We shall wait until we have completed our 'window' and our 'picture' readings before we try to use the text as a 'mirror' on our own times.

PART 2

READING THE OLD TESTAMENT

4

PEOPLES SURROUNDING ISRAEL, AND THEIR GODS

If we want to find out how the biblical writings relate to the religions of the time, we need first to know something about these religions. This chapter offers an overview of the peoples and faiths 'behind the text' of the Old Testament world.

Common ideas

The Bible story spans at least two thousand years, during which the people of Israel interacted with different peoples in different places with different gods. (I use the word 'peoples' rather than 'tribes' or 'nations' because this includes both ethnic and socio-political groups. 'Nations' as we know them in the twenty-first century did not exist in Bible times.) The gods and the beliefs and practices associated with them changed and developed during these years, but there are some characteristics of the religions surrounding Israel that were similar throughout.

- *Peoples believed in many gods.* At any given time, a particular people would have a main god, but they would also believe in other gods. These gods had their own characteristics, and usually ruled over different aspects of life. It was no problem that different people had different gods. Societies were *pluralist*.

- *Gods were associated with particular peoples and particular places.* Often, a god was seen as the god of a particular people or even a particular city. He or she had a temple in that place, and had power in that area. Religions were *territorial* and/or *national.*
- *The king had a special relationship to the god.* He ruled according to the god's laws and led the people in serving the god. He therefore represented the god to the people and the people to the god; and was sometimes seen as divine himself. A victory for the king was seen as a victory for the god. Religions were *political.*
- *Gods were sometimes merged.* It is sometimes difficult to tell the difference between two gods. Sometimes, a god had more than one name; sometimes, similar gods were worshipped in different places and were eventually joined together; sometimes, one people might conquer another, and take over their gods. There could also be a deliberate merging of gods for political reasons. Religions were *syncretistic.*
- *Gods had particular functions.* The most important gods had to do with the aspects of life that most concerned the people: weather, food production, childbirth, war and death.
- *Gods often expressed something in the natural world.* For example, the Egyptian god Hati was the god of the Nile, and the Canaanite god Baal was in control of the rain. There were gods associated with the sun, the moon or the stars. Others were represented by animals.
- *There were stories about the gods.* The peoples explained their world by telling these stories, usually vivid poetic descriptions of battles and sexual exploits. Most peoples had stories about the gods creating the world and the beginnings of their particular kings, cities and ancestors. Several had stories of a great flood.
- *Gods were worshipped in similar ways.* The different gods took different forms and were represented by images. They had priests and temples, and sacrifices were common. These could be animal sacrifices or libation offerings, but there is also evidence of human sacrifice. Then there were various

rites that served the gods and persuaded them to act in ways
beneficial to human beings. These included regular acting out
of the gods' stories, some of which included their sexual
exploits and therefore gave rise to cult prostitution.

- *There were religious experts.* There were people who knew the
  stories of the gods and what they required of the people.
  Then there were those who were qualified to carry out the
  rituals, to tell the future and to help people with everyday
  problems through magic practices. One person could
  combine all these roles.

In general, all peoples accepted the existence of many gods.
They worshipped only those considered to be the gods of their
group or place, and usually considered one god more important
than the others. However, they accepted that other peoples had
other gods, and acknowledged their power in their own spheres.

The peoples

Peoples who feature in the Old Testament came from three main areas.

Mesopotamia

This is the fertile land between the rivers Tigris and Euphrates. It
is the area from which Abraham came, and to which the Israelites
were taken in exile. Its peoples included:

- *Sumerians.* They settled in the south of Mesopotamia many
  years before the time of Abraham. They had myths about the
  creation of the world and of civilization, about human beings
  and their failure, and about a great flood. These are in the
  Sumerian and Akkadian languages. Sumerian society was
  organized mainly in villages grouped around cities to form
  city states, each of which would have a ruling council under
  a king who was the representative of the city's chief god.
- *Babylonians.* These were people associated with Babylon and
  the surrounding area. They included Sumerians and Semites.

Babylon varied in importance and in the area of its rule during the course of biblical history, but it was often a centre of power. For example, Hammurabi (also called Hammurapi), the king of Babylon from 1792 to 1750 BC, tried to unite the whole of Mesopotamia under his rule. He is famous for his laws, since a stone inscribed with 282 of his legal judgments was found in 1902.

The chief gods were Anu, the heaven god, Enlil, the air god and Ea, the god of wisdom. Under these were many other minor gods. However, the city of Babylon had its own god, Marduk (also called Merodach and later Bel), who was considered particularly powerful. He is mentioned in Isaiah 46:1 and Jeremiah 50:2.

- *Assyrians.* These were people from the area north of Babylonia, who originally came from different places. They gained power as far away as Lebanon and Phoenicia under the reign of Ashurnasirpal (883–859 BC, about the time of Ahab, king of Israel) and were a major political and military force until the rise of the Babylonians at the end of the seventh century.

  Their national god was Ashur, with his temple in the capital of Assur. The Assyrian king was considered his representative, and any conquered peoples were treated as his servants. Also important was Ishtar, the goddess of love and war, whose temple was in the other influential city, Nineveh. Nineveh had a great library, where many texts have been found. Some contain stories and discussions that are both similar to and different from those in the Bible.

Egypt

This was a very different civilization, with its economy based on the regularly flooding River Nile. Egypt interacted with peoples in Canaan during the whole of biblical history, and many Semites came to live among the Egyptians at different times. Egypt was ruled by a long succession of pharaohs, who made their capitals in different places. It had hundreds of gods, who were prominent in different places at different times. There were local gods, such as Ptah at Memphis and Amun at Thebes. There were nature gods such as Nut the sky goddess, Geb the earth god and Hati the Nile god. Several gods were represented by animals, or had animal heads. Egyptians were particularly concerned about what happened to them after death. They had elaborate funerals and graves, into which they put things that would help the person in the afterlife. They had stories about Osiris, the king of the dead.

One of the most prominent focuses of worship was the sun. There were several sun gods, or perhaps the sun god was given different names. Well known are Re and Amun. One pharaoh, Amenhotep IV (1379–1362 BC) worshipped the sun god Aton and forbade the worship of other gods. So devoted was he that he changed his name to Akhenaton, the servant of Aton.

Egyptian worship was different from the worship of the other peoples discussed in this chapter, in that temples were isolated and only priests were allowed inside them. It was only during festivals that the gods were brought out in procession. Otherwise, people had their own household gods or worshipped minor gods. The greater gods in the temples were treated rather as if they were human kings: they were awakened with hymns in the morning, washed and dressed, given morning, midday and evening offerings and then put to rest for the night.

Canaan

This is the 'Promised Land', where Israel settled. Its peoples included Aramaeans, Amorites, Moabites, Edomites, Nabataeans and Midianites inland, and Phoenicians and Philistines near the coast of the Mediterranean Sea. Much of what we know about their religions comes from texts discovered at the ancient city of Ugarit, on the coast of present-day Syria. They had many gods, which were worshipped in temples, some of which had similar layouts to Solomon's temple. They had animal sacrifices and libation offerings, and there is also evidence of human sacrifice. They also had a variety of rites to persuade the gods to give blessing.

El was the chief god, worshipped under different names. In Genesis, for example, we read that Melchizedek was priest of El-Elyon, usually translated 'God Most High' (14:18), and the Ugaritic texts speak of Elyon. Some scholars think that this was a separate god, and even that the various names of El found in the Bible originally referred to different gods; but most agree that these are different titles for the same god. The Ugaritic texts speak of El as creator, kindly, merciful, father of men, wise and ancient. He is described sitting as king at the confluence of two streams, giving a picture of majesty and omnipotence. Under him was a pantheon of gods, sometimes called 'sons of El'. He was often called 'bull'.

The god we read most about in the Bible was Baal, the storm god. The word 'baal' means 'master', but comes to mean the specific god Hadad. By the time of the exodus, he was by far the most important god in Canaan, perhaps because, as weather god, he was also the one who ensured fertility. He was the god of the thunder, and was represented as a warrior with a battleaxe or spear. His helmet was decorated with a bull's horns.

Other Canaanite gods mentioned in the Bible include Dagon, the father of Baal, Mot, the god of death, barrenness and sterility, and the three goddesses of sex and war: Asherah, consort of El, Astarte (Ashtaroth), the mother goddess, and Anat, consort of Baal.

An important story tells how Mot attacks Baal, destroys his powers and scatters his body. El leads the mourning for his dead son, but Anat fights. She attacks Mot, kills him and throws his body into a field, where the birds eat his remains. She then revives Baal, and his power is restored through sexual relations with her. Such a story reflects the pattern of rainfall and fertility in Canaan. As god of weather, Baal was alive to bring the crops in October to April, but seemed to die during the dry season in May to September. The story was acted out with temple prostitutes to ensure his 'revival' and therefore a good harvest every year.[1]

In what ways are the religions in your area like the religions of these different nations?

5

Beginnings: Genesis

Genesis is the book that tells us who we are, as human beings and as people groups. It also tells us what has gone wrong with the world, and how God begins his mission to all peoples. This chapter will be the longest in the book. This is partly because Genesis is an important foundation for all that follows; but it is also because I want to explore one book in some depth. I hope that this will offer the reader a model for deeper study of some of the passages referred to later.

Genesis 1 – 11: God the Creator of all peoples

Human beings and peoples

Genesis 1 – 11 introduces a world of peoples. It describes God creating human beings in his own image and putting them in a good land, the sin of the first human beings, the expulsion from Eden and the increase in human wickedness that leads to judgment in the flood. In Genesis 7 and 8 the land and its creatures disappear, and then emerge again, making a new world after the flood. This is our world: a world of human beings who are still wicked, yet to which God is unconditionally committed (8:21–22), and in which he promises blessing and requires justice (9:1–7).

The great fact about this world is the covenant of Genesis 9:8–17. It includes all peoples – in fact, it includes all living beings (vv. 12, 16) and the earth itself (v. 13). There is no exception at all. *The first thing the Bible teaches us about people of other faiths is that they are human beings, in God's land and under God's rainbow, just like us.* Part of the point of the flood story is to show that all peoples have one source: we all come from Noah. The three sections that follow underline this. In doing so, they give us an insight into the world of different peoples on which we are going to focus in our Bible study.

Noah and his sons (9:18–29). This tells us that, even though the peoples are all related to each other, there will be arguments and inequalities among them. Noah's drunkenness is followed by his son's sin, and leads to Noah cursing his own descendants. Even Noah, the one person righteous enough to escape the flood, can provoke the beginning of slavery, which has been one of the things that have most devalued the precious human beings God made!

The table of nations (10:1–32). This gives a more positive view of the peoples. It not only tells us that we are all descended from Noah: it is also organized to show us God's providence and care. It is in three parts: the descendants of Japheth, Ham and Shem. Each part has a similar shape, ending with a similar formula about clans, languages, territories and nations. The names are grouped in sevens and multiples of seven, and the total number of peoples is seventy.[1] Three, seven and seventy are all numbers of perfection and fullness. The whole chapter, then, tells us that this great variety of peoples, each with its own land and culture, is good, and part of God's creation.

The tower of Babel (11:1–9). This sees the division of the peoples as part of God's judgment. When everyone worked together, their sinfulness led them to work for themselves and against God. They wanted to stay together and to develop power for themselves in their own land (v. 4). God therefore confused their languages and scattered them. We see that the differences between peoples will be a barrier to communication and to cooperation. This is obviously true today, when people of different languages, cultures and faiths find it very difficult to understand each other, and we often think that this is a bad thing. In some ways, we are right: the lack of communication is a result of human sin. But there is another side: the division of the peoples is necessary to limit the effects of sin in our world.

Genesis 1 – 11, then, gives us a picture of the world in which we live, and into which God called Abraham. It tells us that *all peoples are made in God's image and are fallen, and that our differences can be both part of God's providence and the results of our sin.* These fundamental truths will underlie all our thinking about people of different faiths, as they underlie all the biblical writings from Genesis 12 to Revelation 22. In fact, Revelation often echoes Genesis 10 as it tells of the variety of peoples, first under God's judgment and in heaven, and then in the new heaven and earth, still with their different languages but now without their territories (Rev. 5:9; 7:9; 10:11; 11:9; 13:7; 14:6; 15:4; 17:15; 20:7; 21:24–26; 22:2).

When you look at the people of different faiths around you, what can you see (a) of the image of God and (b) of the results of the fall? Is this any different from what you can see in Christians in your area?

At first reading, the above is the basic teaching of Genesis 1 – 11 about people of different faiths. However, if we read again, in the context of the beliefs of the peoples surrounding Israel, we learn much more.

Genesis 1 – 11 and the stories from the nations

The chapters appear to tell us very little about the religions of the time. Chapter 10 mentions languages and territories, but not gods. The Babel story probably refers to a temple; but Genesis calls it a 'tower'. Only the obscure reference to the 'sons of God' in 6:2 suggests that anyone believed in any divine figures other than the one God.

Yet the peoples of Genesis 10 had many gods, and their own creation stories.[2] The different stories reflect the different environments in which they were written. For example, some of the Mesopotamians, who depended on rain from heaven to fall on earth, told of creatures being born through the marriage of heaven and earth gods, or through gods watering the ground with their semen. The Egyptians, on the other hand, depended on the yearly flooding of the Nile. As the flood went down, it left mounds of earth teeming with small animals. In Egyptian creation stories a god makes a mound, from which living beings emerge. This is then represented by the temple of the god.[3] In all cases the most powerful god in the story is the god of the particular people who tell the story. He usually has to fight against some kind of enemy.

Some of the most widely known stories were from Mesopotamia. Two of the most complete that we have concern Babylon. They are also the stories most similar to Genesis 1 – 11.

The Babylonian creation epic (Enuma Elish)
'When the heaven gods above were as yet uncreated, the earth gods below not yet brought into being, alone there existed primordial Apsu who engendered them, only Mummu and Tiamat who brought all of them forth.'[4]

Apsu, Mummu (his servant) and Tiamat (his wife) are seas. They mingle to give birth to various nature gods, such as silt, horizon, sky and earth. The latter, Ea, is the most powerful. The new gods anger their parents by making a lot of noise, so Apsu and Mummu plan to destroy them, while Tiamat defends her children. Ea kills Apsu and Mummu, and the gods are preserved. Then things change. Some gods rebel, and persuade Tiamat to fight the gods in revenge for the death of Apsu. Tiamat gathers an army of rebel gods and other creatures, and chooses Kingu as her husband. The battle begins, but even Ea and his brother Anu have no power against Tiamat.

Enter a new champion: Marduk son of Ea. He agrees to fight Tiamat, on condition that the gods make him King. They agree, and he is given supreme authority and defeats Tiamat and her army. Marduk then slices Tiamat's body in two, and makes heaven and earth. Heaven is made from the top half of the body, and in it Marduk makes paths for the heaven gods to follow. Earth is made from the bottom half of the body, with the Tigris and Euphrates flowing out of the eyes.

The gods then plan to build Marduk a house in Babylon. They realize that this is going to involve them in a lot of work, not only in building the house but also, for the lesser gods, in future service of the greater gods. Marduk's solution is to make another creature to serve, so that the gods can rest. So Kingu is killed and human beings are made from his blood. The gods then build Marduk's temple and the city of Babylon as a home for both gods and human beings. The story finishes with the enthronement of Marduk in Babylon.

The Babylonian flood story (from The Epic of Gilgamesh)

This story is told to the hero Gilgamesh, who is two-thirds god and one-third man and is seeking immortality. He crosses the Waters of Death and meets Utnapishti, the only mortal who has ever attained everlasting life, and who tells his story to show that immortality can be given only by the gods.

The gods, advised by Enlil, the chief god, decide to send a flood, but Ea, the goddess of wisdom, warns King Utnapishti to leave his home and build a boat. He follows their instructions, and builds a vessel – details are given of its design and construction. Into it he loads his wealth, all the different kinds of living creatures, his family, domestic beasts and craftsmen. Shamash the sun god tells him when to go into the boat and close the door. The gods of storm and rivers open their waters, and vivid details are given of storms and floods. Even the gods are afraid. The storm lasts for six days, and the boat is then caught on the top of a mountain. After another seven days, Utnapishti sends out a dove, which returns to him. He sends a swallow, which also returns, and then a raven, which does not come back.

Utnapishti then pours out a libation offering, scatters a food offering on the ground and burns incense. The gods smell the offerings, and 'gather like flies'. Ea announces that Enlil will be barred from the offering that Utnapishti has prepared, because he wanted to destroy the human beings. Enlil then arrives, and is furious to find that one human has survived. Ea explains that Enlil was wrong to send the flood because it destroyed people indiscriminately rather than those who deserved it, and that she had therefore warned Utnapishti. Enlil then takes Utnapishti and his wife back on to the boat and makes them gods, so that they will never die.

These stories have some similarities with Genesis, and the book of Genesis reached its final shape after the *Enuma Elish*. Some scholars therefore suppose that the Genesis stories were derived from the Sumerian stories. Some point out that it could be the other way round: the stories in Genesis are obviously much older than Genesis itself, so the Sumerian stories could be based on the Genesis stories. It is also possible that all the stories are based on other stories that have been lost, or that they grew up independently in an area where people shared similar experiences. It is difficult to date the various stories, so it is impossible to say which of these possibilities is true.

If we believe that Genesis was written under the guidance of the Holy Spirit, and that God was revealing himself to humans, we might want to ask a different question. It is likely that the Genesis writer knew the other creation stories, and certainly God knew them. The key question is then how the Babylonian stories help us to understand what God is saying to us in Genesis.

What can we learn from the similarities between Genesis and the other stories?
The stories have similar literary forms, so we can suppose that

they have similar purposes. Clearly, these are not the same purposes as the creation stories of current physical or biological science. They are not interested in the physical development of matter or in the chemical basis of life. They do not even distinguish between 'natural' and 'supernatural' or between 'physical', 'psychological' and 'spiritual'.

Rather, these stories are interested in the wills of those involved in the creation. They offer an understanding of land and of crops and of seasons, and an account of human beings and where they fit in. The end point of all the creation stories is a particular human society, in a particular place, organized for the service of the gods. Much attention is usually given to the temple building that symbolizes all of this.

If we read Genesis 1 – 11 as having similar concerns, we see the following:

- There is only one will that matters in the creation of the world: the one God.
- There are anti-God and anti-human forces, but the one God does not have to fight them: he can control them by a word.
- The cycle of seasons is under his control. There is no need for human beings to persuade him to keep on acting: he has promised to do so.
- Although the end of Genesis 11 introduces Abraham, the people of Israel are until then only incidentally included in the creation story. The society that is the result of the creation process is not a particular people in a particular land, but all peoples, in all lands.
- The building story is not of a temple for God in Jerusalem, but of a tower against God elsewhere.
- The service that is the result of the story is not the worship of a particular God in a particular place: rather, the one God commits himself to the service of humankind.

In summary, while the *Enuma Elish*, like other ancient stories, exalts the chief god of a particular place and people, Genesis exalts Yahweh as the only creator of the whole universe and of all peoples.

What creation stories do people in your area tell? What is the purpose of these stories?

What can we learn from the differences between the stories?
Genesis discounts the other gods. Perhaps the most striking thing about Genesis compared to the other stories is what it leaves out: it has no gods except the one.[5] Many of the gods of the surrounding peoples, their symbols and the things they contol are all under this one God. The sun, the moon, the stars and all the creatures are his, and he is in control of weather, fertility and land.

Genesis gives a different view of the purpose of human beings. The one God does not need servants. Human beings are not created to solve a problem for him, but to be, in some ways, like him, and to receive his blessings. The jobs they are given are also the blessings: that they should have responsibility within creation, and increase in number.

Genesis recognizes anti-God powers. The other stories recount the battles of the gods, but the one God of Genesis has no need to fight. The darkness and the sea and the sea monsters are all there, but they are entirely under God's contol. They are all created by his word, and declared good. In the flood story the destructive power of the waters is recognized, but it can only take effect at God's command and for his purposes. The one same God sends the waters back to their place, and promises to keep them there.

But there is one creature that can effectively fight against God: the human being.[6] Because we are made like God, we can endanger his creation. God has to act to limit the evil we can do. That is why we are locked out of the Garden of Eden, our lifespan is limited (6:3) and our languages are confused (11:1–11). The good news is that God is not only supreme over this potential anti-God force: he is also committed to love us and to give us what we need. This is the message of the covenant with Noah.

God's judgments are for different reasons. In the Gilgamesh flood story, no reason is given for the flood: other flood stories tell us that the humans annoyed the gods by being too noisy. In Genesis, the problem damaging creation is moral wickedness. God does not respond out of annoyance, but out of grief and anger. *This emphasis on God's justice and human sin is unique to Genesis.* Other stories have the world starting from a poor situation and getting better, but Genesis has it created good and damaged through human sin. The contrast between Noah and Utnapishti is interesting here: Utnapishti is a king and a hero, and is finally rewarded with immortality. Noah is just an ordinary person, of whom we learn very little except that he obeyed God. His story ends with his getting drunk, cursing his son and dying.

What do we learn about religion?
Although Genesis 1 – 11 does not discuss the religions of its time, we can learn quite a lot about human religion from it.

Humans need a way to God. Genesis 1 – 3 shows that humans were originally in a healthy relationship with God and creation, and that sin separated them from his presence. This is shown by the cherubim with the fiery sword that guard the way back into Eden. People clearly need a way back, but it will be different from the way they left.

Sacrifice is one way. Three people in Genesis 1 – 11 are said to be righteous: Abel, Enoch and Noah. Two of these offered sacrifices accepted by God. Readers of the Cain and Abel story often ask, with Cain, why his sacrifice was rejected. We are not told, although we know that Cain could have offered an acceptable sacrifice had he done what was right (4:6). Not just any sacrifice will please God, but any person has, it seems, the possibility of offering right sacrifices.

Perhaps the more interesting question is, then, What made Abel's and Noah's sacrifices acceptable? For Abel, we are told that

God did not only accept his sacrifice: he also accepted him. For Noah, the sacrifice was the occasion, and perhaps the reason, for God's covenant with all living creatures. In fact, it seems to be the only reason for that covenant, since God knew that humans would be just as wicked after the flood as before it. If we want God to accept us, we need to know what an acceptable sacrifice is. Genesis 1 – 11 shows that sacrifice is a possible way to please God and that not all sacrifices are acceptable, but it does not explain the mystery.

One thing is clear: God does not need our sacrifices. The Babylonian gods gather round Utnapishti's sacrifice because they are hungry, and it is the human's job to feed them. Genesis says only that the aroma pleased God. God gives Noah and his descendants meat for food: they do not have to feed him (9:1–3).

Religion can cause violence. Because his religious practice – his sacrifice – was rejected, Cain killed his brother. Rather than listening to God, he took revenge on the person whose sacrifice was accepted. The first murder, then, was due to a religious argument.

Babylonian religion is criticized. This can be seen most strongly in the story of Babel. We can compare it to the story of the building of Marduk's temple in Babylon at the end of the Babylonian Creation Epic. While the Babylonians explained the name 'Babel' as 'Door of God', Genesis explains it as 'mixed up, confused'. The story shows the smallness of humans, and the disastrous result of their using religion to claim a place as their own and to make themselves great. It also implies the smallness of Marduk's temple in relation to the one true God. The temple was not, says Genesis, built by the gods with special materials, but by humans with home-made bricks rather than good strong stone. The climax of the story is not Marduk taking up residence in his temple and the praise of his glorious names: it is the one true God coming down to confuse the people. For he sees that the worship of Marduk is, in fact, the worship of the people's own power and interest.

We can make two fundamental religious mistakes. The first is thinking we can become the same as God. God has made us in his image, but we are also different from him, and it is wrong to try to blur the distinction between creature and Creator. This was the serpent's temptation: he told Eve that she would become like God. She and Adam tried to become like God through knowledge. In a different way, there seems to have been a blurring of the distinction between human and divine in the strange marriages of the 'sons of God' and the 'daughters of men' in Genesis 6. Both of these errors had to be severely dealt with.

The second is the opposite mistake: thinking that God is far away and that we can find a way of reaching him. This can be seen in the story of Babel. People thought that God was up in heaven, and that they could build a tower to reach him. They were wrong in two ways. First, they did not realize how high God was – the story pictures him as so high that he could not even see their wonderful tower. Second, they did not realize that God could come down to be among them. They thought that they had to try to reach him.

Genesis offers two pictures of true faith – rest and walking. The other creation stories often give the origins of religious practices and festivals. For example, a yearly festival might involve acting out a story about the coming of rain or crops, in order to ensure a good harvest. In contrast, Genesis 1 – 11 gives the origin of only one religious tradition: the Sabbath. This is not acting out a story to persuade a god to work, but a day of blessing and holiness that recognizes that creation is complete. Because of God's total control, he can rest, and we can also rest. We worship by recognizing that his work is done: rituals and magic are unnecessary.

Genesis 1 – 11 offers another picture of how human beings can relate to God. We are not to try to be like him or climb up to him: rather, God who is different from us chooses to 'come down' to us. We see this in 3:8, in the beautiful picture of God walking in the garden. What is required of us is that we respond by walking with him. Sadly, Adam and Eve were too ashamed and afraid to do this. But Enoch and Noah, two of the three righteous people in Genesis 1 – 11, did respond – they 'walked with him' (5:24; 6:9).

This is Genesis' simple picture of faith. There are no stories of gods, no myths to be acted out, no temples, and no link between gods and peoples or gods and kings. Rather, there is the one God who made all. This one God is not a myth or an idea, but is a real being who has created humans in his own image, and who is able to communicate with them and to come to them. The problem is that humans have rebelled against him, and have created many gods in their images, so that they no longer recognize his moral nature nor wish to meet him. It is into this world, and for the sake of all these human beings with their clans, languages, territories and nations that this real God speaks and acts as he calls Abraham.

How do these ideas about religion help you to understand the religions in your area?

What can we learn about communication?

The Babylonian and Canaanite stories have a very different view of the world than the Bible has. So we might expect the people of Israel to tell very different stories, and to tell them differently. Yet the Genesis writer tells a similar story, similarly. This is, of course, partly because he is telling the story of events that all peoples knew of, such as the flood. But it is also because he shares some of the culture and ways of thinking of the other nations, and God spoke to people through the Genesis writer in terms they would understand.[7]

The writer expressed himself in a way normal to him, and this was how God chose to reveal himself. Into the ancient Near East, God did not send a Greek philosophical lecture, a medieval theological tract, nor a twentieth-century scientific paper, but a creation story. As we have seen, this not only addresses his readers using their own thought forms, but also deals with their urgent concerns.

At the same time, it challenges those who believe the other stories. Some scholars go so far as to describe Genesis 1 – 11 as a 'polemic tract', saying clearly, 'Your gods are no gods. They are creations of the one God, who is also your judge.'

Whatever the historical relationship between the Genesis stories and those of the surrounding nations, we can see the writer of Genesis using

- *familiar literary forms to express ideas* – people would enjoy the language and rhythms of the stories;
- *stories to challenge stories* – anyone could see that the Babel story mocked the story of Marduk's temple;
- *images people would understand* – everyone knew that there were stories about gods battling with waters, so they would immediately see the implications of God's control of the flood;
- *appropriate thought categories* – people would understand the story of the serpent and the fall much better than any abstract discussion of temptation and sin.

Think again about the creation stories people in your area tell. How could you use Genesis 1 – 11 to communicate with them?

For further study.   Hosea uses the imagery of Baal religion to communicate his message.

- Read Hosea, looking out for ideas associated with Baal: fertility, rain, storms, crops etc. Notice how these are used to show that Yahweh is Lord of all.
- An important aspect of Baal was his relationship with his wife, Anat. To ensure a good harvest, Baal worshippers would act this out through intercourse with temple prostitutes.
    - What evidence can you find of this sort of practice in Israel?
    - How does the story of Hosea's wife use the Baal imagery to correct Israel?

Genesis 12 – 50: God calls a family

Why Abraham?
Genesis 1 – 11 tells us about the world of nations: Genesis 12 – 50 tells us about God's mission to that world. It starts with God's command to Abraham to leave his land and his people to go to a new land, and goes on to some of the most important verses in the Bible.

> I will make you into a great nation
>   and I will bless you;
> I will make your name great,
>   and you will be a blessing.
> I will bless those who bless you,
>   and whoever curses you I will curse,
> and all peoples on earth
>   will be blessed through you.
>   (Genesis 12:2–3)

Paul calls the last statement 'the gospel announced in advance' (Gal. 3:8). God's covenant to bless Abraham and his family is not for their own comfort, but for the blessing of all the mixed up, sinful peoples descended from Noah. Abraham is reminded of this after the binding of Isaac (22:18), Jacob is given the same message at Bethel (28:14), and right at the end of Genesis Joseph recognizes that all that has happened to him has been for 'the saving of many lives' (50:20). The Bible is about God's plan to bless the nations. His method is one man and his family.

Other nations have stories of gods choosing their ancestors and kings, but there is nothing similar to this story of God's call of an ordinary person and his family. This means that we cannot compare Genesis 12 – 50 with other stories, as we did Genesis 1 – 11. Instead, we shall read it in the context of what we know about the other nations.

Abraham among the nations

The peoples to be blessed through Abraham were religious. Abraham was brought up among the Mesopotamian religions, and he and his family also lived in Canaan and Egypt. In Abraham we see God calling someone out of a religious family, and starting his mission to a multi-religious world. What can we learn about this world and God's mission to it?

Perhaps the most striking thing is that the different religions are not discussed at all. The Qur'anic story of Abraham has him as a champion of the one God fighting polytheism: he turns away from the worship of sun, moon and stars, preaches against idolatry, and destroys his father's idols (Qur'an 6:74–82; 21:51–71). Jewish commentaries tell similar stories. Reading it, we wonder why the biblical story of Abraham begins with no mention of the religion of his family. It simply tells us where he lived, that God spoke to him and that he obeyed.

Genesis tells us that it was Yahweh who called Abraham, but who did Abraham think it was? The people of Ur, Haran and Canaan had many gods. From the names of Abraham's family, it seems likely that his ancestors worshipped a moon god. But the chief god was El, and this is the name for God most often used in Genesis.

Wenham has analysed the names used for God in Genesis,[8] and showed that El is most often used in speeches, while Yahweh is most often used in the narration of the story. Where Yahweh is used in speech, it is sometimes added to El, and otherwise seems to be used for a specific purpose. For example, 15:7 has God saying, 'I am Yahweh, who brought you out of Ur of the Chaldees'. This echoes the 'I am Yahweh, who brought you out of Egypt' found in many other places in the Pentateuch. Wenham considers all this in the light of Exodus 6:3, where God says to Moses, 'I appeared to Abraham, to Isaac and to Jacob as God Almighty (El-Shaddai), but by my name the LORD I did not make myself known to them.'

Putting all the evidence together, it seems that *Abraham was thinking in terms of El, the god he already knew about, but that it was Yahweh who was calling him all the time.*

How did Abraham respond to God? At first, he simply obeyed, but after he reached Canaan he wanted to worship. We could say that he wanted to make a religious response. God had not told him to do anything religious or given him any instructions about rituals, so he did what he already knew: he built altars and 'called on the name of the Lord'. From Genesis alone, we could not guess what sorts of altars he built, why he built them, or how he worshipped.[9] Genesis later describes him as making vows, offering sacrifices and libations, giving tithes, praying, and cleansing himself. These were all common practices in the worship of El and of other gods. In all this, Abraham was responding to the God who had called him in the ways that were already used in his culture.

But there were ways in which Abraham's worship was different:

- He built his own altars, rather than worshipping at established places. For example, he built an altar near Bethel, but not at Bethel (12:8).
- One aspect of El worship was ruled out spectacularly: human sacrifice. This is clear from the account of the binding of Isaac in Genesis 22.

As his relationship with God grew, Abraham slowly learned how God was like El, but also how he was different from him.

These patterns continue throughout Genesis. Apart from circumcision, God gives Abraham and his family no religious rules. He speaks to them, works for them, encourages them and loves them. They respond, sometimes in faith and obedience, and sometimes in doubt and sin. It is these life responses that are important, but we also see people responding in the normal patterns of human religion. Only slowly does the religion become different from that of the surrounding nations, and it does not really reflect the difference of Yahweh until the time of Moses. What is important in Genesis is not religion, but God's covenant call to a particular family.

Did God call you to religion or to a covenant relationship? If a Hindu, Muslim or a traditional African believer comes to Christ, what sort of religious practice should he or she follow?

El and Abraham's God
To begin with, God does not seem to have told Abraham who he was, or anything about himself. However, he did promise land, blessings and children, and we know that these were things El was believed to give. El was also said to be wise, kind and merciful; and

he was the creator of everything. It is therefore unsurprising that Abraham recognizes Melchizedek's god, El-Elyon – El Most High, Creator of heaven and earth – as his God (14:18ff). God also introduces himself as El-Shaddai – El Almighty (17:1). Some scholars think that this was another name used by the Canaanites. Shaddai is used as a title for God several times in Genesis, and is linked with the idea of God's faithfulness in keeping the promise of descendants.

Abraham, and his descendants after him, learnt that their God would actually do the good things El was said to do. We can see this most clearly in Genesis 22. Even as Abraham thinks that God wants him to kill his own son, he is sure that God will keep his promise. And it is so: not only does he find that God is different from El – he does not require human sacrifice – he also has it confirmed that God acts in his world and can be trusted to keep his promises. The altar he builds is called 'The Lord will provide' (22:14).

Abraham's lessons about God can be summed up in one word: *covenant.* The parallels between God's covenant with Abraham and the treaties between kings or between a great king and a conquered people are well known.[10] Genesis 15 describes a covenant ceremony, but one with a difference:

- It is not between a conquering king and his vassal, but between God and a human family.
- This God is living and awesome.
- He requires nothing of Abraham: instead, he makes an unconditional promise. It is much later, in chapter 17, that he tells Abraham his part of the covenant. This is circumcision, which marks Abraham's family as belonging to God.

Abraham learnt, then, that God was his king, and that he and his family belonged to him and must be loyal to him. But, before that, he learnt that God was the one who took the initiative, and would always keep his promises. He learnt, too, that the covenant was not only for his relations but also for his whole household, including foreign slaves (17:12–13).

Isaac, Jacob and Jacob's sons all had to learn the same lessons. The God of their father was also their God. Unlike El and the other gods, he had *not* given a set of laws to keep. He had *not* given any rituals for worship. He had *not* even said what was 'clean' and 'unclean'. He had called them as individuals and as a family. He would keep his covenant and fulfil his purpose through them, no matter how long it took them to learn their lessons of faith and obedience.

Which of the laws and religious practices of your church were given by God?

What about the other nations?

Abraham and his family lived among other nations, and they were called for the blessing of those nations. What do we see of the nations in Genesis 12 – 50?

Other nations than Israel are Abraham's descendants

Abraham's descendants are not only from Isaac and Jacob. They also include the children of Keturah and other concubines, and Ishmael and Esau and their children. There is also Lot, who was Abraham's ward for a time.

Of Keturah and her children we know nothing but their names (Gen. 25:1–4). Some seem to be ancestors of tribal groups that are little mentioned in the Old Testament. Only Midian becomes significant: sometimes, the Midianites are friends of Israel, like Jethro, Moses' father-in-law, who apparently worshipped God. At other times, they are enemies (e.g. Num. 31:1–12; Judg. 7 – 8).

The descendants of Lot, Ishmael and Esau would turn to other gods, and some would become some of Israel's greatest enemies. Genesis tells us only of their sad origins.

- The Moabites and Ammonites resulted from Lot's neglect of his daughters, and then from drunkenness and incest (19:30–38). The Moabites seduced Israel into worshipping their gods (Num. 25). They and the Ammonites were considered such a danger to Israel's worship that they were excluded from the tabernacle (Deut. 23:3), and they often appear as Israel's enemies.

- Ishmael was born as a result of Abraham and Sarah's difficulty in believing God's promise. He was then separated from Abraham's family because of jealousy. As Genesis 25:18 warns, there would be hostility between the Ishmaelites and Israel.

- Perhaps the saddest split in Abraham's family is that between Jacob and Esau. Genesis 33:16–17 tells of Jacob deciding to live apart from Esau, and 36:6–8 of Esau separating his family from Jacob. The rivalry between the brothers that was rooted in the favouritism of their parents was never really overcome, despite the reconciliation of chapter 33. Esau's descendants, the Edomites, are portrayed as Israel's enemies in many places in the Old Testament (e.g. Num. 20:14–21; 1 Sam. 14:47; 1 Kgs 11:14–22; Ps. 137:7). Like the Moabites, they worshipped gods other than Yahweh, and on at least one occasion the Israelites turned to these gods (2 Chron. 25:14–20).

Why is some of the worst rivalry between the peoples who are most closely related?

Relationships with people outside Abraham's family
If God keeps his covenant with Abraham, we can expect him also to keep his promise to bless all peoples through him. What do we see of this in Genesis 12 – 50?

Abraham does not seem to have been very concerned about blessing others. He lies to Abimelech and to the king of Egypt, and is therefore the cause of God's judgment on them. Far from wanting to relate closely to those around him, he insists on finding his son a wife from his home area. He does not even take good care of Hagar, a foreigner who lives in his own household. He does intercede for Sodom and Gomorrah, but we wonder whether that was only because his own nephew was there. Isaac and Jacob seem to have had no more concern for other peoples; and the story of Jacob's sons' treatment of the Shechemites (Gen. 34) is one of the ugliest in the Bible.

But, if we read carefully, we can see God's concern for the peoples, and their recognition of him. Foreigners are included in the covenant with Abraham's family (17:12), and we see God caring for and speaking to people outside the covenant.

- God spoke to Abimelech, king of Gerar (Gen. 20:6–7). Abimelech simply accepted this – it does not seem unusual that God should speak to him and he respond. This not only shows that someone outside the covenant could hear God: it also shows God rescuing Abimelech from the mess into which Abraham had got him through lying about Sarah. God also rescues the king of Egypt in 12:10–20, and then rescues (presumably) another Abimelech when Isaac lies about Rebekah in 26:1–11. The foreign kings act better than Abraham and Isaac in these stories.
- Later, Abimelech approached Abraham, and asked for a treaty with him. This was because he recognized God's presence with Abraham (21:22ff.).
- Melchizedek was a priest of El-Shaddai. Genesis assumes that he worshipped the same god as Abraham, that he was an apt recipient of tithes, and that he could bless Abraham (14:18–20).
- God's concern for the Egyptian slave Hagar and her son is important. They were part of Abraham's household, and were therefore included in the covenant, but they were not treated well. God spoke specially to Hagar, and she acknowledged him as 'the God who sees me' (16:13–14). It is also clear that God has purposes for Ishmael as well as for Isaac (16:10–12; 21:18).
- We see God's concern for the other women who married into Abraham's family. These include not only his relations Rebekah, Leah and Rachel, but also the Canaanite girl

Tamar. Judah neglects her, and we find the ugly story of her luring him into sleeping with her; but God brings her the blessing of twins, one of whom becomes the ancestor of David and therefore of Jesus (Gen. 38:29–30; Matt. 1:3).

- Perhaps the most significant story here is that of Joseph. The good that results from his being sold as a slave is not only for his family: it is also for the whole Egyptian people and those surrounding them (Gen. 41:57). It is through him that they survive the years of famine. The household of Potiphar (39:5) and the people in the pharaoh's prison (39:21–23) are also blessed. It seems that the presence of one of God's people brings with it the presence of God, and therefore his blessing.

God spoke to people outside Abraham's family. Does he speak to non-Christians today?

What about other gods?

How, we wonder, did Joseph relate to the religion of Egypt? How did he manage to be faithful to God among people who worshipped other gods? As with Abraham and the gods of Canaan, Genesis is strangely silent. Joseph became so much part of Egyptian culture that his brothers did not recognize him. He spoke the Egyptian language and wore Egyptian clothes, and even married the daughter of one of the local priests (41:45, 50); none of this seems to have been a problem. He was able to continue worshipping God, and to tell the Egyptians that his abilities came from God (40:10; 41:16; 25 – 32). The Egyptians were also able to acknowledge this (39:3; 41:38–39). Eventually, Pharaoh also received blessing from Jacob (47:10).

The only mentions of other gods in Genesis come in the story of Jacob.

Laban's household gods (31:19, 30–35) were probably small figures made of clay or stone. They might have been family gods that were like title deeds, representing the family's inheritance.[11] Another possibility is that they were female figures, which were thought to give fertility and help in pregnancy and childbirth. Whatever they were, Genesis does not treat them seriously. These 'gods' can be stolen, or hidden under a menstruating, and therefore unclean, woman. If they were the very figures supposed to help women in producing children, the picture of Rachel sitting on them is funny. The true, living God is the one who gives children, but Rachel had to wait a long time, and had only one son (29:31 – 30:24). Now here she is, sitting on the very 'gods' she hopes will enable her to bear another child – and they cannot even tell Laban where they are!

Worship at Bethel (35:1–7). When God met him at Bethel when he was fleeing from Esau, Jacob swore to return and worship if God took care of him (Gen. 28:20–22). God did what Jacob asked, but Jacob did not go to Bethel when he returned to Canaan. He settled many miles away in Succoth. He did build an altar there (33:20), but it seems that this was not enough. In chapter 35:1 God spoke to him and told him to go and live in Bethel, and to build an altar there. Jacob obeyed, and here we find the reference to other gods. He ordered his whole household to get rid of any foreign gods, and also to purify themselves and wear clean clothes.

If we read this in the light of the rest of the Pentateuch, it is unsurprising: we know that no other gods were permitted where Yahweh was worshipped, and that there were strict rules about ritual purity. Even burying earrings (v. 4) makes sense when we remember that these were made into the golden calf (Exod. 32:2–4). However, this is the only time in Genesis where such things are mentioned. It is also the only time when God commands the building of an altar.

What are we to understand from this? Wenham points out that we need to understand it as following on from chapter 34: the rape of Dinah and the massacre of the Shechemites, an ugly tale, in which no-one acts rightly.[12] Were the 'foreign gods' and the earrings booty from Shechem? Was this worship at Bethel in part to purify the family from the terrible thing it had done? Certainly, Jacob was right in thinking that his sons' actions had made him a 'stench' to the Canaanites (34:30), which meant that the journey to Bethel was dangerous. Perhaps we can see God's command to go to Bethel as Jacob's test of faith, parallel to Abraham's test in chapter 22, or as a call parallel to Abraham's call in 12:1. The danger and the distance meant that obedience was not easy. Yet here, after so many failures by Jacob, God gives him the chance simply to obey: to fulfil his vow and therefore to acknowledge that the Lord is his God.

This, then, is the context for 'getting rid of foreign gods' (35:2). It seems that Abraham and Isaac never needed to get rid of foreign gods, because they accepted the Lord as their God from the beginning. Jacob knew all about his father's God. He had actually met him at Peniel (32:22–32), and his limp must have reminded him of it every day. But, it seems, only at this late stage did he eventually accept this God as his only god, and therefore realize he had to get rid of other gods.[13]

Summary
Genesis 12 – 50 tells the story of God's call to a particular family, but offers no direct discussion of the religions surrounding them. In fact, if we did not know something about those religions, we would scarcely learn anything about them from Genesis. What are we to make of this? Here are some suggestions:

- The other gods are not important. What matters is that the one true living God is active among the people he has made. Like the household gods who could be hidden by being sat on by a menstruating woman, the other gods are nonentities.
- Forms of worship are not yet important. Worship is expected as a response to God, but, within certain boundaries, it is acceptable in the familiar form of the culture to which the patriarchs belong.
- Other aspects of religion, like laws and ritual purity, are also not yet important. What does matter is trust in God and obedience to his specific commands.

In calling out a people from polytheism, then, God did not give a religion. The way to blessing for a multifaith world was not a religion, but a family called to dynamic relationship with the living God.

Paul goes to the story of Abraham when he is discussing how non-Jews – people from another faith background – can be included in the church (Gal. 3). What can you learn from the story of Abraham about mission to a community that already has a different religion? How does this beginning of God's mission to the nations compare to the beginnings of Christian mission in your country?

6

DEVELOPMENT: THE CALLING OF A PEOPLE

God's plan for blessing the nations was not only an individual and his family but a whole people in a land (Gen. 12:1–3). By the end of Genesis, Abraham's family has grown, but is not yet a nation; it owns only one field (Gen. 23), and is away from the Promised Land. This chapter explores how God developed the family into his special nation among nations that worshipped other gods.

As we shall see, Israel's job was to show the nations their God: the one creator God of Genesis, who later revealed himself to Moses as Yahweh (Exod. 3:14). The name Yahweh is derived from the verb to be, and is translated as 'I am who I am' or 'I will be who I will be'. This is a god who will not let human beings define him. He is. He really exists. He is not the embodiment of a nation nor of some aspect of the weather or the universe. He is not limited to any people nor any place. He is not a philosophical idea nor a theological concept. He is not what anyone imagines him to be. He is, quite simply, the only real God who actually exists, regardless of what anyone thinks about him.

Israel had to go through a long process to learn who Yahweh was and what was involved in being his special people. It was hard for her to understand that Yahweh's choice of her did not mean that she was his favourite. Rather, she was chosen by the one God of all peoples for the sake of all peoples. She was one of many similar nations created by God, and so shared the human characteristics of all nations; but she was also different.

A nation like other nations

We can see how Israel was like other nations from their writings. Even the contents pages of such collections as J. B. Pritchard's *Ancient Near Eastern Texts Relating to the Old Testament* (Princeton University Press, 1950) and W. Beyerlin's *Near Eastern Texts Relating to the Old Testament* (SCM, 1978) show that the peoples surrounding Israel had literature parallel to nearly all of Israel's literature.

Stories. We have already considered some of these that seem similar to biblical stories. There are many shared images. For example, we have noted the stories of gods fighting the primeval waters: the Old Testament has frequent reference to God's control of waters, not least in the parting of the sea during the Exodus (Exod. 14) and of the Jordan during the occupation of Canaan (Josh. 3).

Legal texts. Some peoples had lists of laws similar to those in the Pentateuch. For example, the laws of Hammurabi are remarkably similar in form to the biblical laws, and often deal with similar concerns. Here are some examples:

195. If a son has struck his father, they shall cut off his hand.
209. If a seignior has struck a seignior's daughter and caused her to have a miscarriage, he shall pay ten sheckels of silver.
246. If a seignior hired an ox and has broken its foot or cut its neck tendon, he shall make good ox for ox to the owner of the ox.[1]

Historical texts. There are inscriptions and documents that tell of the military exploits of kings under the guidance of the gods. Some include details of building temples and palaces. Others include oracles given to kings, and prophecies about the future.

Lamentations over the destruction of cities, similar to those in
Lamentations and other biblical prophetic books, can also be found.

Descriptions of rituals, incantations and festivals. These include
charms, curses, rituals for specific events and dramatic perfor-
mances of stories of gods, but there are also details of sacrifices
and purification rites. For example, here are instructions about
offerings to some of the Akkadian gods:

> Every day throughout the year, ten fat, clean rams, whose horns and
> hooves are whole, shall be sacrificed in the . . . to the deities Anu and
> Antu of heaven, to the planets Jupiter, Venus, Mercury, Saturn and Mars,
> to the sunrise and to the appearance of the moon. On the sixteenth day
> of each month, ten first-class, fat, clean rams, whose horns and hooves
> are whole, shall – after the sacrificer's hands have been cleaned – be
> offered boiled to the deities.[2]

And here is part of a Hittite purification ritual:

> As a substitute for the king he hands over one ox, and as a substitute for
> the queen's implements he hands over one cow, one ewe and one goat.
> While this is being done, she speaks as follows: 'With whatever evil word,
> oath, curse and uncleanness the god was afflicted, let the substitutes
> carry them away from the god! Let god and sacrificer be free of that
> matter!'[3]

Wisdom literature. This addresses many of the same concerns as
does Israel's wisdom literature. There are proverbs to instruct
both children and kings, poems about innocent suffering, reflections on the futility of life, and love poems. Some of the proverbs
are almost exactly the same as those in the Bible. One of the best-
known examples is the Egyptian *Instruction of Amen-em-opet*,
which, like Proverbs 22:17 – 24:22, is arranged in thirty wise
sayings. Here are some extracts:

> First chapter: Give thy ears, hear what is said, give thy heart to

understand them. To put them in thy heart is worthwhile, but it is damaging to him who neglects them. Let them rest in the casket of thy belly, that they may be the key to thy heart . . . [cf. Prov. 22:17–21]

Second chapter: Guard thyself against robbing the oppressed and against overbearing the disabled. Stretch not forth thy hand against the approach of an old man, nor steal away the speech of the aged . . . [cf. Prov. 17:22–3]

Sixth chapter: Do not carry off the landmark at the boundaries of arable land, nor disturb the position of the measuring cord; be not greedy after a cubit of land, nor encroach upon the boundaries of a widow . . . [cf. Prov. 22:28; 23:10–11][4]

Hymns and prayers. These are addressed to many different gods, but they show the same concerns for blessing, assistance and forgiveness that can be found in the Psalms. They often praise the gods in language quite similar to that of the Bible. An Egyptian prayer to the sun god Amun acknowledges him as the one who releases from oppression:

You, Amun, are the lord of the humble man, you come at the call of the poor.
   I call on you when I am oppressed, and you come quickly, to save me in my wretchedness . . .[5]

Another prayer sees Amun as shepherd:

Amun, shepherd, early in the morning you care for your flock and drive the hungry to pasture. The shepherd drives the cattle to the grass; Amun, you drive me, the hungry one, to food, for Amun is indeed a shepherd, a shepherd who is not idle.[6]

A Mesopotamian prayer to the goddess Ishtar longs for forgiveness:

I called to you, your wretched, exhausted, sorrowing servant.
Look upon me, O my mistress, hear my supplication,
look faithfully upon me, accept my prayer.
. . . Forgive my sin, my iniquity and my offence,
Overlook my transgression and accept my prayer.
Loose my fetters, secure my deliverance,
Guide my path aright, so that I can again go my way
among men radiantly like a great man.[7]

A Canaanite prayer to El calls for help:

Be gracious, O El! Be a support, O El! Be salvation, O El! O El, hasten,
come swiftly![8]

Israel had the same sorts of writings as the other nations had, which used the same sorts of imagery that the other nations used. Her people had the same sorts of concerns and feelings as other peoples had. This is unsurprising: the people of Israel were humans who lived at particular times and in particular places; and the surrounding nations were also humans, who lived in the same times and the same places. Scholars have found parallels to almost every aspect of the Old Testament in the records of the other nations,[9] and some therefore suggest that almost all of Israel's religion has its roots in other, earlier religions. That is, we can understand Israel's faith as that of one nation among many similar nations.

But the Old Testament is different
The Old Testament is also very different from the writings of the surrounding nations. An obvious difference is that it has been preserved and used throughout the centuries, while the other writings are only slowly being dug out of ruins. Why is this? I would argue that it is because, *although Israel was in so many ways like the nations surrounding her, Israel's God was not like their gods.* For all their likeness to Bible passages, a careful reading shows that the

other writings are built on different assumptions about God and humans. The world of the Old Testament text is, therefore, fundamentally different from the worlds of the other texts. This is often most clearly seen where Israel's writings are, apparently, most similar to those of the other nations. Important here are the laws, which determine people's culture, and the temple, which symbolizes the presence and power of a god in a particular place.

The laws of Hammurabi seem similar to Israel's laws, but their context is different. The Code begins with 300 lines in which King Hammurabi lists his own excellences and achievements. It ends with more claims from Hammurabi, including the claim that the laws were given to him by the god Shamash. There follows a short statement about the blessings of the god Shamash for the leader who keeps the laws, and then a long list of invocations of curses from various gods for those who do not keep them.

The historical introduction, the claim that the laws are god given, and the blessings and curses, all have parallels in the Pentateuch. But the biblical account of God's actions in exodus and covenant, the lack of kingship, and the details of the leaders' weaknesses as well as strengths, all contrast with Hammurabi. The balance of blessings and curses is different, as is the monotheism of the Bible compared to the fifteen gods mentioned by Hammurabi. All this shows that Israel's God is different from Hammurabi's gods. As we shall see below, the basis and content of Israel's laws are also different.

All the gods had temples, but Yahweh was different. We have seen that the Babylonian creation story has its climax in the building of Marduk's temple in Babylon. The story of Baal and Anath is based on Baal's need for a house, and human beings are created to assist in building and maintaining it. There are many inscriptions that record a king's building or rebuilding a temple for his god.

The biblical accounts of the tabernacle and the temple have much in common with these stories. They follow similar patterns, and even the detailed descriptions of materials, dimensions and furnishings have parallels elsewhere.[10] The difference in the Bible is not in the structure of the temple nor in the literary nature of the accounts: it is in the God to whom the temple belongs. Solomon's prayer of dedication in 1 Kings 8 makes this clear, especially when compared with other dedication prayers.

Please read 1 Kings 8 now.

First, *God does not live in his temple*. In other accounts, the climax of the story is the god, usually with his wife, entering the temple, usually when the statues are brought in. In 1 Kings 8 it is not God but his glory that comes into the temple (vv. 10–11), and Solomon recognizes the impossibility of confining God to a building (v. 27). The temple is the place where God chooses to have his name honoured (v. 29); but, for the previous centuries of Israel's history, he chose not to have such a place at all (v. 16). The tent with the ark of the covenant was sufficient.

Therefore, second, *God does not need a temple*. In the other accounts, the gods need houses, and the king who builds the temple can expect them to be grateful for the temple and the sacrifices. It is on these grounds that the kings can ask for the gods' blessings on themselves, their land and their people. Here, for example, is part of the dedication prayer of Nabonidus, the father of the biblical Belshazzar, after building Ebabarra, the temple to the sun god Shamash:

O Shamash, great lord of heaven and earth!
When you enter Ebabarra, your beloved house,
When you set up your eternal dais,
For me, Nabonidus, king of Babylon,
The prince who sustains you and gladdens you, and who builds your
    exalted cella –
Look happily on my good works.
Daily, when rising and setting, in heaven and on earth make my
    portents good.
Take my supplications, accept my prayer.

The staff and sceptre of justice which you placed in my hand, may I
    carry forever.[11]

Solomon shares the concern that his god should answer prayer
and establish his throne, but he knows that Yahweh has no need of
sustenance. His prayer is not, therefore, based on what he has
done for God, but on what God has done for Israel and for his
father. That is, *Solomon's prayer is based on God's covenants*.

*How does Solomon's prayer depend on the covenants with Abraham,
Moses and David? Look specially for mention of the other nations.*

Another difference is that *there is no image of Israel's God in the
temple*. This is emphasized in the account of the ark in Exodus
25 – 27. Other peoples had portable shrines, sometimes including
wooden boxes overlaid with gold. But Israel had no image of God.
Rather, her ark contained her covenant documents together with
some manna and Aaron's rod to symbolize God's faithfulness to
his people.

The ark also had cherubim on either side of its lid. These were
not just for decoration. Comparison with other portable shrines
suggests that the ark was similar to the thrones of other gods and
kings. Winged creatures formed parts of the throne, which was
carried on long poles. The king was seated on this throne, with his
feet on a footstool. Clearly, the ark symbolizes the throne of
Israel's God, and its cover – the 'mercy seat' or 'atonement cover' –
is his footstool. But the throne appears to be empty: this god has
no image. Rather, the invisible God is present with his people. The
ark symbolizes only his presence.

At the centre of the Exodus account of the tabernacle is the
incident of the golden calf (ch. 32). Even while Moses is receiving
instructions about the right worship of God, the Israelites are
indulging in false worship. The contrast shows us again how
Israel's God is different from the other gods. Some scholars think
that the golden calf was a god other than Yahweh.[12] However, it is

more likely that the people were intending to worship Yahweh in the form of a calf.[13] From the time of Abraham, people knew Yahweh under the name of El, the chief Canaanite god, who was also known as 'The Bull El'. Aaron says not only that the calf is the god who brought them out of Egypt (Exod. 32:4), but also that the feast they will celebrate will be 'to Yahweh' (v. 6). Of course, he knew that he was doing wrong (v. 22), but it seems likely that many of the people did not yet understand how different Yahweh was from the other gods. The contrast between the calf and its riotous worship and the tabernacle and its strict regulations point to that difference.

A nation unlike other nations

Israel, we have said, is like the nations, but her God is not like their gods. This means that, though Israel may be like the nations, she is also unlike the nations. The Pentateuch tells us what this will mean. We can say it in one word: *holy.* Israel is to be different, like her God.

In Genesis there is no clear separation between the religion of the family of Abraham and the religions of other peoples. They are just one family among many, and there seems to be what Wenham calls a 'bonhomie' with the surrounding religions.[14] However, Exodus indicates direct opposition between Israel's God and the Egyptian gods. We can see the plagues as a competition between God's prophets and the Egyptian magicians, which implies a competition between their respective gods. This is clear from the nature of the plagues, in which Yahweh shows himself as in control of the Egyptian 'gods'.

The Nile turning to blood shows that Yahweh is greater than Hapi, the god of the Nile, and Osiris, whose bloodstream was said to be the Nile. *The death of cattle* shows that Yahweh is greater than Hathor, the mother and sky goddess who was represented by a cow, and than Apis, the fertility god who was represented by a bull. The plagues of *frogs*, *hail*, *locusts* and *darkness* show that Yahweh is greater than Heket, the goddess of childbirth, who was

represented by a frog; than Seth, the god of wind and storms; than
Isis, the goddess of life; than Min, the god of fertility and than all
the various sun gods. *The death of the firstborn* shows that Yahweh
is greater than Osiris, the judge of the dead. We would not know
all this from the accounts of the plagues, but Jethro recognizes it
(Exod. 18:10–11) and Numbers 33:4 makes it explicit.

By Leviticus, the Israelites are being told that they must not
follow either Egyptian or Canaanite practices (Lev. 18:3). When
they reach Canaan, they are commanded not only to conquer the
peoples there but also to destroy them and their religions: 'Break
down their altars, smash their sacred stones, cut down their
Asherah poles and burn their idols in the fire' (Deut. 7:5).

What has changed since the time of Genesis? Has God changed
his mind about the other gods? It seems that two things have
happened.[15]

First, the other religions have changed

In Egypt. At the time of Joseph the Egyptians and their king, or
pharaoh, were friendly to his people and his God. This may have
been at the time of one of the reform movements in Egyptian
religion. We know that there were times when some Egyptians
wanted only one god. There are several hymns to the sun, as the
highest or even the only god; and one king, Amen-Hotep
(1380–1362 BC), changed his name to Akhen-atun (servant of Atun,
a sun god), and insisted on the worship of Atun alone.[16] However,
his religion did not last long, and most Egyptians seem to have
continued to worship many gods.

It is difficult to tell how the Egyptian ideas of one god relate to
the influence of Joseph and the Israelites in Egypt, not least
because scholars are not agreed about dates. What is clear from
the Bible is that there was a great change in attitudes among the
Egyptians by the time of Moses, when the pharaoh was hostile to
both the people of Israel and their God.

We would not expect a king of Egypt to accept the god of
Israel as the only god; and we would not expect the king of one

nation to worship the god of another nation. However, kings usually allowed foreign groups to serve their own gods. This pharaoh is not even willing to do that. He is, perhaps, afraid of the power of the Israelites, or angry that the god of a subject people should tell him to do anything. Whatever his reason, he refuses to recognize Yahweh's demands of Israel (Exod. 5:2). The result is, as we have seen, a competition between Israel's god and the pharaoh's gods.

Exodus does not actually discuss the gods of Egypt: we would not know anything about them except their impotence from the Bible alone. Exodus appears to recognize only the human dimension of the gods. It is not that the Egyptian gods are real beings who are at war with Yahweh. Rather, it is human beings who are using these gods to fight Yahweh. It is, perhaps, this that makes their practices so abominable at this time.

In Canaan. In Abraham's time the high god El was the main Canaanite god. He had many of the characteristics of Yahweh and, as we have seen, the Bible has no problem in using his name for God, although it rejects some aspects of him. By the time of the exodus, the worship of Baal seems to have taken over.[17] Since Baal was god of fertility as well as weather, there were many rites and, in particular, sexual practices associated with his worship. The Bible sees these as an abomination.[18] Canaanite religion had become focused on immoral and therefore destructive practices. There was a time when Abraham's family could live as part of the surrounding nations with their religious practices, but there was a time when God's people would have to make a break.

Genesis 15 hints at a change in Canaan, when Abraham is told that his descendants will not receive the Promised Land until much later because 'the iniquity of the Amorites is not yet complete' (15:16). Their iniquity would mean that Israel had to become separate from them, but it would also mean that they would have to be judged. Deuteronomy explains that the conquest of Canaan would bring together two things: judgment on the Canaanites and the fulfilment of God's promise to Abraham.

It is not because of your righteousness or your integrity that you are going in to take possession of their land; but on account of the wickedness of these nations, the LORD your God will drive them out before you, to accomplish what he swore to your fathers, to Abraham, Isaac and Jacob. Understand, then, that it is not because of your righteousness that the LORD your God is giving you this good land to possess, for you are a stiff-necked people. (Deut. 9:5–6)

Second, Israel has changed

If the surrounding nations have become worse, have the Israelites become better? As the above passage from Deuteronomy makes clear, the Israelites thought that the answer was 'yes', but they needed to learn that the answer was 'no!' The passage goes on to remind them of how they 'provoked the Lord to anger in the desert' (v. 7) with the golden calf. It was not only the Canaanites who could worship idols and indulge in revelry!

What, then, had changed? *The Israelites had become a people: God's own people.* They are first called God's people from the burning bush, when God says, 'I have seen the misery of my people' (Exod. 3:7). From then on, this is how the Israelites are described.[19] The battle with Pharaoh is not only to show that Yahweh is greater than all the other gods: it is also Yahweh's battle for his people. 'Let my people go!' he says. To this point, God is the god of Abraham, Isaac and Jacob: the god of the family he has chosen. Now, the family has become, as promised, a people, a nation: the Old Testament again and again identifies Yahweh as the one who brought Israel out of Egypt, and Israel as the people of the exodus.

God's first instruction at Sinai reminds them that their purpose is for the blessing of the nations:[20]

Thus you shall say to the house of Jacob, and tell the people of Israel: 'You yourselves have seen what I did to the Egyptians, and how I bore you on eagles' wings and brought you to myself. Now therefore, if you will indeed obey my voice and keep my covenant, you shall be my treasured possession among all peoples, for all the earth is mine; and you shall be to me a kingdom of priests and a holy nation. (Exod. 19:3–6)[21]

Israel is God's special people, because of what he has done for them. However, the context of this is that the whole earth with all its peoples belongs to God. Israel's job is to be obedient. Her function will then be twofold among the other nations. She will be

- A 'kingdom of priests'. The priests had tasks: teaching the law (Lev. 10:11), handling sacrifices (Lev. 1 – 7) and blessing the people (Num. 6:22–27). If Israel is to be a priesthood among the nations, she should bring them knowledge of God and his laws, show them how they can have forgiveness of sin and fellowship with God, and bring the nations God's blessings.
- A 'holy nation'. That is, she will reflect God's character of holiness. Holiness here is not just an aspect of God: it is his very essence. For Israel to be holy, she will have to be different from the other nations as God is different from their gods. The rest of Exodus 19 begins to tell them what this means. The people must be cleansed and consecrated, for God is so pure that no-one can survive his presence without his invitation and without being purified according to his instructions.

This is the call that both makes Israel different from the other nations and requires her to live differently from the other nations.

A holy nation

What Israel's holiness means in practice is detailed in the rest of Exodus, Leviticus and Numbers. Within these books there are only occasional specific references to the religions of the other peoples, such as the sweeping denunciation of Leviticus 18 quoted above. We shall have to turn to what we know about these other religions in order to understand how Israel was to be different.

Exodus–Numbers contains the account of Yahweh's actions in taking Israel as his people, the laws by which he expects them to organize their society, details of the tabernacle, worship and sacrifice, the choice of priests and their consecration and duties, and categorization of clean and unclean / holy and common things. All these are aspects of God's covenant with Israel, as is made clear by the structure of the book of Deuteronomy, which reviews the earlier events.

As we have seen, the surrounding nations also had laws, places of worship, sacrifices, priests and ideas of ritual purity. These, too, were understood in the contexts of the stories about how the gods created human beings and founded nations. If Israel was to be a nation among other nations, she too needed a story, a law and a way of worship, and God met these needs.

Other nations also had covenants. These were not with their gods, but with kings who conquered them: they related the history of the conquering king's relationship with the people, his requirements of them, and the consequences of obedience and disobedience. The various biblical covenants contain all the ingredients of such treaties. This points to the first great characteristic that distinguished Israel among the nations: *Israel had no human king. Her king was Yahweh.* The other nations had kings that were believed to represent their god, and sometimes even to be divine themselves. Israel's covenant is made directly by Yahweh, at his initiative. Moses is a prophet, and not a king. The holy nation is under the direct rule of God.[22]

Deuteronomy tells us that if she kept the covenant, other nations would look at her and say, 'Surely this great nation is a wise and understanding people' (4:6). In what ways, then, was life in Israel to be different?

Her laws were different
First, they are based on the character of Israel's different God. The stories of other gods are full of pride, battles, sexual exploits and other all-too-human sins and weaknesses. Israel's God does not only command righteousness: he is also completely righteous. *Israel is to be holy because he is holy* (Lev. 19:1).

Second, the laws are based on different ideas about human beings. Israel can reflect God's holiness because human beings were made to reflect the image of God. In contrast, the surrounding nations saw humans as made to serve the gods. Israel's laws therefore give more importance to human beings than do the Mesopotamian laws, which emphasize instead the importance of property.[23] The laws are not given for God's benefit, but to enable human beings to relate to him, to each other and to their environment.

Third, Israel's God is one and is not in competition with any other spiritual being.[24] There is therefore no need for him to show partiality towards the people who worship him. Israel's laws forbid the worship of the gods of other peoples, but they also insist on the rights of foreigners.

Her worship was different

Israel shares many forms of worship with the surrounding nations, but on a different basis. We have seen how her tabernacle has no image of her God, because Yahweh is really present among his people. We can also learn that God's holiness, and the fact that human beings are in his image, imply different reasons for worship.

We saw from Genesis 1 – 11 that human beings were made 'in the image of God', to 'walk with him'. But we have become separated from God and need a way back to him, and one possible way is sacrifice. Here, in Leviticus, God gives details of sacrifices that will please him. These have two basic purposes – dealing with sin, and sharing fellowship;[25] and sin has to be dealt with first. We cannot share fellowship with God unless sin is dealt with, because Yahweh's holiness requires purity. To come anywhere near to Yahweh without purity and without his specific invitation is not so much impossible as *dangerous*.

This contrasts with the surrounding nations, where sacrifices were thought of as feeding the gods to persuade them to supply human needs.[26] In Israel, worship was a response to the faithful

God of the covenant, who does not want us to feed him but has given a way of returning to fellowship with him.

Her food was different

One of the themes of Leviticus is the idea of ritual purity, which can be found in most religions, including those of the ancient Near East.[27] It is necessary to be 'clean' in order to worship. Some things make people 'unclean', and purification is needed in order to make them 'clean' again. The food laws (Lev. 11, 17) are one aspect of this.

The Mesopotamian and Egyptian instructions about worship tell the priests to be clean because they are serving the gods' food, and should be courteous. Sometimes, it seems that the gods also need to be purified: 'Wash (your hands), wash your hands, You are the god Enlil, wash (your hands).'[28]

For Israel, purity is an aspect of holiness. Only clean things and clean people can enter the presence of the holy God. The laws envisage the whole of the Israelite camp as a holy place, but the tabernacle is particularly holy, and at its centre is the most holy place. The strictest purity regulations apply to the one person permitted to enter the most holy place: the high priest.

In the contexts of the other faiths around Israel it is interesting to note what things can make Israelites unclean. They include sexual relations within marriage and death as well as food. These are not wrong in themselves: sexual relations are part of God's good creation, and handling dead bodies is a necessary part of life. Why, then, are the Israelites required to purify themselves after these things, and why are priests so restricted in who they can marry and who they can mourn (Lev. 21)?

The clue can be found in the fact that the division between 'clean' and 'unclean' is also described as a division between 'holy' and 'common'. Some things were appropriate in the context of common life, but had to be excluded from worship in the tabernacle. Again, we ask why they should be these particular things. The answer seems to be that these were the things that stopped

Israel from worshipping like the surrounding nations, and from joining in the worship of other gods (Lev. 20:23–26).

- Worship included feasting. Israel's food restrictions prevented people from joining in the feasts to other gods.
- Other peoples had various rituals around death, some of which were specifically forbidden to Israel (e.g. Lev. 19:28). Making contact with the dead 'unclean' excluded death from the place of worship, and stopped Israel from developing a cult of the dead.
- One of the worst aspects of other religions was, according to the Bible, the sexual practice linked with fertility cults. In fact, the strict commandments about keeping apart from the practices of Egypt and Canaan (Lev. 18:1–3, 29–30) are in the context of forbidding certain sexual relationships, some of which were practised by other peoples. Requiring purification after even legitimate sexual relationships prevented Israel from developing fertility rites in her worship.

Israel's holiness laws, then, are not only symbolic, or good for hygiene. They also have specific purposes relative to the surrounding faiths. On the one hand, the tabernacle, the priesthood, the sacrifices and the worship express Israel's relationship to her God in forms appropriate to her cultural context. On the other hand, the details prevent her from joining in the worship of other gods, and forbid forms of worship that cannot be adapted for the worship of the Holy One. In all this, they reflect the one holy God, for this is Israel's purpose among the nations.

In what ways are Christians in your area like non-Christians? In what ways are they different?

Holy people and resident aliens
There were many non-Israelites living among God's holy people. Some came out of Egypt with them (Exod. 12:20); some arrived

later. Some, like Ruth, accepted Israel's God, intermarried with the descendants of Abraham, and became completely integrated into Israel. Some, like Rahab's family, accepted Yahweh but retained their identity as *gēr* – 'aliens' (New International Version), 'foreigners' (Good News Bible), or 'strangers/sojourners' (Authorized Version). Some *gēr* kept their previous gods. If Israel was a different, holy people, how should she treat these non-Israelites?

The principle is clearly laid down in Deuteronomy 8:17–22: God's people are special, but God is not partial. Foreigners, like orphans and widows, were at a disadvantage in Israel's society. God's people are told to take special care of them. In fact, the great commandment to 'Love your neighbour as yourself' is given twice in the 'holiness code' of Leviticus 19. In verse 18 it refers to fellow Israelites, but verse 33 is about loving the *gēr*.

For further study. Look up 'aliens', 'foreigners' and 'sojourners' in a concordance. In Exodus–Deuteronomy, where were the *gēr* to live within the framework of Israel's laws, and where were they treated differently? On what conditions could they join Israel's worship? What do the prophets teach about justice for the *gēr*?

Who are the 'gēr' in your community?

7

GOD'S NATION AMONG THE NATIONS

The Pentateuch tells how God called Israel as his covenant people for the nations. The rest of the Old Testament is the record of how they continued to live among the nations. Throughout the record, we see God keeping his covenant. The question is, How will Israel live? Will she keep the covenant given on the mountain, or will she continue the golden calf pattern of the valley?

The choice is clearly set out in the last chapters of Deuteronomy, as Israel prepares at last to enter the Promised Land.

> See, I set before you today life and prosperity, death and destruction. For I command you today to love the LORD your God, to walk in his ways, and to keep his commands, decrees and laws; then you will live and increase, and the LORD your God will bless you in the land you are entering to possess.
>
> But if your heart turns away and you are not obedient, and if you are drawn away to bow down to other gods and worship them, I declare to you this day that you will certainly be destroyed. You will not live long in the land you are crossing the Jordan to enter and possess. (Deuteronomy 30:15–18)

Their welfare in the land depends on loyalty to Yahweh.

Deuteronomy 28 – 29 shows that their relationship with other nations also depends on that loyalty. If they keep the covenant, they will live at peace, and defeat anyone who attacks them, and 'all the peoples on earth will see that [they] are called by the name of the LORD' (28:10). If they break the covenant, all their relationships with the nations will go wrong. They will lose their land, and in exile they will worship other gods (28:64). This, too, will be seen by the nations (29:22–28). Whether Israel is obedient or disobedient, God will speak to the nations through them; but disobedience will bring all sorts of trouble on Israel.

Some people say that, to live at peace with people of other faiths, we need to recognize their gods and even to pray with them. Deuteronomy tells Israel that she will live at peace only if she refuses to worship other gods. What questions does this raise in your mind?

At the time portrayed in Deuteronomy Israel is a people, but she is still without political power and without land. As the above discussion indicates, the land will be central to what follows. This chapter explores some key aspects of the story of Israel's land and power: chapter 8 returns to the blessing for the nations.

A dangerous triangle

All land and power is God's. In the beginning he created the whole earth. He put people into it, and it was by his authority that they had dominion over it. Genesis 2 tells how God put two particular people into a particular piece of land. Verses 15–16 explain that dominion meant looking after the land, and required acknowledgment of God's sovereignty through use of the fruit of the land. Written into creation, then, is a triangle of people, land and power – human beings by their very nature need a place in which to live, and in which they have responsibility. At the centre of the triangle is God, who made the people and the land, and who is the source of all power:

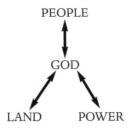

Genesis 3 tells how this triangle very quickly went wrong. The power that the human beings had was God given, and they should have wielded it only under God, acknowledging that the land is his, and in right relationship with him and with each other. Instead, they took power into their own hands. They wanted to put themselves alongside God rather than under him, and they decided to use the fruit of the land to gain power for themselves. I would like to describe this as turning the triangle upside down:

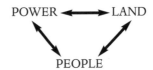

This makes the triangle *dangerous*. In fact, the power for good and evil in human hands was so dangerous that God decided to limit it by expelling the people from that land.

As sin continued, we see Cain exiled from the land, and then the land covered and restored through the flood. Eventually, God recommits himself to the people and the land and all that is in it (Gen. 9:8–11). Then, in Genesis 10, the people multiply and become peoples, each with its own language and its own land (vv. 5, 20, 31). The ordering of Genesis 10 makes it clear that all these peoples are ordered under God's providence – the territories are clearly God's provision for the peoples, just as Eden was God's provision for Adam and Eve.

Sadly, just as Adam and Eve took power for themselves, the people took power for themselves. Genesis 11 starts with the story of Babel – of a people deciding to stay within a particular piece of land, and to build a name for themselves there (v. 4). The centre and the symbol of their enterprise was the tower they tried to build up to heaven. It was a *religious* enterprise, using religion to develop the power to keep the people in the land:

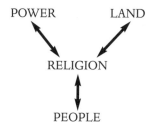

Putting religion at the centre of the triangle makes it so dangerous that God has to act again in judgment. This time he confuses the people so that they can no longer share the power, and he scatters them out of the land where they want to stay.

We have seen that the Babel story is an obvious reference to the great temple of Marduk in Babylon where, as in other ancient places, the god was closely linked with the particular people, land and king. In other words, such ancient religions saw their gods as legitimizing the triangle of a particular people taking power over a particular land, and the god's temple was the greatest symbol of this. *This was normal for the peoples of the time, but Genesis diagnoses it as a result of sin.*

Israel was tempted to fall into this natural human sin. God gave his people a land. He had warned them that if they broke the covenant, he would remove them from the land; but it was going to take the exile to teach them what that really meant. Until then, and even afterwards, they were tempted to think of the land as their right and Yahweh as their national god.

Conquest: God–people–land

The book of Joshua tells of the conquest of the land and the destruction of the Canaanites and their gods at Yahweh's command. This might suggest that Yahweh was like the gods of the other nations, 'for' his people and 'against' everyone else. Some Christians therefore ask whether they should fight people of other faiths. Others are so offended by this picture of God that they wish Joshua was not in the Bible.

I have sometimes been in the second group. I have really struggled with writing this section, and have asked God how he could possibly have told Israel to destroy whole towns, including babies. I have come to accept not only that this book is in the Bible, but also that it is an essential part of the story of God's mission, and has very important teachings for us today. However, we need to read Joshua carefully, and in the context of the rest of the Bible, to find out what those teachings might be. It is important to remember that *the conquest is unique*. It is the only time when Israel is told by God to take land. Elsewhere, she is told to fight her enemies, sometimes she takes land and, after the exile, God returns her to the land; but this is a unique settlement of God's people in the land he has chosen for them. It is also important to remember that *the Messiah was given the name 'Joshua'* (Matt. 1:21). Joshua is not only about the establishment of a people in a land, but is also about the awful reality of God's holiness and judgment. As God committed himself to an alternative to the judgment of the flood after Noah's sacrifice in Genesis 8 – 9, so the second Joshua will be the sacrifice that brings an alternative way of holiness.[1]

Joshua is about land

At creation God gave people land. People have always needed, and still need, land to cultivate and places to live. God has always been the one in charge of allocating land to all peoples. In fact, Paul chooses this as an important point in his main recorded sermon to non-Jews (Acts 17:24–26; cf. Amos 9:7). God's covenant with Abraham recognizes both the human need for land and God's ownership of all land; and Joshua tells of the fulfilment of God's promise. One of the most repeated ideas in the book is that God gave the land.

But *it was a very long time before Israel got her land*. It was promised to Abraham, but we get right to the end of the Pentateuch with the Israelites owning only one field, and then they have 400 years in Egypt and 40 years in the desert. This shows that it is possible to be God's people without a land, and that there are more important things than entering the land. It also shows that the timing of the conquest was important, which takes us to another key aspect of Joshua.

Joshua is about judgment

Expulsion from land was part of God's judgment for the very first sin (Gen. 3:23–24), as it was later part of his judgment on Israel's sin. Joshua sees the conquest of the Promised Land as God's judgment on its inhabitants. The timing of the conquest was, then, not only important for Israel: it was also for the sake of the Canaanites. In Genesis 15:16, Abraham was given the reason for the delay: 'the iniquity of the Amorites has not yet reached its full measure'. *Israel was not allowed to take the land until it was the right time for its inhabitants to be judged.* The destruction commanded in Deuteronomy 8 is not a random destruction of idols and idolaters by God's favourites. It is, at the same time, God using Israel as his instrument of judgment and meeting her need for land.

God's judgment is terrible, but it is just. A careful reading of Joshua shows this.

The destruction was carefully limited. Israel was only given a certain amount of territory (Josh. 1:4); and within it there were other peoples to whom God had given land (Deut. 2:9–25). Total destruction was carried out only in cities, where the rulers and traders lived (Deut. 20:10–18). Comparison with the book of Judges shows that Joshua's conquest was far from complete: what God gave Israel was a foothold in different parts of Canaan.[2]

There was nothing like the total ethnic cleansing that we might expect from Deuteronomy 8 or Joshua 10:40.

Israel destroyed only those who opposed her. The Canaanites did not have to accept destruction: some of them acknowledged Israel's God and accepted conquest instead (Josh. 2, 9 – 10:19). In the covenant renewal after Ai it is clear that there were 'aliens' among the Israelites (8:33), who probably included Canaanites as well as people who had come from Egypt. God does not judge people just because they have the wrong ethnicity.[3]

Many twenty-first-century Christians see the total destruction of Joshua as bloody and barbaric. For the time, it seems to have been remarkably civilized. Other ancient records of war are at least as bloodthirsty. For example, a Moabite inscription describes a victory over Israel:

> I killed all the people in the city as an atonement for Chemosh . . . I took it and slew them all: seven thousand warriors and old men – together with women and old women and maidens – for I had it consecrated for Ashtar-Chemosh.[4]

Other early literature has gods exulting in killing. The Baal myth describes Anat, the Canaanite goddess of war:

> She mows down the cities, she shatters the inhabitants of the coasts, she annihilates the men of the sunrise. Beneath her, heads lie like balls, hands fly over her like locusts, the hands of shield-bearers like hacked-off stubble. Soon the heads towered up to her back, the hands stretched up to her lap. She bathes her knees in the blood of soldiers, her rings in the life-blood of the shield-bearers.[5]

God's justice is summarized in Joshua 11:20, which contains the difficult idea of God hardening people's hearts. Paul's discussion of this in Romans 9:16–18 has been the subject of many commentaries, and I will not try to do better than them. Suffice it to say that this hardening of hearts is clearly part of God's judgment on wicked people. In this case the form of the hardening was enmity towards Israel, which meant that Israel had to fight them, and that the destruction ordered by God was seen to be just.

A friend who read this section commented, 'I still have a real problem with God ordering violent conquest. Was there no other answer? What about God being a god of peace?' What do you think about her questions?

Joshua is about holiness

All this can help us to see the story of Joshua and its violence in its context, but we need to go further. This book is in the Bible, and we need to find out where it fits into God's plan to bless the nations. Killing people does not look very like blessing them! As I have struggled with this question, I have come to the conclusion that the key is *holiness*.

Joshua is about Israel's holiness. The main reason given for destroying all signs of other religions and refusing intermarriage with the Canaanites was to keep Israel from the temptation of wrong worship (Deut. 7:4). The passage goes on to explain, 'For you are a people holy to the LORD your God. The LORD your God has chosen you out of all the peoples on the face of the earth to be his people, his treasured possession' (Deut. 7:6). The Israelites then have to be reminded that they have not been chosen because they are any better than other nations, but only because of God's covenant and sovereign love, and that they themselves will be destroyed if they are unfaithful (vv. 7–10).

More importantly, *Joshua is about Yahweh's holiness.* An idea Joshua often repeats is 'destroy them totally' or 'devoted to destruction' (Deut. 7:2, 26; Josh. 7:12 etc). This translates words from the Hebrew root *ḥērem*, which means 'irrevocably given to God'. It could apply to items entirely dedicated to God's service in the tabernacle, but also to things that were destroyed in that service. As we have seen anything unholy that enters the presence of Yahweh is destroyed because of his absolute holiness. The judgment on the Canaanites was that they were given over to God. Their sinfulness meant that the result was destruction.

It is not only the Canaanites who are devoted to God. Israel too has to be consecrated before entering the land (Josh. 3:5ff.), and the ark, which symbolizes Yahweh's holy presence, has to travel a whole kilometre in front of them (3:4). When Israelites trespass against Yahweh's holiness, they too are destroyed – as the tragic story of Achan shows (Josh. 7). It also shows that if Israel does not act according to God's holiness, she will be treated the same way as the Canaanites who oppose God, and be defeated.

Joshua, then, is the story of the holy God giving his holy people a land, as part of his plan for blessing all nations. It is never Israel that takes the initiative, but God. He gives them the land, and he delivers the nations over to them. The land belongs to God, Israel belongs to God, and the nations belong to God. It is his holiness that demands the destruction of the unholy, whether among the Canaanites or within Israel.

Perhaps the key to the whole book is Joshua's meeting with the angel just before his first battle, in 5:13–14. 'Are you for us or for our enemies?' he asks. The answer is, 'No!' The commander of Yahweh's armies is not on the 'side' of any nation: Yahweh is God of Israel and Canaanites alike. And he has a message for Joshua: 'The place where you are standing is holy.' This may seem puzzling as a message, but it sums up the whole of what we have said above. The holy God is choosing this particular land and this particular nation to demonstrate his holiness.

Is the place where you live Christian territory? Muslim territory? Secular territory? To whom does the land belong? What needs to be cleansed of other gods for you to be holy? You, your family, church, tribe, nation . . . ?

The kings: gods and political power
The conquest shows a holy God with a holy nation, different from other nations. The books from Judges to Chronicles show how Israel keeps on trying to be like the other nations. As Moses and

Joshua warned, they turn after other gods, and they try to worship Yahweh as if he were like the other gods. They also choose to have kings, so that they can compete with the nations in political power.

When Israel was made a nation at Sinai, she was given no king. When she settled in Israel, she still had no king. As Gideon explained when the people wanted to make him king, 'I will not rule over you, nor will my son rule over you. The LORD will rule over you' (Judg. 8:23). Israel did not have a king like the other nations because Yahweh was her king.

Having no human king was, in some ways, a problem: there was no-one to enforce the law, and 'everyone did as he saw fit' (Judg. 17:6; 18:1; 19:1; 21:25). But it was not this that made the Israelites want a king. The other nations had kings who represented the god and led the people into battle. In 1 Samuel 8:5, 20 we read that Israel wanted a king because she wanted to be like the other nations in this way.

The background was both corruption in Israel's priesthood and severe pressure from the Philistines (1 Sam. 4 – 7). The capture and return of the ark should have taught Israel that they needed repentance and sacrifice rather than a king to win their battles.[6] While Samuel was alive the Israelites were able to trust Yahweh to help them. As he had aged and his sons were not trustworthy, they began to panic and demanded a king.

Yahweh's response is interesting (8:7–9). He gave them what they asked for, but first warned them of the consequences. They were not only changing their leadership, but rejecting his kingship, and that was just like serving other gods. Further, their king might win battles, but he would also treat them as the other kings treated their people. The other nations saw the people as servants of the gods, and therefore as servants of the kings that represented the gods. So Israel's king would treat his people as servants and oppress them terribly.

The people continued to insist that they wanted a king, and repeated that they wanted to be like the other nations. So they got their king. And what was Yahweh's response to Israel's monarchy?

Not surprisingly, he kept his covenant. He let Israel go the way she chose, but directed the whole process of finding the first king. More than that, he chose to use Israel's kingship to bless her and to bless the nations. He made a further covenant with David and his descendants, and eventually sent Jesus the Messiah as the true King of Israel.

Was Israel wrong in wanting a king? So strong is the idea of kingship in the Old Testament that many commentators see a contradiction in Samuel's opposition to it,[7] and suggest that there are two conflicting sources of 1 Samuel.[8] Another possibility is that the Israelites' mistake was to insist on having a king for their own reasons and at the wrong time: that they should have waited for God's own timing and God's choice of David. For our study, the important point is that, in choosing to have a king, Israel wanted to be like the nations in power politics. Among the other nations,[9] kings claimed to be appointed by their gods and were sometimes described as the son of the god or the shepherd of the god's flock. They ruled on behalf of the god, administered his laws and maintained his temple. They waged wars in the name of the god, with the help of the god, in order to extend the rule of the god. This gave them rights over the peoples they defeated. The gods of the enemy were conquered as the enemy was conquered, and so the conquered people could be mutilated and be treated as vassals. So close was the relationship between the king and the god that it is sometimes difficult to distinguish between them in ancient writings.

In Israel, too, we see kings appointed by God, building God's temple, shepherding his people, ruling according to his law, and fighting in his name. In all this she was, as she wanted to be, like the other nations. Some commentators say that this was necessary: Canaanite society was changing fast, with the coming of the Iron Age and the military pressure from the Philistines. A more organized government was needed than that of the time of the judges, so perhaps the monarchy was necessary to Israel's survival. There is a sense in which Israel had to be like the nations, because she was a nation. The problem was that, as she was warned, she often became too much like them, and fell into the wrong worship and abuse of power that produces the 'dangerous triangle' described above.

The reign of David shows us the possibility of a kingship in which the triangle is the right way up. The king's power is clearly distinguished from God's power, the king subjects himself to God by listening to the prophets, and there is a clear distinction between David, the warrior who established political security, and Solomon, the wise man who built the temple (1 Chron. 28:3). However, the history of Israel's monarchy shows how often the king took religion and power into his own hands. The very first king lost his throne because he took the priest's role by offering a sacrifice before a battle (1 Sam. 13:1–14). It seems that Yahweh will not permit one person to join religious and political leadership.

As the history unfolds we see that kings and wrong worship are, all too often, linked. The books of Kings and Chronicles character-ize each king's reign by his worship and morality. In the southern kingdom of Judah some kings are faithful to Yahweh, but few actu-ally lead the people into right worship. In the northern kingdom every king leads the people astray. The beginning of this was Jeroboam's attempt to set up Yahweh worship in his area (1 Kgs 12). He knew that other kings had their palaces near their temples, and ruled in the name of their gods. He was afraid that his people would go and worship in Jerusalem, and give their allegiance to the king there (vv. 26–27). He therefore decided to set up two places of worship in his area, and to put golden calves in them. It was these calves that were to be a constant temptation to wrong worship.

Was he deliberately leading the Israelites to worship other gods? It seems not. Like Aaron (Exod. 32:4) he said, 'Here are your gods, O Israel, who brought you up out of Egypt' (1 Kgs 12:28). As there, Yahweh is being represented by the image of the calf: he is being worshipped as if he were like other gods. This is underlined as Jeroboam builds shrines on the high places, as did the Canaanites. He institutes his own priesthood, his own festival and his own sacrifices. He led his people to worship Yahweh in his own way, to keep his own power; and that, according to the Bible, is as bad as worshipping other gods.

The books of Kings and Chronicles tell us how the kings' unfaithfulness leads Israel into unfaithfulness and eventually into exile. As in the case of Jeroboam, the wrong worship may be from a concern to keep power. As in the case of Ahab, it may be through marriages into powerful foreign families. In each case, the king acts like the kings of other nations, and Israel becomes like them where she should be holy like her God.

What role has political power played in establishing religions in your area? What role has religion played in establishing political power?

Exile: gods–peoples–land

The first six books of the Bible tell of the promise of land, and its fulfilment in Israel's settling in Canaan. Most of the rest of the Old Testament takes us in the opposite direction: it is focused on the exile, the consequence of not being holy in the land. The historical books tell of the unfaithfulness that led to exile. The pre-exilic prophets warn of exile. The exilic prophets explain the exile, and then speak of return. Esther and Daniel tell of the Jews living in exile. Ezra, Nehemiah and the post-exilic prophets tell of the return from exile. Even the first six books prepare for the exile, as they warn of the consequences of disobedience.

Why is the exile so important? For our study of religions it is important because it demonstrates that *Israel's God is not like the gods of the nations, because he is not a national or territorial god*. The exile breaks the ties between god, king, people and power that support the dangerous triangle. It also has significance for *God's mission to his world*, as it forces Israel to live among the nations.

The ancient kings believed that they conquered nations because their gods were powerful. We see this in Sennacherib's challenge to Hezekiah in 2 Kings 18:19–35, 2 Chronicles 32:10–15 and Isaiah 36. The threefold repetition emphasizes its importance.

> Has the god of any nation ever delivered his land from the hand of the
> king of Assyria? Where are the gods of Hamath and Arpad? Where are
> the gods of Sepharvaim, Hena and Ivvah? Have they rescued Samaria
> from my hand? Who of all the gods of these countries has been able to
> save his land from me? How then can the LORD deliver Jerusalem from
> my hand?' (2 Kgs 18:33–35)

The Bible tells us that Yahweh saved his people and judged
Sennacherib, but, outside the Bible, Sennacherib's own account of
the siege of Jerusalem does not recognize this. He acknowledges
that he did not manage to make Hezekiah submit to him, but
focuses on his attacks on the surrounding villages, the siege and
Hezekiah's eventual sending of tribute to him.

> Hezekiah himself, whom the terror-inspiring splendour of my lordship
> had overwhelmed . . . did send me later, to Nineveh, my lordly city,
> together with 30 talents of gold, 800 talents of silver, precious stones,
> antimony, large cuts of red stone, couches inlaid with ivory . . . and all
> kinds of valuable treasures, his own daughters, concubines, male and
> female musicians.[10]

Other Assyrian inscriptions equate the 'terror-inspiring splendour' of the king with the 'terror-inspiring splendour' of his
god, so that the conquest of the one is also the conquest of the
other.

All three biblical accounts agree that Sennacherib's challenge is a
challenge to Yahweh (2 Kgs 19:22; Isa. 37:23–24), and that Yahweh
saved his people and judged Sennacherib (2 Chron. 32:21–22; Isa.
37:26–27, 36–38). However, they do not agree with Sennacherib that
the exile is a result of Yahweh's weakness. Ashur did not give
victory to his chosen king, Shalmaneser: Yahweh used Shalmaneser
as his instrument for judging Israel. Similarly, it was not Marduk but
Yahweh who gave victory over Judah to Nebuchadnezzar. It was
not that Yahweh was weaker than the other gods, but that his
people had broken the covenant, and that his holiness demanded

they be removed from their land. He is the sovereign Lord over Assyria and Babylon as well as over Israel.

And so the Israelites went into exile. This raised new questions for them about the other religions. To this point, their questions had been about how they should worship, and the main issue had been whether they would remain faithful to Yahweh. Now, they were no longer in their own land or under their own rule. They had to think about other issues:

- Can we live as Yahweh's people if we don't have a temple, if we don't have power, if we don't have land?
- Yahweh is not like the other gods. We are beginning to understand more about him; but what does this say about the other gods? What are they?
- Yahweh's rule can be seen in the defeat of his people as well as in their victories. How, then, will we see his ultimate victory?

These questions are dealt with in the prophet Jeremiah's letter to the exiles (Jer. 29:4–9), in the book of Esther, and in Isaiah 40 – 66. Jeremiah 29 tells us that living faithfully without land and without power was possible, provided the Israelites remained faithful to Yahweh and worked for the good of the peoples among whom they were sent. Esther recognizes the possible problems of being a religious and ethnic minority, but shows Yahweh's almighty power to save. Isaiah declares the sovereignty of Yahweh over both the nations and their gods. All these are worth further study, but we shall focus on one book that deals with all the above questions: Daniel.

Daniel begins by posing the problem: sacred vessels from the temple have been taken to the temple in Babylon (1:1–2). This symbolizes the apparent defeat of Yahweh by the Babylonian gods as well as Israel's exile from her land. The rest of the book reveals Yahweh at work in Babylon, showing both Israelites and Babylonians – and everyone else – that he is not defeated, but is lord of all.

The visions of chapters 7–12 give an apocalyptic glimpse of Yahweh's lordship, and of his commitment to Israel; but the stories of chapters 1–6 are just as clear. The wisest men of Babylon have to admit their limitations, and that their 'gods do not live among men' (2:11). Belshazzar discovers how dangerous it is to dishonour the sacred vessels from Jerusalem (ch. 5). Again and again the kings have to acknowledge that Yahweh, and not they, rules (2:47; 4:1–37; 6:25–28).

So Daniel shows the rule of Yahweh, the uselessness of other gods and the limits of human wisdom, and utterly breaks the Babylonian people–power–land links with religion. But it is important to see the role of four young Jewish men in doing this. Daniel, Shadrach, Meshach and Abednego are Yahweh's missionaries to Babylon. It is through their holy lives that Yahweh's glory is shown, and that blessing comes to those Babylonians who want to receive it – to the wise men whose lives are saved in chapter 2, and to Nebuchadnezzar himself as he eventually acknowledges Yahweh. Like Esther, *Daniel answers a resounding 'Yes' to the question of whether God's people can live and worship without power, temple or land, at the very heart of a nation with a faith very different from that of Israel.* This makes it an important book for understanding mission to people of another faith.

Daniel was able to say to the king of the nation that had taken him into exile, 'I have never done anything wrong before you' (6:22). How does this challenge and encourage Christians who live as a minority, under the rule of people of a different faith?

For further study.   Read Daniel 1 – 6, and look for how Daniel and his friends adapt to the Babylonian culture, how they make themselves different from the Babylonians, and how they interact with the Babylonians.

Note:

- The new names in 1:7 include the names of the Babylonian gods Bel and Nebo.

- The Babylonian wisdom and literature would have included religious stories and rituals.

Back to the land

Yahweh was the one who used other nations to send his people into exile. Isaiah 45 and the books of Ezra and Nehemiah tell us that he was also the one who brought his people back to their land, and that he used foreign kings to do so.

If Yahweh is the God of all places and peoples, and if the Jews can serve him in any place, why did he bring them back to Jerusalem? There are two related reasons. First, Yahweh is always faithful to his covenants, even when his people are unfaithful. It is through the return that both Israel and the nations see his faithfulness and his authority. Second, it was part of Yahweh's plan. It was still his intention to bring blessing to all nations, and to do it through Israel. Haggai and Zechariah, who prophesied when the Jews were resettling Jerusalem, understood that Yahweh intended to do something far greater than ever before, and that this would be acknowledged by all nations (Hag. 2:1–9; Zech. 2:10–13; 8:20–23; 14:1–21). For this to happen, Israel would have to be holy in true worship and righteous actions. The books of Ezra and Nehemiah show how Israel tried once again to be holy, while living among people of other faiths.

The number of Jews who returned to the land was small – only about 50,000 (Ezra 2:64–67; Neh. 7:66–69). The leaders were, no doubt, familiar with the prophecies of Ezekiel and Jeremiah, which explained the reasons for the exile. They were also acutely aware of Israel's past sins, and wanted to prevent future unfaithfulness. One way they did this was to remind the people of God's laws; but they also realized that part of the problem had been their trying to be like other nations. They therefore emphasized separation in a way that had not been seen since the time of Joshua.

We see this *first in the building of the temple*. Some of the local people wanted to help, but were refused (Ezra 4:2). They claimed to be worshippers of Yahweh, and there is no reason to doubt that they were telling the truth. Some may have been Jews who were left behind during the exile. Others were foreigners who had been moved to Samaria when the people of Samaria were moved to Assyria. 2 Kings 17:24–40 tells how these people were taught to worship Yahweh, because he was the local god. They seem to have been quite happy to do this, but had also continued to worship their own gods.

The Jewish leaders refused the offer of help: it was the Jews' job, they said, to do the rebuilding. No reason is given for this except that the Persian king had commanded it. When the temple was finished, local people who had 'separated themselves from the unclean practices of their Gentile neighbours in order to seek the Lord, God of Israel' (Ezra 6:21) were welcomed to the Passover celebrations.

Were the leaders right to exclude the local Yahweh worshippers from helping with the temple? Why, we wonder, did the leaders not explain that the local people could not worship both Yahweh and other gods, and give conditions by which they could join in? Why wait until the Passover? As with so much of the Old Testament, we are not told, although the writer of Ezra seems to approve Ezra's actions. Perhaps he was just acting practically: Ezra 4:1 suggests that those who wanted to help with the temple did not really want to help but to hinder.

We see the separation most clearly in the ruthless *getting rid of foreign wives* (Ezra 9 – 10; Neh. 13). When the Jewish leaders first approached Ezra about this, they seem to have thought that the basic problem was racial purity (Ezra 9:1–2). However, neither Ezra's prayer (9:6–15) nor the later prayer of Nehemiah (Neh. 13:23–27) makes this point. Ezra speaks only of the wrong practices of the other peoples (Ezra 9:11, 14) and of unfaithfulness to Yahweh (9:10ff.; 10:10). Nehemiah mentions the problem of language (13:24) and points out that foreign marriages led even such a king as Solomon into sin (13:26–27).

The Old Testament records some marriages to foreigners that were obviously blessed by God. Tamar, Rahab and Ruth all followed Yahweh, and are ancestors of David and therefore of Jesus. Interracial marriage cannot, in itself, be the problem. Rather, the need is for Israel to remain a distinct people, and to be faithful to Yahweh. The foreign wives could lead Israelites into worship of other gods, prevent their descendants from communicating in their language, and therefore lead Israel away from Yahweh's purposes for her.

It is interesting to ask whether Ezra and Nehemiah's attempts at holiness worked any better than did, for example, Josiah's reforms.[11] By the time of Jesus there were many Jews who were very exclusive not only about whom they would marry but also about whom they would visit; and Jesus was unimpressed by that kind of holiness. It is also interesting to note another intermarriage from the time of the Persian kings. Esther was forced to marry a non-Jew, but she was able to keep her identity and her faith in a totally non-Jewish situation. Is holiness, then, to be found in living in the land and separation from the surrounding peoples? Or is there another sort of holiness that does not depend on where people live or whom they live among?

What sort of holiness is it that can bring blessing to the nations? Do you have to keep separate from sinners to stay righteous? How can we witness to people of other faiths if we keep apart from them?

8

GOD, GODS AND NATIONS

All peoples on earth will be blessed through you.

Genesis 12:3

Abraham and the other patriarchs may have had good relationships with other peoples, but the rest of Israel's history seems to give a negative view of the nations and their religions. The law is largely about Israel differing from the nations, and therefore about her *not* worshipping or living like them. Israel's history is largely about her struggles with the other nations. They are often her enemies, and their gods are, it seems, Yahweh's enemies. Does this contradict the idea that God called Israel to bless the nations?

Certainly, the focus throughout the Old Testament is Israel's relationship with Yahweh. The covenant with David (2 Sam. 7) does not even mention the other nations. However, this does not mean that the nations are forgotten in the time of the kings. The covenant with David does not cancel the covenants with Noah, Abraham and Moses. This becomes obvious in the prophetic visions of the future, such as Isaiah 40 – 66, Psalm 96 and Zechariah 16, which see the nations coming to Israel and to her God.

We need to see the battles between Israel and the nations in their wider context.[1] In God's universal purposes it seems that they were one of the things that would show all nations, including Israel, Yahweh and his righteousness (e.g. 2 Sam. 22:48–50). Perhaps that is why the Old Testament gives them so much space. However, they do not represent the whole of Israel's relationship with the nations. The historical books cover a long time and many different situations. Many reigns are recorded briefly, with no mention of battles, which implies that there were long periods of peace. Sometimes the nations also helped Israel. We shall look at positive interactions during the reigns of David and Solomon, and in the wisdom literature.

Further, the exile challenged the links between nations, lands, kings and gods. This suggests that a battle with a nation is not necessarily the same thing as a battle with her religion or her god. We shall look at the relationship between religion and judgment. We shall see that the real battle against false religion was not with the other nations, but within Israel. This is confirmed by the New Testament's choice of Old Testament material about foreigners.

David and Solomon

David was the king who established Israel as a real political force among the nations. He freed Israel from Philistine rule, captured the Canaanite city of Jerusalem, and conquered Edom, Moab, Ammon and parts of Syria (2 Sam. 8; Ps. 60:6–9). His son Solomon reigned in splendour over the widest kingdom that Israel has ever known. Together, they show the Jews at their most powerful and secure point in history. A close reading shows that this was not only a time during which foreigners respected Israel, but a time when many were blessed through Israel.

The reign of David

David's military conquests might make us suppose that he was against the other nations, but this is not so. He had friendly rela-

tions with the kings of Tyre and Hamath (2 Sam. 5:11; 8:9–10) and
he went to the Philistines when Saul was persecuting him (1 Sam.
27). He had also received hospitality from Nahash, one of the
Ammonite kings. When he came to the throne, he not only
thought how he could show kindness to Jonathan's son (2 Sam.
9:1): he also tried to show kindness to Nahash's son (2 Sam. 10:1–2).
Sadly, Nahash's son did not accept the kindness, and war ensued;
but the repeated word 'kindness' implies David's sense of indebt-
edness to the royal houses of both Israel and Ammon. In Hebrew
this 'kindness' is *ḥesed* – Yahweh's covenant love.

After David had established Israel among the nations, he had to
deal with a group of foreigners who were living among the
Israelites – the Gibeonites, with whom a treaty had been made at
the time of the conquest. Saul had tried to get rid of them – we
would say, he had tried ethnic cleansing (2 Sam. 21:2). Yahweh was so
angry at this that he sent Israel three years of famine. David had to
do justice by allowing the execution of seven of Saul's descendants.

The books of 1 and 2 Samuel, which tell of David's conquests,
focus much more on his relationships than on his battles. It is
remarkable how many of these are with foreigners in the land of
Israel.

There were foreigners among his fighting men:

- David's personal bodyguards were Perethites and Kerethites
  (2 Sam. 8:26; 1 Chron. 18:17), and there were 600 Gittites who
  served him. These all came with him when he fled from
  Absalom (2 Sam. 15:18), contrasting the loyalty of the
  foreigners with the treachery of David's own son.
- There were foreigners among David's mighty men listed in 2
  Samuel 23, including Eliphet the Maacathite (v. 34), Zelek the
  Ammonite (v. 37) and Uriah the Hittite (v. 39).
- There were foreigners among David's overseers listed in 1
  Chronicles 27, including Obil the Ishmaelite (v. 30), Jaziz the
  Hagrite (v. 31) and Hushai the Arkite, who is called 'David's
  friend' (v. 33; see also 2 Sam. 16:16).

There are a number of stories about specific foreigners:

- Doeg the Edomite is the only one who appears to be against
  David and against Yahweh (1 Sam. 21:7; 22:18–22). He betrays
  David and carries out Saul's order to kill the priests.
  However, he does this out of loyalty to Saul.
- In other cases the foreigner's faithfulness to Yahweh contrasts
  with the unfaithfulness of the Israelites. For example, Uriah
  the Hittite's integrity contrasts with David's sin (2 Sam. 11:1 –
  12:12); and Ittai the Gittite's loyalty and Hushai the Arkite's
  friendship contrast with Absalom's treachery and enmity
  against his own father (2 Sam. 15:19–23; 15:32–37; 16:15 – 17:17).
- The books of Samuel finish with the story of another righteous foreigner, Aruanah the Jebusite, who offers his land to
  David for the building of an altar.

There were many foreigners living among the Israelites, and, as
we saw in chapter 6, God was concerned that they be treated
justly. Many reached high office. Many turned to follow Yahweh,
and were more faithful to him than were some of the Israelites.

Solomon and the nations

My house will be called a house of prayer for all nations.

Isaiah 56:7

We saw how Ezra and Nehemiah excluded the Samaritans who
wanted to help build the temple. Solomon's temple was quite
different. He actually asked the king of Tyre to help with the
building project (1 Kgs 5:3–6; 2 Chron. 2:3–9). Tyrean and Israelite
craftsmen worked together in preparing for building (1 Kgs 5:18),
and Solomon brought a half Israelite, half Tyrean, craftsman from
Tyre to do the brass work (1 Kgs 7:14; 2 Chron. 2:13–14).

Next came the dedication of the temple, and Solomon showed
his understanding of God's wish to bless the nations. He asked
God to hear and answer different sorts of people who came to the

temple. He included the foreigners, who would hear about Yahweh and come to worship. Solomon asked God to hear them, 'so that all the peoples of the earth may know your name and fear you as do your own people Israel' (1 Kgs 8:43; 2 Chron. 6:33).

And foreigners did come to Jerusalem. They brought blessings to Israel by their gifts, and received blessing as they found out about Yahweh. We read that 'the whole world sought audience with Solomon to hear the wisdom that God had put in his heart' (1 Kgs 10:24; cf. 2 Chron. 9:23). The climax of the Solomon story comes in 1 Kings 10 and 2 Chronicles 9, with the visit of the Queen of Sheba. We read of the splendour of Solomon's court, of the queen bringing great riches to Israel, and at the same time receiving blessings as she hears Solomon's wisdom and witnesses the worship of Yahweh. What a picture of God's blessing Israel and the nations through her!

Sadly, this did not last. These good relationships with the nations were not produced by Solomon, but were based on the relationships and stability built up in the time of David. They were a result of David's faithfulness to Yahweh and Yahweh's faithfulness to David, and they lasted only as long as Solomon was also faithful. Solomon married women who worshipped different gods and, towards the end of his life, *he* started to worship their gods. This angered Yahweh, and, as a result, God raised up enemies against Solomon, and, after Solomon's death, took most of the kingdom away from his descendants (1 Kgs 11). Never again did Israel live united in the Promised Land, as a blessing to the nations.

Solomon's wisdom led to blessing for the nations, but his marriages with foreigners led him to unfaithfulness to God. Nehemiah would neither let foreigners help with building the temple, nor let Israelites marry non-Israelites. How did their actions depend on their circumstances? What can you learn from these examples for your circumstances?

The wisdom of the nations
Two things made Solomon such a remarkable king: God's

covenant with his father, David, and the wisdom that God gave him. We have seen that the Old Testament is mostly about God's relationship with his covenant people. The Pentateuch tells of the establishment of the covenant, the historical books tell the story of Israel's unfaithfulness and God's faithfulness to the covenant, and the prophets are God's messengers to his covenant people. But the Old Testament also contains another set of writings: the wisdom literature, which scarcely mentions the covenant.

In chapter 6, we saw that some of the biblical writings have close parallels in the writings of the different nations. What is interesting for our study is that the closest parallels are in the wisdom literature:[2] Proverbs, Job, Ecclesiastes and the Song of Solomon. For example, Beyerlin's collection, *Near Eastern Texts Relating to the Old Testament*,[3] includes an Akkadian dialogue on the unrighteousness of the world that raises many of the issues of Job and Ecclesiastes, a Sumerian poem about man and God that is sometimes called 'The Sumerian Job' and a Babylonian poem, 'I will praise the Lord of Wisdom', which also echoes the poetry of Job.

As we have seen in chapter 5, it is not always easy to see which writings came first, and which way influence works. However, when we come to the Proverbs, it seems clear that Israel did use the wisdom of other nations. The passages from the Egyptian instructions of Amen-en-opet quoted in chapter 6 are so similar to Proverbs that both must surely have the same literary source.

This should not surprise us. 1 Kings 4 tells us that Solomon's wisdom had two sources. God gave him wisdom (v. 29), but he also used his wisdom to describe what he observed around him (v. 33). Solomon spoke thousands of proverbs (v. 32), but this does not mean that he made them all up himself. Ecclesiastes tells us how 'The Preacher' worked: 'He pondered and searched out and set in order many proverbs. The Teacher searched to find just the right words, and he wrote what was upright and true' (Eccl. 12:9).

In 2 Chronicles 1:10 Solomon asks God for 'wisdom and knowledge', which might make us expect that he wanted God to put things into his mind. However, the prayer in 1 Kings makes it clear that he was not asking for an encyclopaedia of ideas and information, but 'a discerning heart to govern your people and to distinguish between right and wrong' (1 Kgs 3:9). This is what God gave him (1 Kgs 3:12; 4:29).

All the nations had wise men, who collected and memorized wise sayings, meditated on them, and passed them on. This wisdom was part of the basis on which society was built, and was what the rulers needed if they were to govern justly. This was Solomon's reason for asking for wisdom (1 Kgs 3:8–9; 2 Chron. 1:10). God's supernatural gift of wisdom enabled Solomon to search human wisdom, and to choose from it what was good.[4] It is possible that the other wisd om literature as well as the Proverbs represents non-Israelite writings that the inspired writers recognized as good, and rewrote in the context of their knowledge of Yahweh.

What can we conclude from all this? We might start by suggesting that all truth comes from God, and that what I have called 'human wisdom' is just another way of describing what theologians call 'general revelation'. An interesting question would then be, 'Where did the non-Israelites get ideas that agree with the Bible?' However, I do not think we can find the answer to that question in the Bible, perhaps because it is a question about people of other faiths, and not about what God requires of us. For our study, a more important conclusion is that *the wisdom literature shows the Bible's engagement with the human search for right living and thinking.*

The Bible does not dismiss human wisdom as worthless or useless.[5] As we compare the Egyptian proverbs and the biblical Proverbs, we can see much agreement. The Bible here says to the Egyptians, 'You are right': there are human beings who do seek for truth and righteousness, and it is possible for them to find quite a lot of wisdom for themselves. While the other books of the Old Testament show us the sinfulness of Israel, the wisdom literature shows us a good side of human nature.

Further, the Bible takes the concerns of the surrounding nations seriously. The questions of how to live, how to relate to people, and how to deal with the realities of suffering and death are important. However, the best wisdom recognizes its own limits. Both ancient and modern wisdom know that there are questions about suffering and justice and eternity that no amount of human searching can answer. Biblical wisdom also recognizes these limits. While Proverbs tells us how to live the good life and prosper, Ecclesiastes recognizes that the good life and prosperity are not enough. Job argues with the 'wisdom' of his comforters, and shows that all their thought cannot produce satisfactory explanations of innocent suffering.

So biblical wisdom does not stand by itself, but in the context of the whole story of God's interaction with human beings. Israel always interprets her wisdom in the light of her knowledge of God. Proverbs tells us where wisdom begins: with the fear of the Lord. Ecclesiastes tells us where it finishes: in the same place. Job tells us the only satisfactory answer to the puzzles of the world: encounter with the god who made it and us. And this is not just any god: this is Yahweh, who brought Israel out of Egypt. As Wright and Goldingay point out, 'Non-Israelite insight is set in a new context within the religion of Yahweh.'[6]

The Bible presents wisdom as something public and available to everyone. It calls out to everyone – in the streets, on the heights, in public squares and at the city gates (Prov. 1:20–21; 8:1–3; 9:3). But wisdom is also something we must seek: we have to apply ourselves to it, long for it, and hold on to it (Prov. 2:1–3; 3:1; 4:7). For it is not the only voice shouting for our attention. The call of folly is also public (Prov. 9:13–15). This means that, while people in every nation may find wisdom, they may also find folly. Israel did not accept all the proverbs of Egypt, and there are many aspects of the writings of the surrounding nations that she rejected.[7]

Israel and the nations can agree on much wisdom, but wisdom is not sufficient in itself. The problem is not only that it may be mixed with folly: it is that, in the end, wisdom is not what matters most. Human beings were made for the relationship with Yahweh that comes through his covenants. What the Bible has to offer the world is not superior wisdom, but Yahweh saving his world. Yet, in the context of the story of God's salvation, there is room for some of the wisdom of the nations.

It was not only the ancient nations that had wisdom. Present-day religions such as Hinduism, Judaism and Islam also have wisdom traditions, as do Christianity and Confucianism. John Eaton has explored wisdom in the Bible and other traditions,[8] and has found a number of common themes such as discipline, attentiveness, humility, love, the limits of understanding, the givenness of life, work, trust and the knowledge of God. What kind of 'wisdom' is common in your society? Where can you say, 'This is right'? How might the biblical wisdom literature speak to people in your community today?

Religion and judgment

> Stop bringing meaningless offerings!
>> Your incense is detestable to me.
> New Moons, Sabbaths and convocations –
>> I cannot bear your evil assemblies.
>> (Isaiah 1:13)

How does religion affect God's judgment? Isaiah 1 tells us what he hates. The surprise is that it is not pagan ritual in worship of some other god, but Israel's worship of Yahweh, based on the rituals he himself gave them. Why does this religion disgust Yahweh? Because those who practise it are doing evil (Isa. 1:15–31). Worship without faithfulness to other aspects of God's law stinks.

What about people outside the covenant community? What does God think of their religion? One of the questions raised by current theology is that of the salvation of people of different faiths. If Christ is the way of salvation, will God condemn people to hell if they follow a different religion? This section offers some insights from the Old Testament prophets that can help us begin to answer this question.

The Old Testament has very little to say about what might

happen to individuals after death, but plenty to say about God's judgments of whole peoples before death. It is important to remember that these books of the Bible were written for Israel, and that they therefore deal only with the nations in relation to Israel. *These books of the Old Testament tell us only what Israel needed to know, and not everything we would like to know.*

Amos: Judging Israel among the nations

The main thing Israel needed to know about God's judgments was that she herself would be judged. Amos makes this very clear. It begins with the roaring and thundering of God (1:2) against the nations. Damascus, Gaza, Edom, Ammon and Moab: all will be judged. Why? For the vicious ways they have treated Israel. Israel needs to know that their crimes against humanity anger God, and that he will deal with them. But that is not all Israel needs to know. Amos 2:4–8 declares judgment on Judah and Israel in the same language used for judgment on the nations. What is different is the *reason* for Israel's judgment. They have disobeyed God's laws, they have followed other gods, and they have oppressed the poor.

There is no suggestion that the other nations will be judged for disobeying God's laws or for worshipping the wrong gods; and no mention of how they dealt with their poor. Why will God judge Israel for all this?

> You only have I chosen
>   of all the families of the earth;
> therefore I will punish you
>   for all your sins.
>   (Amos 3:2)

Israel seems to have thought that, because she was chosen, she could expect God to judge the other nations and be lenient to her, but the truth was just the opposite. She has extra responsibility. She is reminded again of this in 9:7–8.

'Are not you Israelites
   the same to me as the Cushites?'
   declares the Lord.
'Did I not bring up Israel from Egypt,
   the Philistines from Caphtor,
   and the Arameans from Kir?

Surely the eyes of the Sovereign LORD
   are on the sinful kingdom.'

This is an interesting passage. Its main purpose is to remind Israel that she is not God's favourite, and to underline the fact of her judgment.[9] But it also reminds us that God is god of all the nations. We are not to think each nation has its own god who looks after it. It is the one Lord who is responsible for all.

Other prophets frequently remind us of this, as they tell of God using the nations to judge Israel. He gives one nation to another in conquest (e.g. Jer. 21:7; Ezek. 29:19), and kings are described as his servants, both for judging and for saving Israel. For example, Jeremiah describes Nebuchadnezzar, king of Babylon, as God's servant in conquering many nations (25:9; 27:6–7; 43:10) and Isaiah calls Cyrus, king of Persia, God's shepherd, anointed to bring Israel back from exile (44:28; 45:1).

Judging the nations

The Old Testament focuses on the judgment of Israel, but there are also many passages about the judgment of the other nations. In the context of our questions about the salvation of people of different religions, it is helpful to ask *why* the nations come under God's wrath.

Throughout the prophetic books, God's judgment on the nations for their *vicious treatment of Israel* is the most frequent theme (e.g. Isa. 10:7; 34:8; Ezek. 25:6; Ob. 1:10–14; Nah. 3:19; Zeph. 2:8–10). Jeremiah uses the word 'vengeance' when he describes these judgments (50:15, 28; 51:6, 11, 36). This is, perhaps, because

Israel needed reassurance that God would act justly on her behalf;
but it is also, I would suggest, because she needed to know that
vengeance was in God's hands, and not in hers.

Other reasons given for judgment include general *wickedness*
(Isa. 13:11), *spreading terror* (Ezek. 32), *amassing riches* (Jer. 48:7; 49:4;
Zech. 9:3–4) and *complacency* (Jer. 48:11–12; 49:31). Nahum has a
graphic description of the lies, plunder, sorcery and witchcraft
Nineveh used to enslave other nations (3:1–4), and for which she
would be judged.

Pride is often mentioned (Isa. 23:9; Jer. 48:29; 50:31–32; Ob. 1:3). It
seems to be the greatest religious sin of the various nations,
because it is seen as a *declaration of independence from God*, or even a
direct challenge to him.

- Ezekiel 26 – 28 deals with Tyre. She is judged because she has
  rejoiced over the defeat of Israel (26:1–3), but also because of
  her boastful attitude (27:3). More seriously, her king thinks
  that he is a god (Ezek. 28:2): judgment will show him how
  wrong he is (28:6–10).
- Isaiah deals with two different ways in which the Assyrians
  defied God. Assyria is 'the rod of God's anger' (10:5), so she
  was obeying Yahweh when she attacked Israel, but she
  wanted to follow her own agenda and destroy Israel (v. 7). She
  thought it was her own strength that had given her victory
  (vv. 13–14). It is this that Isaiah sees as defiance. The picture he
  uses is that Assyria was God's tool, and that the tool suddenly
  turned round and tried to wield its maker (v. 15)!
- Isaiah 36 – 37 deals with the more direct defiance of
  Sennacherib, who mocks Israel for depending on Yahweh
  (36:4–20).[10] He is told that he has insulted the holy one of
  Israel (37:23–24): here, defiance of God's people is also
  defiance of God.

In summary, the prophets tell us that the nations are judged for
obvious wickedness, for war crimes in relation to Israel, and for the

arrogance that makes itself equal to God. This reassures us that God will not overlook wickedness, that he will vindicate his own people, and that Yahweh is the Creator God of all the nations.

What about the nations' gods?

None of the above reasons for judgment relates directly to the nations' religions. Although the prophetic books contain a great deal about Israel's idolatry, they say little about the other nations' worship of their gods. In several places it is pointed out that these gods cannot save (Isa. 16:12; Jer. 46:15; 51:17–18), and the later parts of Isaiah mock them as lifeless and useless.[11] But what about judgment?

The judgment of a nation is sometimes seen as the defeat of her gods (Isa. 19:1; 21:9; Jer. 50:2; 51:49; Ezek. 30:13). Jeremiah sees it as punishing both gods and kings (46:25; 51:44, 47, 52) or as putting the gods to shame (48:13; 50:2). Nahum speaks of the destruction of Nineveh's idols (1:14). Clearly, Yahweh is supreme over them all; but what is interesting for our study is that there is hardly any suggestion that the nations are punished because they worship these gods. In a passage headed 'Woe to the Chaldeans' in my English Standard Version, Habakkuk 2:18–19 says clearly, 'What profit is an idol? . . . Woe to him who says to a wooden thing, awake!' Yet even this is part of a general judgment on the unrighteous (v. 4), and commentators discuss which parts are mainly directed towards the Chaldeans, and which towards Israel herself.

Two other relevant passages are the judgments against Moab and Babylon in Jeremiah 48 and 50 – 51.[12] Moab is judged as the people of Chemosh, and the judgment on Babylon is seen as humbling Marduk and Bel and Nebo. There are three relevant verses:

> In Moab I will put an end
>   to those who make offerings on the high places
>   and burn incense to their gods.
>   (Jeremiah 48:35)

Woe to you, O Moab!
> The people of Chemosh are destroyed.
> (Jeremiah 48:46)

A drought on her waters!
> They will dry up.
> For it is a land full of idols,
> idols that will go mad with terror.
> (Jeremiah 50:38)

Of these, the second simply describes Moab as 'the people of Chemosh'. As in 48:7, which describes Moab's exile as Chemosh's exile, this is the link between people and their gods we have frequently observed. The other two verses suggest the possibility of peoples being judged because of their idolatry, but their primary thrust is Yahweh's defeat of the other gods. Nahum 3:4 suggests that sorcery and witchcraft are reasons for judgment, but otherwise it seems wrong religion is not an important criterion for the judgment of people outside the covenant.

In summary, the prophets told Israel that the other nations would be judged mainly for their pride, for their sinful actions and for their bad treatment of God's people. However, the prophets also assured Israel of Yahweh's sovereignty above all other gods. The other gods are seen as useless, and under God's judgment; and one of the results of judgment will be putting them to shame – that is, all peoples will see their uselessness.

In what ways does Paul's discussion of judgment for Jews and non-Jews in Romans 2 reflect the teaching of the Old Testament prophets?

Blessing for the nations?

God's judgments on Israel were necessary because God is holy, and his people must also be holy. But the judgments did not mean that God hated his people: they were part of his covenant love. Several of the prophets tell us that God was grieved when he had to judge Israel (e.g. Hos. 11:8); and their messages of judgment are always accompanied by promises of restoration.

What about the nations? Can we see God's judgment on them also as part of his intention to bless them? The vast majority of the messages about the nations are about their judgment, but a careful reading shows that God has compassion on them also, and intends to restore and bless many of them.

First, Jeremiah's lamentation for Israel is not the only lament in the Old Testament. Jeremiah also laments for Moab (48:31–32, 36), as does Isaiah (15:5; 16:11); and Ezekiel laments for Egypt (30:1–5; 32:2) and Tyre (27). Some of these laments are commanded by God, and some seem to express his lament as much as the prophet's lament. The riches of the nations are a reason for their judgment if they are gained by oppression and if they accompany complacency, but there is also great beauty in the nations such as Tyre and Egypt, and their destruction causes anguish to the prophets and, we infer, to God.

Second, one of God's purposes in judging both Israel and the nations is that all peoples will come to know about him. Ezekiel often points this out in the context of the judgments on different nations (25:7, 11, 14, 17; 26:6; 29:6, 16, 21).

Third, as in Jeremiah 12:14–17, God may intend to restore nations after judging them, provided they learn his ways as shown to Israel and listen to him. There are specific promises of restoration for Moab (Jer. 48:47), Ammon (Jer. 49:6), Elam (Jer. 49:39) and Egypt (Ezek. 29:13), and Jeremiah 51:9 tells of God's longing to heal even Babylon. Most striking is Isaiah's treatment of Egypt in 19:18–25. This speaks of true worship of Yahweh being established in Egypt, and of Yahweh healing the Egyptians and answering their prayers. The chapter ends with a future blessing from Yahweh himself: 'Blessed be Egypt my people, Assyria my handiwork, and Israel my inheritance' (v. 25). Yahweh claims Egypt and Assyria as well as Israel, and blesses them.

These prophecies were all given to Israel, and are what Israel needed to know. She needed to know that God would deal with her enemies, and that they as well as she would be judged. However, she also needed to know that God wanted his glory to be seen by the nations, and that he had plans to bless them as well as to judge them. As always, the blessing is in their coming to Yahweh.

All these passages are about God's judgments on nations. The only individuals dealt with are the kings, who, as we have seen, are linked with the gods and the nations. Does God deal this way with groups of people today? What does the Christian church need to know about God's judgments?

What really matters?

One of the difficulties in asking what the Old Testament has to say about people of different faiths is that it says a great deal. It has many different kinds of literature, written by many different people in many different situations. And these refer to many different peoples who worshipped many different gods. One way of finding out what is most important in the Old Testament is to turn to the New Testament.

The Gospels mention Old Testament non-Israelites in several places. This is usually to teach the religious people that they are not God's favourites, and that God does not hate the other nations. In fact, it has always been his intention to bless them.

Rahab, Ruth and Uriah are mentioned in Matthew's genealogy of Jesus (Matt. 1:5). Rahab was a harlot, in the first city Joshua conquered, but she recognized Yahweh's people and she and her family were saved. Ruth was from one of Israel's greatest enemies, the Moabites, but she came into Israel and God blessed her so much that she became the great-grandmother of David. Uriah was the faithful foreigner who was murdered after Israel's greatest king, David, stole his wife.

Jesus tells the Pharisees that the *Queen of Sheba* and the *people of Nineveh* will actually judge them (Matt. 12:38–42; Luke 11:29–32). The Pharisees have the Scriptures, and they have the Messiah among them, but they neither recognize him nor repent. The queen did not have Yahweh's revelation, but she travelled all the way to Israel to see Solomon and hear his wisdom. The people of Nineveh repented when Jonah preached to them.

Jesus also speaks of towns that did not repent: *Tyre* and *Sodom* (Matt. 11:21–24; Luke 10:13–15). These were renowned for their pride and wickedness, and for God's severe judgment on them (Ezek. 26 – 28; Gen. 19). Yet, says Jesus, some of the towns of Israel are even worse. Tyre and Sodom would have repented if they had had the opportunity to see the Messiah, but the Jewish towns Chorazin, Bethsaida and Capernaum rejected him.

The widow of Zarephath and *Naaman the leper* are both mentioned by Jesus in Luke 4:24–27. The people in Jesus' home town thought they knew about the Messiah, and that he would come to save them. Jesus angered them by reminding them of two stories that merit further study.

The story of the widow comes during the reign of Ahab, who with his wife Jezebel led Israel to worship Baal and 'did more to provoke the LORD, the God of Israel, to anger than did all the kings of Israel before him' (1 Kgs 16:33). One of the things that people hoped to get through the worship of Baal was rain for their crops. But, as a result of their Baal worship, Yahweh withheld the rain, and sent Elijah to tell Ahab what he was doing. So Israel suffered a terrible famine: as Jesus said, there must have been many Jewish widows suffering at that time. 1 Kings 17 then tells us of one person whom God provided for, and called to provide for Elijah: this was not a powerful man like Ahab, but a poor widow. And she was not an Israelite. Israel was suffering under God's judgment, and God sent the blessing of food to a foreigner. He not only kept her alive: he also spoke to her through Elijah, and miraculously restored her dead son.

This story is not only significant in showing us a Gentile whom God blessed when Israel was under his judgment. It also shows us a pagan woman who accepted God's prophet when Israel was worshipping the pagan god.[13] Elijah's competition with the Baal prophets in 1 Kings 18 is one of the strongest statements of the uniqueness and supremacy of Yahweh in the Bible. But beside it stands this tender account of Yahweh's care for an insignificant individual.

Naaman was the commander of the army of the king of Aram (2 Kgs 5:1). This king was, presumably, Benhadad, who was one of Israel's persistent enemies, so his army commander must have been in the forefront of some of the battles against Israel. However, 2 Kings shows no personal hostility towards him. Rather, it says that he was a valiant soldier and that God was working through him. But he had leprosy, and God used a young Israelite girl who had been captured in battle to send him to the prophet Elisha for healing.

At first, Naaman was reluctant to admit that there might be anything special about Israel (2 Kgs 5:12). Then he was healed, and made a most remarkable statement: 'Now I know that there is no god in all the world except in Israel' (2 Kgs 5:15). We have seen non-Israelites acknowledging Yahweh's greatness before, but this goes further: there is no other god. Here is a foreigner who was much quicker to understand this than was Israel. He therefore realized that he would have a problem going home.

It is interesting that his problem did not have to do with the fact that his people were at war with Israel. The beginning of the chapter reminds us that fighting against Israel was not necessarily fighting against Yahweh: on the contrary, Yahweh had given victory to Aram through Naaman (2 Kgs 5:1). What worried Naaman was worship. He knew he would have to go into Rimmon's temple with the king of Aram, and he realized that he could not worship both Yahweh and Rimmon. Elisha reassured him, simply saying, 'Go in peace' (2 Kgs 5:19).

While the widow of Zarephath challenges us in the context of a religious battle, Naaman challenges us in the context of physical battles. He shows us God's concern for an individual in the enemy ranks. He shows us a valiant and honest man whom God used to defeat Israel.[14] He shows us a Gentile with a remarkable under-standing of the uniqueness of Yahweh. And he shows us the possibility of someone who serves Yahweh even when going into the temple of another god.

Jesus' use of the Old Testament is, as always, masterly. He sees that the people are going to reject him, and uses these stories both to warn them of what they are about to do and to tell them that others will receive him. He does this by reminding them of God's graciousness to Gentiles at times when Jews were rejecting him.

The main reasons that the Jews wanted to be separate from Gentiles were religious and political. Jesus chooses one situation of religious confrontation and one of political confrontation. In each case, Israel receives something important through a Gentile; and the Gentile is blessed by coming to know Israel's God. With the coming of Jesus, God's blessing was at last coming to all the nations.

'He came to that which was his own, but his own did not receive him. Yet to all who received him, to those who believed in his name, he gave the right to become children of God' (John 1:11–12). How do Naaman and the widow of Zarepheth illustrate this principle?

We can summarize this section, and perhaps the whole of this chapter, by saying that God treats all peoples as human beings. He made them, so he is their Lord, whether they acknowledge him or not. They are made in his image, so they are able to hear and respond to him, and there are good things in their writings. But they are also fallen, so there are wrong things in their beliefs as well as their actions. They deserve judgment, but God wants to bless them. And so, through his chosen people Israel, he does bless them.

So the end of our Old Testament studies takes us back to the beginning. As in Genesis, it is not our religious label that matters, but our human interaction with the living God.

PART 3

READING THE NEW TESTAMENT

9

SETTING THE SCENE: THE WORLD BEHIND THE TEXT

The world into which Jesus came was just as much a multi-faith world as that of the Old Testament. It was still a world of many gods, associated with peoples and places and political powers, and with laws and rituals and stories and sanctuaries. But there were also differences. First, the Middle East had been under Greek rule and was now under the Romans. The westerners had brought with them new religious and cultural ideas, as well as different ways of governing subject peoples. Second, this was after the Jews had returned from Babylon, but God's promises of restoration had obviously not yet been fulfilled, so they still considered themselves to be in exile. There was an expectation that he would act soon to vindicate himself and his holy people among the nations.

The New Testament world was home to people from all over the vast areas conquered by Alexander the Great in the fourth century BC. There were many gods and goddesses with their devotees, temples and myths. There were also people who distanced themselves from popular religion and followed various schools of philosophy.[1] The Jews had to work out what it meant to be holy in the new cultural, religious and political setting. How could they live as God's special people among people of other faiths? How would God rescue them from people of other faiths who were oppressing them, and fulfil his mission of blessing all peoples?

These are some of the issues for us in this book. They were the urgent issues for the Jews of Jesus' time and for the first Christians, so they are also some of the main issues the New Testament deals with. Before going on to see how it does this, we need to explore further the tensions and beliefs among first-century Jews, and their attitudes to non-Jews.[2]

The tensions

The New Testament world exhibits all sorts of tensions arising from the interplay between religion, power, peoples and territories that we have so often seen in Old Testament times. These developed during the intertestamental period, as can be seen from the Jewish books written during that time. The most important are collected in the Apocrypha.

Political tensions: who rules in the land?

First, from about 332 BC, Israel was conquered by the Greeks under Alexander the Great. Next, when Alexander died (323 BC), his empire was divided into two parts: the Seleucid empire ruled from Syria, and the Ptolemaic empire ruled from Egypt. These two empires fought over Israel for nearly two hundred years. Eventually, after twenty-five years of armed struggle (167–142 BC), the Jews gained independence, and were at last able to govern their own country. But, by 63 BC, the power struggles within the Jewish people were so bad that the competing leaders appealed to the Romans for help, which led to the Romans taking power.

By the time of Jesus, Roman rule was well established. Israel was ruled for the Romans by King Herod, who claimed to be a Jew but was in fact an Idumaean.[3] He was succeeded in AD 4 by his three sons, who divided the country between them (see Luke 3:1). There were several attempts to overthrow the Romans during this time. In AD 26 the emperor appointed Pontius Pilate as procurator, to take over from Herod's son in Jerusalem. After the death of Jesus, some Jews continued to fight for their political freedom, until Jerusalem was captured by the Romans in AD 70. The temple was destroyed and most of the Jews were scattered.

Cultural tensions: how does culture affect religion?

The old empires of Assyria, Egypt, Babylon and Persia had shared much of Israel's culture. Their gods were different, and that had always been a temptation to Israel. But, on the whole, those empires recognized that different peoples had different gods, and permitted each people to live as they wished. Alexander the Great thought differently. He tried to unite his vast empire by making everyone share his culture. This was called 'Hellenization', from the Greek word for 'Greece' (*Hellas*). It included democratic government, speaking Greek instead of local languages, a gymnasium (sports centre) in every city, recreation centres for young people, and schools that taught Greek literature, arts and philosophy.

This was all different from the Jewish culture; and it was attractive to young people. Most peoples were able to accept it, but it divided the Jews. One of the biggest problems was the athletics competitions in the gymnasiums, where the athletes had to run naked. Such competitions often led to immorality of various sorts. Perhaps even more seriously, people were ashamed of their circumcision, and even tried to remove its marks. It is not surprising that religious Jews feared they might lose all that they had struggled for over so many centuries.

Social tensions: religion, power and wealth

Under the Greeks, the high priest was also the leader of the Jewish council or Sanhedrin, which governed the community, so that *religious and political power were joined*. Throughout this period there were battles between parties who supported Greek culture and parties who rejected it, represented by their chosen high priests. There were two, and sometimes three, people claiming to be high priest at any given time: the king decided whom to appoint. With position came power and wealth for the high priest and for others who cooperated with the Romans.

Power was also exercised by religious people over 'sinners', and the richer Jews of New Testament times do not seem to have been any more eager for social justice than those rebuked by the prophets in Old Testament times. The New Testament reflects a society of powerful and powerless, rich and poor: Roman citizens and others, land owners and day labourers, tax collectors and debtors, masters and servants, freemen and slaves.

Theological issues

Perhaps the main question the Old Testament leaves us is how Israel can ever be holy and righteous.[4] But it also raises other issues, without answering them, such as the world of spiritual powers, and what happens after death.[5] We know these were of concern to the peoples of the time because ancient literature gives them so much space. These questions were all discussed in intertestamental times, because the various tensions made them much more urgent.

Future hope

When the wicked flourish and the good suffer, we ask when justice will be done. As the Jews were subjected to different rulers after the exile, they hoped for a new community: the kingdom of God.[6] This was predicted in, for example, Daniel 2:44. It would mean blessing for righteous people, judgment for unrighteous people, and transformation for the whole world.

How would this kingdom come? One idea was the Messiah. There are many references to the king as anointed ($m\bar{a}\check{s}\hat{i}a\d{h}$) in the Old Testament (e.g. Pss 2:2; 20:6; 18:50), and to the king still to come (e.g. Isa. 7:10–17; Mic. 5:2–4; Jer. 23:5–6; Hag. 2:21–23). So it is perhaps surprising that the intertestamental literature says little about the coming Messiah, and that there is no one clear idea of what he will do. What is clear is that he will bring victory to the Jews, rebuild the temple and establish a righteous kingdom that will extend over the whole earth.[7] Most Jews were expecting this to happen quite soon, bringing social and political as well as religious freedom.

Righteousness

People wanted to make sure that they would be part of the new kingdom: to be the righteous ones who would be blessed. The key question was, then, 'Who are the righteous ones?' Even within one intertestamental book[8] there can be apparent disagreement on this. For example, 1 Enoch 10:21 has Gentiles as well as Jews sharing in blessings, but 1 Enoch 83 – 90 has the Jews in the kingdom and the Gentiles separated from them.

The question then arises whether all the Jews are righteous, which implies the question of what is a true Jew. Who will be included in God's covenant promises? What was involved in keeping the covenant? How should Jews be different from non-Jews? How should they relate to their enemies? The different answers to such questions gave rise to different parties, described in the next section.

Resurrection

Generations went by without the Messiah appearing. As Ecclesiastes observes, the righteous and the unrighteous all die. Another question was, therefore, whether and when they might receive their respective blessings and judgments. An obvious answer was that this would happen after death.

The first clear reference to this is in Daniel 12:2.[9] Other Old Testament books have future hope for peoples on earth: Daniel here suggests that there is hope for individuals after death. Other prophets also refer to individual judgment. A key chapter is Ezekiel 18, which gives details of God's justice for both the righteous and the unrighteous. The intertestamental literature builds on these ideas.

The writings agree that God is Lord of death as well as of life, and that he will eventually judge all people justly. They disagree as to how this will happen: most expect a physical resurrection, but some see it as purely spiritual. Some say that all people will be resurrected: others that the righteous will rise, and the wicked will be destroyed. Some speak only of the Jews: others say that all peoples will be raised. On the whole, however, the expectation was of a physical resurrection that would enable people to be part of the kingdom of God on earth.

Angels and demons

The discussions about good and evil in Job and in Daniel are the context for the Old Testament's clearest descriptions of the spiritual powers (Job 1; Dan. 12). Some of the intertestamental writings build on such ideas, and describe the world of angels and demons.

Some Jews began to see God as completely transcendent, far above human knowledge, and not involved in the world. It was the angels, they thought, who bridged the gap between God and human beings. 1 Enoch and Jubilees give many details of the ranks, names and functions of the different angels.[10] There were also beliefs in rebellious, fallen angels, who were demons or 'satans' (adversaries).

Such beliefs seem to be as much influenced by Babylonian and Persian ideas as by the Old Testament. They were syncretistic – that is, they mixed together ideas from two different faiths. It is possible to trace a direct line to another form of syncretism that threatened the early church: Gnosticism. This took various forms, but was based on the ideas that secret knowledge (*gnōsis*) was needed for salvation, and that 'matter' was evil and 'spirit' was good (dualism).

Full-blown Gnosticism did not appear until the second century AD, by which time it included Greek and Christian as well as Jewish ideas. During the twentieth century some scholars thought that Gnosticism was in the world behind the New Testament text. They even believed that the first Christians got their ideas about Jesus as, for example, the light and the redeemer, from the Gnostics. Now, as much more is known about first-century

Judaism, it is thought that Gnosticism developed much later. Scholars are discovering that they can understand the New Testament without Gnosticism.[11] For our purposes, however, it will be helpful to remember that Gnosticism did develop and did use Christian ideas, and that its beginnings could probably be seen during New Testament times.

Which of these theological issues are important for Christians thinking about other faiths?

Who are the true Jews?

By the time of Jesus, several groups represented different ideas of keeping the covenant, and of dealing with Greek culture and with Roman occupation. That is, they had different answers to the questions 'Who are the true Jews?' and 'How should Jews relate to other peoples?'

The Pharisees tried to follow the example of Ezra and Nehemiah. They believed that the exile was the result of disobeying the law, so they wanted to keep every detail of it – oral as well as written. They only bought and sold from each other. They refused to eat in the homes of non-Pharisees, in case they became unclean. That is, they tried to keep separate from people who might not keep the law.

These Pharisees were mainly lay people, from the lower-middle and working classes, so they were popular with the ordinary people. But they were also close to the upper-class 'scribes', who were the professional students of the law. Thus they had influence at all levels, and the majority of Jews saw their way as faithful Judaism.

The Sadducees were the priestly party, who controlled the temple. They were mostly from rich and noble families, and therefore not close to the ordinary people. They were not so strict as the Pharisees, and they considered the written law as more important than the oral law, and the Torah (Genesis–Deuteronomy) as the most important part of the written law. They rejected some of the ideas not in these five books, such as the resurrection of the body, the final judgment, angels and demons. It was they and the Pharisees who formed the Sanhedrin.

The Essenes are not mentioned by name in the New Testament, but some scholars think that they influenced John the Baptist and even Jesus himself. They were even stricter than the Pharisees. They avoided pleasure, wealth and sometimes marriage, and kept the cleanliness laws very strictly. They saw themselves as the true priests and the true Israel, and tried to keep pure by withdrawing from ordinary life.

Some, like the famous community at Qumran, lived in the desert, because they thought the world was corrupt and they must go to the wilderness to wait for the Messiah. Others lived in groups in the cities, so their influence was widespread. They supported a different high priest than did the more powerful Sadducees, so they influenced *political* tensions. Their *religious* influence was to make personal piety more important than the temple, the land of Israel and Jerusalem. What mattered was the true priests – all the believers – worshipping God wherever they lived.

Each of these *religious* groups represented different ways of relating to the *political* tensions. The Essenes chose the way of *withdrawal*: they had their own communities, which had as little as possible to do with the Roman occupiers, or even with other Jews. The Sadducees mostly chose the way of *cooperation*: they received their power from the Romans, and did not want to upset them. The Pharisees chose the way of *cultural protest*: they insisted on being different by keeping their own religious and cultural ways and defying the Romans where necessary.

In addition, there were those who chose the way of *armed resistance*. *The Zealots* were revolutionaries who wanted to get rid of the Romans by armed force. There were several groups of Zealots, and some scholars think that Judas Iscariot and the 'sons of thunder' as well as Simon the Zealot were members of these. Another nationalistic group were the *Herodians*. We know little

about them except that they supported the kingship of Herod, and
that they saw Jesus as a threat to the Jewish nation (Mark 3:6; 12:13).

Most of the people did not belong to any of these groups. They
were just trying to live their lives and serve their God in a very
difficult situation. They did not know how God's victory would be
won, but some, like Anna and Simeon (Luke 2), were expecting it
and waiting for it.

*Withdrawal, cooperation, cultural protest, armed resistance . . . Where
can you see Christians relating to political powers, and to people of other
faiths, in these ways today?*

What about the nations?

The Pharisees and the Essenes chose different ways of separating
themselves from the Gentiles, and even from other Jews. The
Zealots wanted to fight the Gentiles. Even the Sadducees, who
cooperated with the Romans, did not want to include Gentiles
into the people of Israel. They agreed with the Romans to exclude
Gentiles from the temple. What had been the 'court of the
Gentiles' became the place where animals were kept and money-
changers did their business (see Mark 11:15–18). It seems as if Israel
was no more ready to bless the other nations than in Old
Testament times.

However, this is not the whole story. First, people believed that
Israel's restoration would bring God's rule among the Gentiles.
They knew the psalms and the prophecies about the nations, and
were expecting them to come to Israel either to serve God or to
be judged by him. Second, most of the Jews did not live in Israel.
It is thought that, at the time of Christ, there were about 3 million
Jews divided equally between Palestine, Egypt and Syria, and one
and a half million more scattered through Asia Minor, Europe
and Asia. We can compare this to about 42,000 in Israel at the
time of Ezra (Ezra 2:64), and 180,000 at the time of the
Maccabees. Even if there were many Jews who did not return to
Israel, this means that the total population of Jews had grown

very rapidly. This was not only because of the birth of children, but also because of conversion.

The New Testament gives a picture of religious Jews making 'proselytes'. That is, they called people to follow the God of Israel, circumcised them, welcomed them and then considered them part of the Jewish people. The Jewish historians Philo and Josephus also tell of conversions, and even of discussions about whether proselytes needed to be circumcised. There were clearly some Jews who believed that God wanted Israel to share her knowledge of him with other nations; and there were some among the nations who recognized the call of the one true God.

Missionary methods included calling people from idol worship, living holy lives, and discussions showing the goodness of the laws of Moses. Sadly, some conversion was also through military might. The book of Esther records people joining the Jews out of fear (Esth. 8:7–14), and towards the end of the second century BC both the Idumaeans and the Ituraeans were conquered and forced to accept the Jewish religion, although this did not necessarily mean they were recognized as full Jews. Herod was an Idumaean, and many regarded him as a foreigner and not a proper Jewish king.[12]

The world behind the New Testament text is one in which Jews had many different attitudes to the surrounding peoples and their religions and cultures. They also had different ideas of their mission as Jewish people. As a result of the mission of some, the Jewish community worldwide included people from many different ethnic, linguistic and cultural backgrounds, as well as with different social, political and religious views.

In what ways is the world you live in like the New Testament world?

10

A NEW PEOPLE

The New Testament arises out of and speaks into the world described in chapter 9. It is a world full of religious tensions and different faiths, which means that every page of the New Testament is relevant to our study. As the gospel message challenged first-century Jewish thinking at every point, it can challenge not only our thinking about people of other faiths but also our thinking about ourselves and our own faith at every point.

As is well known, the New Testament deals with the obviously religious questions of its time by showing that the fundamental problem of sin is dealt with through the Messiah's coming, cross and resurrection, and that the people of God can be holy through the one Holy Spirit of God. The gospel challenged the thinking of all religious parties about the law and about relationship with God. It showed how empty the sort of self-righteousness that can be gained through religion is (e.g. Phil. 3:1–11), and made people face the fact of universal sin (e.g. Rom. 1 – 3). The New Testament therefore offers many resources for responding to those who seek to please God through religious rules.[1] We might say that it offers a unique diagnosis of human problems, which lies behind all the discussions about whether people of other faiths can gain salvation.

What is salvation? What did the different groups of Jews of Jesus' time want to be saved from? What do your neighbours from other faiths want to be saved from? What do you want to be saved from?

The questions of law and grace and original sin have been discussed throughout Christian history. In this chapter we shall focus on another way in which the New Testament challenges all religions: it shatters ties between religion and territory, and between religion and power, even more strongly than did the exile. It also shatters ties between religion and the Jewish people and their culture.

These are the ties that support the dangerous triangle of people, power and land that has always characterized so much religion. It is the cross that shatters them, as it offers radical answers to the old questions: What about the nations? Who are the true Jews? What is the kingdom of God? It opens the way to blessing for all peoples, it shows weakness as true power, and it inaugurates a people whose identity does not depend on state or land. It points to a new creation, in which people will live in a new land, with God among them as their king – the 'triangle' with God at its centre and turned the right way up for ever (see p. 98).

However, the New Testament does not simply spiritualize everything. When Jesus says, 'My kingdom is not of this world' (John 18:36), he is actually speaking to the representative of Caesar's kingdom. He does not deny that his kingdom challenges Caesar's: rather, this is a different kind of kingdom. We might picture Caesar's kingdom as filling a two-dimensional plane. The kingdom of God is not, then, a separate kingdom within that plane, but a third dimension that intersects with every point on it.

As you read, please remember that the non-Jews were, to the Jews, people of other faiths.

What about the nations? Breaking the religion–people–culture ties

The New Testament announces that, at last, God's blessing to the nations has come. What Paul calls the gospel announced 'in advance to Abraham' (Gal. 3:8), in Genesis 12:3 is fulfilled in Jesus Christ.

We could follow this theme through the whole New Testament. Revelation shows the ultimate judgment and salvation of the nations, as it speaks of the 'tribes and languages and nations' of Genesis 10, now, strikingly, without territory (e.g. 5:9; 7:9; 11:9; 13:7; 14:6). The epistles are addressed to new Christians learning to live and think, worship and witness, in a multi-faith world. Acts relates the history of mission to that world. The Gospels tell the story of Jesus, and all in their different ways address the question of how non-Jews will be included in God's kingdom.

Matthew sets the tension at the very beginning, when he presents Jesus as the Son of David and of Abraham, and then tells how the Magi – foreigners of a different faith – recognize him as King of the Jews while the Jewish leaders are indifferent and their king tries to destroy him. The question of the relationship between Jews and Gentiles, and their responses to Jesus, is a theme throughout the book, reaching its climax in Jesus' declaration of his authority over all and command to make disciples of all in 28:18–19.

Mark has little to say explicitly about the Gentiles, but his Gospel bears the marks of being written for them. Its climax is arguably the Roman centurion's declaration 'Surely this man was the Son of God!' (15:39).

Luke is the first part of Luke-Acts, which tells the story of the mission to Jerusalem, Judea, Samaria and 'the ends of the earth' (Acts 1:8). It therefore gives attention to Jesus' interactions with non-Jews, especially the despised Samaritans.

John is different. It does not refer much to non-Jews, but clearly presents Jesus as the universal life-giver, from the cosmic dimensions of the prologue to the catch of 153 fish, apparently representing all the nations, after the resurrection.[2] Non-Jews appear explicitly in chapters 4 and 12. The first is a Samaritan woman. It is in the context of a discussion about her religion that Jesus first declares himself to be the Messiah (4:26), and she becomes an effective witness to her people. The incident in chapter 12 is even more significant: it is the desire of some Greeks to see Jesus that signals the turn of the Gospel towards the cross.

Up to this point, John has been pointing forward to something he calls 'the hour', and insisting that it has not yet come (2:4; 7:6; 7:30; 8:20). Now, in 12:20, some Greeks want to see Jesus. They do not go directly to him, but to Philip. Perhaps they were aware of the divisions between Jews and Gentiles, and uncertain about whether Jesus would receive them. Philip seems to have been uncertain too, because he goes to Andrew and they go to Jesus together. Jesus' response is amazing. It is not 'I won't see them because they are Gentiles', but neither is it 'Bring them to me!' It is, instead, 'The hour has come!' (12:23)

This seems to have nothing to do with the Greeks, and we are not told whether they saw Jesus or not. John is not telling this incident to give us the story of the Greeks, but to show that the coming of the Gentiles was the sign of Jesus' 'hour'. And what was the 'hour'? It was the time when Jesus was glorified, when he fell into the ground and died, when he was lifted up, and when he drew all people to himself (12:23, 24, 32). It was the cross.

And that, of course, is what the New Testament tells us about the non-Jews. It was God's plan to include them in his kingdom, but it could happen only through the cross. The death and resurrection of Jesus stand at the centre of the New Testament's interaction with people of different faiths, as they do at the centre of everything else. The cross is the cost of the covenant that God offers to all peoples.

Working this out was not easy, because including the Gentiles disrupted the ties between religion and a particular people and culture. Galatians shows how strong these ties were, and how the early church had to struggle to deal with them.

The questions were whether Gentiles had to become Jewish in order to share God's blessing, and whether Jewish Christians should keep to their God-given cultural taboos. The specific points of concern were circumcision and ritual purity: Should Gentiles be circumcised? And could Jews eat with Gentiles? These questions go right to the heart of the gospel (Gal. 1:6–10).

Galatians 2 tells how the Christian leaders realized that the Gentiles did not have to be circumcised: this definition of God's people was no longer necessary, since both Jews and Gentiles needed the salvation brought by Christ. Neither did Jews have to become uncircumcised: they were still Jews.[3] Ritual purity seems to have been a bigger problem, which even Peter stumbled over; but it is clear that the early church eventually decided that he was wrong. The Gentiles did not have to become Jews; neither could the Jews keep all the old religious rules.

These answers would have been a surprise to many Jews. The rules were God given, and the Jews had been severely punished for breaking them. They had been judged for trying to be like the other nations (e.g. Ezek. 20:32ff.), and Moses had nearly lost his life because his children were not circumcised (Exod. 4:24–26). Why, then, were the God-given religious rules no longer necessary, and even dangerous to the gospel?[4]

The law was given to mark Israel as God's people. It is important to remember how it did this: it took the various human institutions of the time, and transformed them so that Israel would reflect the character of her God. Thus Israel could be a nation like the nations around her, but everything about her would show that her God was not like their gods. All this was, says Paul, temporary: Israel needed this religious framework only until both she and the other nations could be transformed through her Messiah.

Paul goes back to Abraham, and explains that he lived and received God's promise of blessing for the nations long before the rules were given. It seems that his study of Abraham took him to the same conclusion that we reached in chapter 5. To begin with, Abraham was not given any religious practices: he simply worshipped in the way he already knew. God's priority was to call Abraham and his family into a relationship with himself. Other aspects of religion, like laws and ritual purity, were not yet important. What mattered was trust and obedience – in Paul's language, faith (see pp. 76–77). *Paul is applying God's way of mission as seen in Genesis to the new situation of mission to the Gentiles.*

The new people of God should still be different from other peoples, but their mark is not circumcision. It is 'faith working through love' (5:6, English Standard Version). In some of his letters, Paul tells Christians how to organize their lives: how to relate to their previous religion, to organize their worship, and to order their households: he follows the pattern of keeping the human institutions of the time and transforming them.[5] Here, however, he deals with none of this, perhaps because he does not want his readers to think that he is replacing the old laws with new ones. Instead, he gives the basis for all our actions: loving our neighbours as ourselves, through the Holy Spirit at work within us. This is why the food laws had to be broken: they could divide Jewish and Gentile Christians and so break the law of love.

What about Gentile religious practices? Paul sees them as slavery, just like Jewish religious practices (4:8–16). In wanting to observe Jewish practices, the Gentiles are going back to where they were before. It seems that *all* religious practices are liable to have the same result: to enslave us to religion, when we should be free in Christ. In summary, Galatians refuses to link faith in Christ with any one culture or set of religious rules.

Israel had to have laws and ways of worship, because she was a human nation like other human nations. Christians have to have some rules and ways of worship, because they are human beings. How can we make sure that we do not become enslaved to our religion?

The true Jews, a people without nation or land

> You are a chosen people, a royal priesthood, a holy nation, a people
> belonging to God, that you may declare the praises of him who
> called you out of darkness into his wonderful light. (1 Peter 2:9)

Exodus 19:6, situated between Israel's deliverance from Egypt and
receiving the law, summarized Israel's calling and mission (see pp.
89–90). First Peter 2:9 echoes this verse, and shows Israel's calling
and mission fulfilled in Christ. The calling is still to be God's
special people among other peoples with other faiths, but this is a
new kind of people.

First Peter 1 explains *the origin of the new people*. As Israel was
chosen, so the new people are chosen (1:2). As Israel was called to
be holy, the new people are called to be holy (1:15). But, where
Israel was given birth by its rescue from Egypt, the new people are
given birth through the cross and resurrection (1:3).

Who is this new people? 1 Peter 2:4–10 tells us: it is composed
of people who were previously 'not a people'. Peter emphasizes
the fact that they were not necessarily Jews. In fact, many of the
Jews rejected their Messiah (vv. 7–8). Those who believe and trust
in him are not only God's new 'treasured possession' (Exod. 19:5;
cf. 1 Pet. 2:4), but also the new temple where God dwells (v. 5).
The blessing God gave to the descendants of Abraham is now, as
he promised, available to all peoples.

What about the land? What Peter does not say is as important
as what he does say here. He makes no mention of land: the new
people are not called out of the land of Egypt into the land of
Canaan, but out of darkness into light (1 Pet. 2:9). Israel's inheritance was the Promised Land, but the new people's inheritance is
in heaven (1:4–5). They are 'to live among the pagans' (2:12), as
'aliens and strangers in the world' (2:11). Clearly, *the new people is
not a nation like Israel*.

Peter's political advice is that the new people should be obedient citizens of the state in which they live (2:13–17). Their first
allegiance is to God as citizens of heaven, but this citizenship does

not require a Christian state. Rather, they should accept state authorities as part of their service to God.

This is, perhaps, surprising, since the state in which they live is not at all friendly to their faith. It follows the pagan religions, and treats its king like a god. It even persecutes Christians. If ever there were an argument for Christians to try to change the government in order to live in security, it would be here. Or perhaps it would be in a situation where a country has been occupied by a foreign army, which is oppressing people and trying to change the way they worship. That would be like Israel at the time of Jesus. He refused to fight the state, and, says Peter, Christians are to follow his example, whatever the cost (1 Pet. 2:21).

Why, we may ask, should the new people not be a nation? Why should they not seek to rule in their land so that they can establish God's laws? After all, as we have seen, religions are usually linked to places and nations and rulers. Part of the answer is that they are a different kind of people, fighting different kinds of battles. But part of the answer is that the Messiah is for all peoples. Imagine what would have happened if he had decided to bring a political rule to all peoples, as the devil suggested to him in the desert (Matt. 4:8–9)! Imagine what would have happened if the new, universal, people had wanted land! We would have had conquest, as in Joshua, but it would have been the conquest of the whole world. I want to suggest that if a religion is to be for all peoples, it will either say that land does not matter, or it will seek to conquer all lands.[6] The new Joshua had to be different from the old Joshua if he were to save the world rather than destroy it. He did not come to save people from their enemies, but from their sins. His sword was very different from the sword the first Joshua (Heb. 4:8–16) had wielded.

1 Peter 2:9–12 comes between the telling of how God has formed his new people and the instructions on how they are to live, just as Exodus 19:3–6 comes between the story of the exodus and the giving of the law. It is not surprising, then, that we find the exodus ideas of a chosen people, a royal priesthood and a holy

nation in it. Verses 9b–12 reminds us that this *calling* is for the purpose of *mission*. Israel was to glorify God among the nations: *the new people are also to glorify God among the nations*. Like Israel, they are to do this by being holy; and, like Israel, it is this call that makes them different from other peoples. The rest of the epistle explains something of what this will mean.

According to 1 Peter, what are the marks of the new people of God?

The kingdom of God and the kingdom of Caesar

From beginning to end the New Testament proclaims God's kingship. From the beginning, Matthew 'celebrates the coronation of the saviour, the God-with-us King'.[7] By the end of Revelation all the kingdoms of the world have been judged, and bring their wealth to the throne of God and the Lamb in the New Jerusalem.

The Sermon on the Mount lays Matthew's foundation for understanding the kingdom of God. As the Jews were expecting, it fulfils the law and the prophets. What would have surprised Jesus' hearers would have been his omissions: there is no mention of an ethnic, political or national kingdom, a particular social order or culture, or even of particular religious practices. This is clear in the Beatitudes:

- The first three (Matt. 5:3–5) offer the blessings of kingdom, comfort and land. All these are things that the Jews expected on return from exile. They did not yet have them, and they expected the Messiah to bring them. Jesus says that he does bring them, but they are different. The kingdom is not of this world, but of heaven. The comfort is not for exile, but for mourning. The land now seems to be the whole earth, and it will be inherited by meekness and not by military power.
- The next three (vv. 6–8) tell us what kind of religion will both meet our needs and bring us to God. It is not religion that follows laws, but religion that longs for righteousness. It does not say, 'I am right and you are wrong,' but recognizes my

own need for mercy and shows mercy to others. It is not
ritual purity that allows us into God's presence, but purity of
heart.
- The last three tell us the political implications of being God's
  own people. The kings of Israel were sometimes called God's
  sons (e.g. 1 Chron. 17:13). Here Jesus says that God's sons, and
  members of his kingdom, are not the people who fight for
  land, but the people who make peace; not the people who
  have victory, but the people who are persecuted.

The last beatitude is a repeat of the eighth, with two extra
verses to explain it, so it must be important. Persecution, and not
conquest, is the mark of the kingdom of heaven.

*Nationalist religion, political religion, legalistic religion . . . How could
a God-given religion go so wrong? What might be the results in
your context of living by the Beatitudes in relation to people of other
faiths?*

From the temptations to the cross, Jesus consistently refused
political power. It was on the cross that, as all four Gospels record,
we see Jesus as 'The King of the Jews'. Jesus redefined God's
kingdom through laying down his life to redeem a new people. As
he explained to Pilate, his kingdom is 'not of this world' (John
18:36).

But Jesus' kingdom did challenge Caesar's power and Pilate's
power and all other 'this-worldly' powers. King Herod, in
Matthew 2, was right to see Jesus as a challenge to his authority.
Caiaphas was right to see Jesus as a threat to the temple and the
nation (John 11:48). Jesus did prevent his followers from fighting
for Jewish rule in the land of Israel. The temple was destroyed,
and the people did lose even the power they had in their land for
nearly two thousand years.

By the end of the New Testament it becomes clear that all
political power will be threatened by the new kingdom.

Revelation shows the power of God's kingdom over all other kingdoms. And whose is that power? The vision of heaven begins with
a throne (Rev. 4), and a voice that declares the triumph of the most
powerful beast: the Lion (5:5). The writer looks, and sees not a
powerful lion, but a Lamb – and the Lamb has been slain (5:6).

Again, it is the cross that defines the kingdom. The kingdom
overrules in all the history of the nations, and results in the final
destruction of the dangerous triangle, with its political and religious power (17:1–6), its autonomy (18:7), and its economic glory
(18:11–17). The final vision is a new land, to which all the kings of all
the nations will come (ch. 21). There will be no more temples
(21:22). The peoples will be under the direct rule of God in the
renewed land (22:1–5). The triangle will be the right way up, forever.

This raises a question important for relating to the many situations where politics and religion are linked: *If Jesus' kingdom is 'not
of this world', in what way does it interact with the kingdoms of the
world?* We shall look briefly at this question through Acts, which
can be seen as the New Testament parallel to Joshua's conquests,[8]
and Revelation, which glimpses God's final triumph.

Acts tells the story of the expansion of the heavenly kingdom
from Jerusalem and Judaea and Samaria to the ends of the earth.
The gospel moves from Jerusalem with its temple, which was the
symbol of Jewish religion in its land, to Rome which was, quite literally, the centre of Caesar's kingdom: I want to argue that Acts
shows us how the expansion of the heavenly kingdom led to
increasing interaction with the earthly powers, starting in
Jerusalem and ending in Rome.

Acts starts with Jesus speaking to the disciples 'about the
kingdom of God' (1:3). They ask, 'Will you now restore the
kingdom to Israel?' which means, 'When will we get power in our
own land?' Jesus responds with the promise of a different kind of
power, of people and of land: the *power* is the power of the Holy
Spirit, the *people* are his witnesses, and their *land* is not only
Jerusalem and Judaea, but also Samaria and the rest of the earth
(1:8). The coming of Holy Spirit power in 2:1–12 reverses the

Genesis 11 judgment on Babel – not by inviting people to build their religion to gain power in their land, but by enabling people from every land to hear the good news of Jesus Christ. This sets the pattern for the rest of the book.

Acts 8 tells of the persecution that pushed the witnesses out of their land into the rest of the world. What leads to the persecution? It is all to do with the temple, with power, with land and with law. The healing and preaching that provoked the persecution were at the temple (3:1, 2, 8, 10, 11; 4:1; 5:12, 21, 25, 42). The believers' prayer recognizes the political powers that join together against God and his Messiah (4:24–29). They know that God is ruler of all, but they do not pray for political power. They ask for boldness and miracles; and the power they receive is Holy Spirit power (4:11). One of the marks of the church was the selling of land (4:34–37), and the first judgment on believers is for abuse of proceeds from the sale of land (5:1–11).

It is not surprising, then, that the opposition focuses on the questions of power (4:7) and the temple (6:13–14). Underlying this seems to be the same concern that led to Jesus' crucifixion: that the Jewish people and the power of their leaders in their land were under threat. Stephen's defence in Acts 7 is a direct answer to these concerns. It uses some of the ideas we have seen in our Old Testament studies to challenge nationalistic religion: the temple and the land were not gained until late in Israel's history; David was not permitted to build the temple; the Jewish people had not kept the laws that identified them as God's people.

Stephen is saying that the temple was unnecessary. People saw temples as ensuring the presence of a god among his people in their land, and therefore as symbols of power. Stephen reminds the Jews that their God is not like that (7:49–50), and so confronts religion that builds the power–people–land triangle. So powerful is the triangle that the response is the stoning of Stephen. Yet, even as he is stoned by the representatives of earthly power, he is filled with Holy Spirit power and sees Jesus in his power at the right hand of God.

The pattern continues. As the witnesses go out, the Holy Spirit kingdom shows its power over increasing areas of land. For Paul, this means not only renewed conflict over the temple (Acts 21 – 22), but also steadily increasing interaction with the representatives of political power, from Jewish and Gentile leaders in Iconium (14:5), through the magistrates' court in Philippi (16:22ff.), the city officials in Thessalonica (17:6–9) and the proconsul's court in Corinth (18:12–16) to the public assembly in Ephesus (19:23–41).

Paul's commission was not only to take the gospel into new cultures and areas: it was to carry the name of Christ before the Gentile kings (Acts 9:15). So the whole of the last quarter of Acts deals with interactions with political authorities.[9] Paul speaks in front of the Roman commander in Jerusalem (21:30 – 22:29), the Jewish Sanhedrin (22:30 – 23:11), two Roman governors at Caesarea (24:1 – 25:12), and eventually to King Agrippa and his court (25:23 – 26:32). The underlying motif is the movement towards Caesar and towards Rome. It is as a Roman citizen that Paul interacts with Roman justice (23:25–28), it is to Caesar that he appeals (25:11), and it is Rome that is his final destination (28:14).

Acts clearly shows us the heavenly kingdom encountering the earthly kingdoms over ever-widening territory and at ever higher levels of power; but at every stage it is the gospel encounter and not the political encounter that is emphasized. It is clear that Holy Spirit power is different in kind to Caesar's power; yet it interacts with Caesar's power at every point.

Yet Paul and the other disciples live in the two dimensions of Caesar's kingdom as well as in the third dimension of God's kingdom. It is as members of the Jewish community that Peter and John stand before the Sanhedrin: it is as a Jew that Paul addresses the Jews (21:39), and as an obedient Roman citizen that he stands before governors and kings.[10] Citizenship matters. In fact, it is our life in the two dimensions that makes the contact point for the third dimension. It was as a Roman citizen that Paul was able to speak to governors and to kings.

However, Paul seldom confronts the earthly powers on their

own terms.[11] When he stands before the authorities, it is not as a diplomat or as a politician, but as a prisoner. When he speaks, it is not about earthly powers but about Christ. When he finally arrives in Rome, there is no suggestion that he actually sees Caesar or interacts with his kingdom or challenges his lordship: rather, Acts finishes with him preaching the kingdom of God and teaching about the Lord Jesus Christ.

As Pilate understood that Jesus had committed no crime against Caesar, so Festus and Felix realized that Paul had done nothing punishable by Roman law. None of these leaders knew what to do with the prisoners in front of them, because these prisoners simply did not fit into the leaders' expected categories. The kingdom of God was not 'of their world'.

Revelation is addressed to Christians living as small minorities under a regime that was often hostile. It offers them no hope of political power or freedom: instead, it gives them a glimpse of how the heavenly king is dealing with and will deal with the earthly kingdoms. It shows them the true nature of power in God's final triumph. Most relevant for our study, it shows them the true nature of the oppressive earthly powers.

Two Old Testament pictures are used: Babylon and beasts. Babylon reminds us of the link between religion and power that was so dangerous at Babel, of the power wielded over Israel, and of the barbarity mourned in Psalm 137. The beast reminds us of Daniel, the book that so clearly tells of God's power in the centre of Babylon.

What makes a religion beastly, and puts it under God's judgment? Revelation 13 and 18 tell us: the mark of the beast is what gives access to trade (13:16–17); and it is the abuse of wealth, power and self-sufficiency that are judged (18:2–7, 11–17), just as it was for the nations surrounding Israel in Old Testament times. It is when a religion becomes associated with economic interests, a totalitarian state or a powerful political leader, that it becomes 'beastly' – less than human. It can persecute God's people, it can be cruel and unjust, and it can try to replace God's rule with its own. Both

Daniel and Revelation show that this is not just a human problem. This sort of religion is likely to have its origin in Satan's plans. The battle between such a religious regime and God's people on earth is equally a battle between spiritual powers.

The good news is that, as we are assured of God's victory over Satan, we are also assured of his righteous judgment of these regimes. Alongside God's judgments go his mercies. Both Daniel and Revelation assure us that those who remain faithful will be saved, even if they are martyred. They will be members of the New Jerusalem.

Where do you see religions linked with land and power in the world today? Where does the Holy Spirit kingdom meet the political powers in your country?

11

FACING SAMARITAN RELIGION

The New Testament writers faced different aspects of religion. Judaism raised questions of nationalism and ethnocentrism, and of a focus on laws. The Gentile faiths raised questions of the worship of false gods, and of political religion. The beginnings of Gnosticism raised questions of experience-based religion that loses ethics, and of a mystery that is available only to the chosen few. All the religions raised the problem of occult practices and, to varying extents, politicized religion. For Christians in many contexts today, some of the most important questions are raised by a less influential people: the Samaritans. There is not much about them in the New Testament, but what there is matters, because they raise issues that are most likely to spoil relationships with people of other faiths: prejudice and hostility. It is also through the Samaritans that we can best see the Lord Jesus Christ himself interacting with people of a different faith.

The Samaritans and Jews were long-standing rivals. There were several violent clashes between the two communities during New Testament times. Such was the mutual hostility that Jews travelling from Galilee to Judaea would walk a very long way to avoid

Samaria. As John explains, 'Jews do not associate with Samaritans' (John 4:9). Why was this?

The origins of Samaritan religion are said to go back to the division of Israel into northern and southern kingdoms, and Jeroboam's golden calves in the north, whose capital was Samaria (1 Kgs 12). From that time on, the worship of Yahweh in the north was marred by the presence of these images. Then, when the Samarian Jews were exiled to Assyria, the Assyrian king brought foreigners into the area. 2 Kings 17 tells of how they continued to worship their own gods, but were attacked by lions. They therefore decided to worship Yahweh, but also continued to worship their own gods. At the time of Ezra they wanted to help build the temple in Jerusalem, but were not allowed to, probably because of this mixed religion; but they were allowed to join the Passover worship if they completely put away all other gods.

We know little about the inhabitants of Samaria during intertestamental times, but it is clear that, by the second century BC, they were *separate* from the other Jews and that there was a great deal of *enmity and suspicion* between the two communities. As Luke 17:18 shows, many Jews thought of the Samaritans as foreigners. However, they worshipped only Yahweh, opposed religious images, and kept strictly to the laws of Moses. They had some particular beliefs, but first-century Judaism was so varied that most of them can be found in other Jewish groups. For example, they accepted only the Pentateuch scripture, but so did the Sadducees.[1]

It might seem, then, that the enmity between Jews and Samaritans arose more from political and social struggles than from religious or ethnic differences. The biggest religious differences that they had their own temple, their own priesthood, and their own text of the Pentateuch. These may seem small differences to us, but temple, priesthood and Torah were the key symbols of Israel's national and ethnic identity. These were what Ezra and Nehemiah had worked so hard to establish when they returned from exile, and they were what so many Jews were fighting for and hoping for at the time of Jesus. As we have so often seen in our study, religion, ethnicity and politics go together. The different temples symbolized the deep division between the two communities.

From a Jewish point of view, then, Samaritan religion was the religion of a despised minority. It was similar to Jewish religion, but it had some errors that made it into a rival, and there was a history of enmity that had led to strong feelings of hostility. It is in this context that we can understand the revolutionary acts of Jesus and the Holy Spirit in relationship with Samaritans.

John 4:1–42: Jesus spoke to a Samaritan woman

John gives a great deal of space to this part of Jesus' mission, which affected not only the woman but her whole community. It follows the cleansing of the Jerusalem temple, Nicodemus the Pharisee's struggle to understand Jesus' teaching about the new birth, and John the Baptist's testimony about Jesus. Now, Jesus decides to travel back to Galilee and, rather than avoiding the Samaritans, he goes through Samaria. He then crosses barriers of prejudice and tradition to ask a Samaritan woman, ostracized even by her own community, for a drink of water.

This chapter has often been used as a model for personal evangelism, and for mission to people of other faiths. For example, Christian women seeking to reach Muslim women point out how Jesus spends much time with one outcast woman, sees and meets her needs, and through her reaches a whole village. Much can be learnt by reading the story in this way, but its place in John's Gospel, and the content of the discussion between Jesus and the woman, make it clear that this is not only a story about breaking down barriers. It also teaches us about the place of the Samaritans in God's plans. It is to this Samaritan woman that Jesus first announces in John's Gospel that he is the Messiah (v. 26). We learn, with Jesus' disciples, that Jesus is the Saviour of the world, and not just of the Jews (v. 42).

Nicodemus, the educated male Pharisee and council member, found Jesus' teaching about new birth difficult to understand, and

John does not tell us how he responded until after the crucifixion (19:39). In chapter 3 we are told only that he came to Jesus at night, presumably because he was afraid of showing a public interest in him. In contrast, this nameless, outcast, Samaritan woman not only understands the implications of Jesus' theological discussion: she immediately bears witness to her whole community.

The Jews thought the Samaritans had the wrong temple. John has already shown us in 2:13–24 that the Jerusalem temple was corrupt. In the conversation with the Samaritan, Jesus acknowledges that the Jews are, in a sense, right, because God has chosen them to bring his salvation. But in another sense they are wrong: in the end, neither temple matters, but 'worship in spirit and in truth' (4:24). The questions about religious practice are the wrong ones. What is needed is a whole different approach – a new birth.

Are there any people that Christians in your area think of as the Jews did of the Samaritans? What are the reasons for the hostility and suspicion? How can John 4 speak into your situation?

Luke-Acts: the Samaritan mission

Luke is one of the New Testament writers most interested in mission. His history of the early church tells us that, between reaching Jews and going to the ends of the earth, the gospel had to go to the Samaritans. This is not only in the announcement of mission in Acts 1:8: it is also what actually happens in Acts 8:2–8.

We might wonder how Jesus' disciples felt when they heard that they were to be witnesses in Samaria (Acts 1:8). Certainly, they did not go there until forced to flee from Jerusalem (Acts 8:1–8). What happened when they got there is significant: God did miracles, and the Samaritans were ready to listen and to receive the gospel with great joy. The Jerusalem church sent Peter and John to find out what was happening, and God sent the Holy Spirit to the Samaritans so that everyone could clearly see that they too were included in God's kingdom. The Jewish Christians had to learn again the lesson of John 4: that the Samaritans might be even more eager to respond to Jesus than were the Jews. This should not be a surprise to anyone who has read the first part of Luke's writings. The Samaritans appear three times in his Gospel.

Jesus experienced their prejudice against Jews (Luke 9:51–56)

On his way to Jerusalem he chose to go through Samaria, rather than taking the normal long route around it; but the Samaritans did not want him. Jesus' disciples responded to prejudice with their own prejudice and anger. Their question 'Do you want us to call down fire from heaven to destroy them?' reminds us of Elijah's competition with the prophets of Baal in 1 Kings 18. Jesus rebuked them. Some manuscripts of Luke's Gospel tell us what he said: that the disciples did not know what was pushing them to speak like this, and that he had come to save and not to destroy. Jesus met prejudice with love. He did not want to fight back, but wanted to find a way of redeeming the situation.

This incident comes at a very significant point in Luke's Gospel: it is the first thing that happens after Jesus sets out for Jerusalem and the cross. It is immediately followed by teaching on the cost of following Jesus. As the coming of the Greeks is the signal in John's Gospel that Jesus' hour has come, so here turning towards the cross is accompanied by opposition from the Samaritans.

Jesus challenged Jewish prejudice against Samaritans (Luke 10:25–37)

In this well-known parable Jesus deliberately chooses a Samaritan as the hero and two Jewish religious leaders as the villains. The despised Samaritan, Jesus suggests, may keep the heart of the law better than the best Jewish law-keepers. More than that, he challenges the basis of the legal expert's thinking: it is impossible to keep God's laws, he implies, while we think of some human beings as our neighbours and put others into a different category.

Jesus included a Samaritan in his healing ministry (Luke 17:11–19)

Leprosy was so unclean that the Jewish lepers were no better able to stay among Jews than were Samaritans. And, with something as terrible as leprosy, the religious details that separated Jews and Samaritans were insignificant. Jesus did not stop to ask whether the lepers had the right religion or ethnicity. He simply healed those in need: the religious difference did not matter. To emphasize this, Luke tells us that the Samaritan actually responded better than the others. He appreciated what Jesus had done, perhaps because he had not expected to be included. It is Jesus himself who points out that the only one who said 'Thank you' was a foreigner.

Jesus dealt with prejudice among his own people and against his own people. How did this prepare the disciples for their future mission? How can the church in your area be prepared for mission across barriers of prejudice and hostility?

12

FACING THE GENTILE RELIGIONS

The New Testament is not a theological textbook on other faiths, but it does tell us something of the history of God's dealings with people of different faiths, through the story of the first Christians and their writings. The challenges that faced them were not so different from the ones that face us. This chapter explores how they met the challenges of mission, teaching converts and planting churches in the context of the various Gentile religions of their time.

The challenge of mission: Acts

Acts begins with the commission to witness in 'Judaea and Samaria and to the ends of the earth' (1:8). If it took persecution to persuade the believers to go to Samaritans (8:1–4), it took a direct intervention of God to persuade them to go to Gentiles. That is why the story of Peter and Cornelius is told in detail twice, in Acts 10, and again when Peter tells his story to the other apostles in Jerusalem. Cornelius is described as 'God-fearing': he worshipped God, prayed regularly, and gave to the poor; but he was a Gentile who had not converted to Judaism.

Acts 10 shows how God deals with him; but the focus is on how God deals with Peter.

Cornelius was the person from 'another faith', yet God heard his prayers. In fact, his prayers and almsgiving came to God like the scent of a sacrifice (10:4). In response, God sent Peter, so that not only Cornelius but all his household could hear the gospel. Then God confirmed his work by sending the Holy Spirit in a spectacular way. The message is clear: God hears people's prayers and wants to save them, even if they are not part of his covenant people.

Peter was the Jew, and the foremost follower of Jesus, but he did not understand what God wanted. He thought that ritual cleanliness was more important than preaching the gospel. He was surprised that God wanted to speak to Cornelius (10:34, 47). He was even surprised that God wanted him to go to Cornelius' house (vv. 27–29). Again, the message is clear: God's concern for people was much greater than Peter's. Cornelius' salvation was much more important than ritual purity. The gospel is for all people: the problem is that we may not be willing to share it.

After Peter's lesson, and the acceptance of the Gentile converts by the Jerusalem church, Acts tells of God's mission to the Gentiles through Paul. He went to Jews first, but little by little we see more contact with Gentiles. There are some particularly important encounters with people from the Gentile faiths.

Lystra: meeting a different world view (Acts 14:8–28)

Up to this point Paul and Barnabas go first to the Jews in every city. Here, for the first time, the contact starts with the Gentiles, and is recorded in some detail. It is interesting that the mission starts in a similar way to that in Acts 3, with the healing of a lame man. However, what follows is quite different. In Acts 3 the Jews immediately give glory to God, and Peter is able to tell them the gospel, starting from their previous knowledge of the Scriptures and the life of Jesus. Here in Lystra the Gentiles do not worship the God of Israel. They do not know the Scriptures, and they do not know the story of Jesus. They do know the Greek gods, with Zeus as the chief and Hermes as his messenger. There were stories about these gods visiting human beings together. So, when Paul and Barnabas healed the man, the crowd interpreted the event through what they already knew. They thought that Barnabas was Zeus, and Paul was his messenger. It is not surprising that the priest came to offer sacrifices to them.

However, it does seem to have surprised Paul and Barnabas (v. 14). But it also gave them an opportunity to explain the miracle.

Read what Paul says in verses 15–17, and compare this with Peter's sermon in Acts 3:12–26. What did the Jews already know that the Gentiles did not know?

In Lystra, Paul does not even mention Jesus. He has to start much further back, to the idea of one creator god, and to explain that he and Barnabas are human beings. The crowd is right that Paul is a messenger, but he is the messenger of the one God, and not of Zeus. Like Isaiah, Paul describes the objects of their worship as 'worthless things', while the one God is real, living and active.

People from different religious backgrounds may interpret the same event in different ways. If people do not know about God as their Creator, they may not be ready to hear about Jesus. The history of the people at Lystra did not prepare them to receive the gospel in the same way as Israel's history prepared the Jews. While the Jews could build on what they already knew, the Lystrans had to discover that some of their beliefs were wrong.

Athens: meeting the philosophers (Acts 17:16–34)
The people of Athens recognized all the Greek gods; but Athens was also a centre of philosophy. Many understood the gods in philosophical terms. The Areopagus was a place where they met to discuss their many ideas. Two groups were prominent, both of which were seeking happiness in an uncertain world. The *Stoics*

believed that the universe was governed by Reason, or *logos*, which could be identified with God. Human beings could be happy only if they accepted that they had to live according to this Reason. That is, they had to see what was 'natural' and to live by it. The *Epicureans* were materialists. They believed that the world was nothing but a collection of moving atoms, so that death was the end of everything. They believed that gods existed, but that they lived in a different sphere and had nothing to do with human beings. Their aim was to reach peace and happiness by controlling their desires and enjoying friendships.

Acts 17 is often used to show what Paul accepted and what he rejected from the Athenian religion, and as a model of how to preach in the centre of another religion.[1] It is therefore instructive to look at it in detail.

Paul's reaction to what he saw. He was 'provoked' (Revised Standard Version) or 'greatly distressed' (New International Version) when he saw the many images of the different gods. He therefore started to talk to people. He seems to have spoken to anyone he could, anywhere he could, whenever he could. What he said is described as 'reasoning'. This suggests that he was using the method of the philosophers rather than his normal preaching style.

The Athenians' reaction to Paul. They were curious. They realized that he was bringing new ideas, and that was what they liked to discuss (17:25). However, these ideas were so strange that they did not understand them, so they took him to their debating place, and gave him a chance to speak.

Paul's sermon. As in Lystra, Paul did not preach the message he normally used for the Jews. Instead, he started with the Athenians' own beliefs, and then challenged them.

- He tells them what he has learnt of their religion. When he says, 'I see that you are very religious', he is making an observation. We do not know whether he intended to commend or to criticize them.

- He chooses something in their religion that is incomplete. The altar to an unknown god showed that the people recognized that there was something that they did not know.
- He tells them that he knows what they want to know. Only then does he tell them where they are wrong: the God whom they do not know is the Creator, and does not have to be served like their gods.
- In all this he is discussing things that concern the philosophers: What is the relationship between the gods and the world? What is the relationship between the gods and the *logos*? What is the relationship between their philosophies and popular religion?
- He quotes from their own poets, and uses Stoic thinking to help them to understand (17:28).
- He challenges them. Now they know about the unknown God, they need to turn from their former worship and serve this God.
- He then chooses one part of the gospel about Jesus: the coming judgment proved by the resurrection of Jesus.

It is interesting that the resurrection was one of the topics of discussion between Stoics and Epicureans, and that Paul's message about resurrection was what they were curious about – they seem to have thought that 'Jesus' and 'resurrection' were two new gods (17:18). It seems that Paul's whole sermon was designed to respond to their interest. He carefully started from within their way of thinking, and moved towards showing them that his message was quite different. He was not proclaiming another god like theirs, but correcting their ideas of god and introducing a whole new concept – of resurrection and judgment – not only as an interesting idea, but as a personal challenge.

And they responded. Some mocked, but others were interested, wanted to hear more, heard more of the gospel and believed.

Ephesus: a religious centre (Acts 19)

The other Gentile mission that Acts describes in some detail is that to Ephesus, one of the chief cities of Asia Minor. Ephesus was famous for its temple to Diana or Artemis, and also for its magic. In particular, it was known for the 'Ephesian names' – secret, magic words reputed to have great power.

When Paul arrived in Ephesus, he first had to complete the mission to the Jews there that had been started by Apollos (18:24–26). After three months' teaching in the synagogue, he experienced opposition and decided to move to a more public place. There he spoke to Gentiles as well as Jews every day for two years. As in Athens, it is not said that he 'preached' but that he 'discussed' or 'disputed' (19:8–9). The Greek word is *dialegomai*, from which we get 'dialogue'. Whatever Paul discussed, and however he did it, the result was that 'all the Jews and Greeks who lived in the province of Asia heard the word of the Lord' (v. 10). The picture is of a centre where people can come to learn, discuss and ask questions, and from which people travel and tell others about what they have learnt. We can imagine Paul's message being passed from person to person, just as an interesting item of news might be spread. Even those who did not believe it could have passed it on. There were also many healings and miracles and signs of the power of Jesus over other powers.

The 'dialoguing' happened peacefully, but the overall effect of Paul's mission was civil unrest (vv. 25–41). This does not seem to have been because Paul and his companions preached against the local religion: in fact, the city clerk defended them by saying that they had not 'blasphemed our goddess' (v. 37). It does not even seem to have been a direct spiritual opposition, although the story of the Jewish exorcists in verses 13–16 reminds us of the spiritual battle that must have been raging. The main problem was that the religion at Ephesus was closely connected to the city's finance. Where previous opposition had been due to Paul's message, the opposition at Ephesus was due to the threat to peoples' *wealth*. The fear that he might be taking away Diana's glory seems to have

been secondary to the fear that he might be taking away the craftsmen's money (vv. 25–27).

Mission and magic (Acts 8:4–25; 13:6–12; 16:16–21; 19:9–22)
Religion is often associated with magic and sorcery. That is, it uses
spiritual powers opposed to God. Magic was part of the Gentile
religion in Ephesus. But Acts also shows us magic in Samaritan
religion in 8:4–25, and in Jewish religion in 13:6–12. The Jewish
magician Elymas opposed the apostles, but the Samarian, Simon
Magus, wanted to use the Holy Spirit for his own purposes – he
even thought he could buy the power of Christ. His clash with the
apostles came after he had been baptized. In both cases, the
verdict is severe:

> May your money perish with you . . . Repent of this wickedness . . . you
> are full of bitterness and captive to sin. (8:20–23)

> You are a child of the devil and an enemy of everything that is right! You
> are full of all kinds of deceit and trickery. Will you never stop perverting
> the right ways of the Lord? Now the hand of the Lord is against you. You
> are going to be blind . . . (13:10–11)

Neither Simon nor Elymas seems to have repented, but, in
Ephesus, many did turn from magic, and destroyed all that had
been associated with it (19:18–20). However, this did not happen
until the danger of abusing the name of Jesus was demonstrated.
In 19:13–16 we find some Jewish exorcists who try to use the name
of Jesus, and are overwhelmed by the spirit they are trying to cast
out. We cannot buy the name of Jesus, and we cannot use it for
our own purposes. Neither can we use it safely, unless we have
turned to him and away from all other powers.

There is one other story in Acts that is relevant here. This is not
about a magician, but about a girl who could tell the future (Acts
16:16–21). She was possessed by a spirit that recognized Jesus and
his servants. We learn little about the girl, except that she was a

slave. We can assume that she wanted to be free from her masters and from the spirit – at least, Paul released her in the name of Jesus. Acts does not blame her, but her owners, who used her to get money for themselves. As in Ephesus, so in Philippi: it is the loss of money more than the message of the gospel that provokes a riot.

In summary, Acts shows us different faces of Gentle religion. In Lystra the misunderstandings were so great that Paul and Barnabas did not get very far in explaining the gospel. In Athens Paul was able to get further because he could relate to the thinking of the philosophers. In Ephesus a long period of discussion and explanation led to great blessing and thence to opposition. In all these *speaking* about the gospel was important, and Paul spoke differently in each place. In Lystra and Ephesus *healing* was important, but in Lystra it was completely misunderstood. In Ephesus *dealing with magic* was important, but magic could also be found in Jewish and Samaritan religion, and even in someone who had received Christian baptism.

Paul had different levels of success in different places. What were the main things opposing the gospel in each place? How did Paul deal with them? What did God do?

The church in a Gentile world

We have seen that the inclusion of the Gentiles brought questions about culture, which are dealt with in principle in Galatians. In practice, there was much still to be worked out. Converts had to find out what they could keep from their own culture, what they had to reject, and what they could transform. There were pressures on the new Christians to mix their faith with ideas from other religions; and there were also occult influences to be faced. Some of the epistles deal with such issues.

Ephesians speaks of the power of the Holy Spirit and the name of Christ in the context of a city famous for its magic and powerful names.[2] It shows how the gospel deals with all the powers of darkness, and how Christians can stand firm in the face of the occult.

Colossians deals with syncretism – mixing Christian faith with ideas from other religions.[3] Gnosticism is a syncretistic religion that uses ideas from Judaism, Greek religions and Zoroastrianism as well as Christianity. Although Gnosticism did not emerge until the second century AD, some of the ideas out of which it grew can be seen in the false teaching in Colossae. They seem to have grown out of the changing world of both Jewish and Christian thinking.[4] Colossians tells the Christians how to discern which ideas from the other religions they can use, and which they must reject. The test is Christ: Do the new ideas help us to appreciate his greatness? Do they recognize the total sufficiency of his incarnation, death and resurrection? Do they encourage lives lived to his glory? Colossians also tells us that his power is sufficient to deal with all fears and needs that the other ideas claim to meet.

Syncretism and magic are two very important issues in multi-faith contexts, and Ephesians and Colossians have much to teach us, but I shall give the limited space here to another epistle. 1 Corinthians deals with some of the urgent practical questions asked by a new church in a religious Gentile context. Chapters 8–10, which deal with the question of food offered to idols, offer a focus to develop basic principles for Christians living among people of other faiths.

What is appropriate for God's people? (1 Cor. 8 – 10)

Food is an important subject for interfaith relations. Every major faith has some sort of food laws – except Christianity. In our study of how the gospel went to Gentiles, we have already seen Peter's lesson about food in Acts 10, and his reluctance to eat with Gentiles in Galatians. In principle, it was decided, the Gentiles could keep their culture and the Jews should eat with them. In practice, there were difficult decisions to be made. The council of Jerusalem in Acts 15 agreed that the Gentiles could keep everything except 'food sacrificed to idols, blood, the meat of strangled animals and sexual immorality' (v. 29). These were the things considered necessary to keep fellowship between Jewish and Gentile Christians: three of them have to do with food.

The mixed Jewish–Gentile Antioch church was happy with this ruling (Acts 15:31). But, as the church became established in thoroughly Gentile environments, things were not so easy. 1 Corinthians deals with a number of issues that arose in a new cultural and religious context. At its heart is a long discussion about food. We shall take time to look at this discussion in depth, since it raises a number of issues important for any new church in the context of a non-Christian religion. The basic question is, 'How can we *both* relate to our neighbours of other faiths *and* remain loyal to Christ?'

This raises questions about the other faith: how should we interpret it, and how do its various adherents interpret it? It raises questions about personal motivation: Are we looking for comfort and status, or are we ready to follow Christ in the way of the cross? It raises questions about relationships within the church: How will my action affect my brothers and sisters in Christ? And it raises questions about relationships with society: How far should we take part in the various activities of our community, and how should we show our loyalty to the state? 1 Corinthians is one of the richest resources in the whole Bible for Christians trying to live holy lives in a multi-faith society, because it is addressed to Christians who had asked for help to do just that.

The Greek city of Corinth had been destroyed in 132 BC and rebuilt as a Roman colony in 44 BC.[5] It was a wealthy centre of culture and trade, which was based on the structure and morals of Roman society but attracted people from many nations. It was a centre for the cult of emperor worship, and managed the nearby 'Isthmian Games' in honour of the emperor. These included music and poetry competitions, athletics and chariot races, and were accompanied by religious celebrations and feasts.

This resulted in a society of 'competitiveness, pragmatism and pluralism'.[6]

Competitiveness. Status was important in Roman society: people of higher and lower status were treated differently in Roman law. For example, a lower-status person could not take legal action against a higher-status person, and only the highest-status people would be invited to attend feasts at the games. In Corinth it was possible to change status by getting the right education, meeting the right people, becoming rich or being religious. So there was competition in all these areas. For example, there was great rivalry between teachers who wanted to attract the most and richest students (in Greek, *mathētēs*, or 'disciples'). There was then rivalry between the students of the different teachers.

Pragmatism. People's actions were often based on what worked rather than on what was right. If they wanted high status, what worked was what gave them public recognition. That is, it was what other people saw that mattered. For example, there was a strong tradition of rhetoric (public speaking), and what worked there was the style of dress and of speech – truth was not so important.

Pluralism. The different peoples living in Corinth had different religions. We have mentioned the imperial cult, but there were also Jews there, and temples to Demeter, the earth goddess, to Asklepios, the healer, and to the Egyptian gods Isis and Serapis. All except the Jews had their images, sacrifices and feasts; and devotees worshipped individually except at festival times.

The church in Corinth was just as mixed as the rest of the population. It included both Jews and Gentiles, and, although many of the Christians were of low status, some were high-status people (1 Cor. 20:26). It is not surprising that people from such different backgrounds had different ideas about how to deal with the challenges of following Christ in Corinth, and that they wrote to Paul for help. The problems of division (1 Cor. 1 – 4), morality (1 Cor. 5 – 7) and idolatry (1 Cor. 8 – 10) in the church reflected Corinthian 'competitiveness, pragmatism and pluralism', and all these aspects of society affected Christian fellowship and worship (1 Cor. 11 – 14).

In each case, Paul points the Corinthians to Christ crucified. Worship of other gods might not have been the cause of the competitiveness and the pragmatism in Corinth. They are the results of sin, going right back to Adam and Eve, who wanted to compete with God. However, a society whose gods are figures of power, fertility and healing is likely to reflect these gods. The cross both deals with the underlying sin and demands very different attitudes.

The chapters that deal with food are 8 – 11. The main issue is *eidōlothyton* – the food associated with idols that had been forbidden in Acts 15. This may have been straightforward for the Jewish Christians, who would never have entered pagan temples and probably knew little about what happened there. Their tradition was to eat specially killed kosher meat, and even the Roman authorities recognized this, decreeing that Jews should have access to kosher meat in special parts of markets. For the Gentiles this was not always a possibility. Further, Paul had told them that they should not avoid associating with non-Christians, and had specifically included idolaters (1 Cor. 5:9–10). This seems to have confused some of them. We can imagine them asking how they could possibly associate with idolaters and at the same time follow the Jerusalem instructions about food.

What counted as *eidōlothyton*? Even to decide this, we need to ask about the nature of the idols, what was done with the food, the contexts in which it was eaten, and the meanings given to it by different people. Each of these questions would have been seen differently by different people. And, as for so many other aspects of the world behind the New Testament, we have limited information about what they would have thought.

The word *eidōlon* in the Septuagint translation of the Old Testament referred to the images of pagan gods that the Israelites were forbidden to worship and that were mocked by Isaiah. Some first-century rabbis were so against images that they forbade any kind of statue. Others thought that an image was nothing but a piece of wood or stone until or unless it was worshipped, so that they could even allow Jewish craftsmen to make images that would later be worshipped.

In Greek there is a word – *agalma* – for a statue, but it is not used in the New Testament. An *eidōlon* is more often a ghost or an image or even a dead body. It is not real, in that it is not the thing itself but a representation of it. The word is sometimes used of images of gods, but also of images of human beings. There were many different ideas about the images of gods. Some people thought that they had real power, and even expected the god to speak through the image. Some thought they were nothing, and mocked the very idea that a god could be like his image. Some saw images as representing different aspects of one greater truth. There was a range of opinion between these extremes, and attitudes also varied according to the particular god represented.

In Corinth a major influence was the Roman imperial cult, which is sometimes called 'emperor worship'. However, this is confusing, as the emperor was never strictly considered divine until he was dead. Even then, he was not, in Roman thinking, a god. The Latin for 'god' is *deus*: the dead emperors could only be proclaimed *filius divus* – divine son. People offered sacrifices in front of some emperors' images even when they were alive, but it can be argued that this was not really worship, as they never expected a supernatural blessing or response. It was merely a way of showing thankfulness and respect. It was also a sign of loyalty to the state. The problem was that Greek did not have a separate word to translate *divus*, so *filius divus* was translated *huios tou theou* – son of god.

What about food offered to these *eidōla* (plural of *eidōlon*)? Again, there was a wide variety of practice. The most likely background to 1 Corinthians is that of sacrifices offered to a god, whether as part of the imperial cult or in one of the other temples. The priests would carry out a ceremony including prayers, and then slaughter the animal and divide it into three parts. A small part was burnt in front of the image. A bigger part was offered on a table in front of the image. The largest part was distributed to people. The latter might be eaten inside or outside the temple. It might be used for a feast, or it might be taken home or to the market. The meat from the table and whatever was left of the burnt offering was eaten by the priests and others of sufficient status to be invited.

What did this food mean? The food from the god's table was 'food offered to idols', but what about the main part of the meat? Had it actually been sacrificed to the god? And what did it mean to eat at one of the feasts? In some cases, and for some people, it meant some kind of fellowship with the god. In other cases, such as the emperor cult, it is doubtful whether the meat was offered to a god at all. Most people simply accepted the feasts as part of their way of life, and did not think much about their meaning.

There were many other dimensions to the problem. The different temples had different structures, which could include banks, markets, museums and libraries. Feasts could be in the inner or the open part of a temple; they could be at the games or in a gymnasium or public hall. They could be social occasions or acts of political loyalty. They offered privilege to the high-status people, who got the biggest portions and the best places. For the lower-status people, they might offer the only opportunity to eat meat at all.

Among Hindus, Buddhists, people of traditional religions, Christians and even Muslims, there are still many different attitudes to images of deities and of heroes and ancestors and prophets and saints. Is it always possible to separate the religious and social meanings of what people do in your context?

It is not surprising that the Corinthian Christians had different ideas about how they should relate to these social and religious aspects of their society, and therefore had to ask for advice. In his response, Paul summarizes the positions taken in the Corinthian church: the 'weak', who would have nothing to do with idol meat, and the 'strong', who were happy to eat it even in a temple. No doubt Paul knew how complex the issues were, but he does not discuss them as we have done. He simply sees individuals who fear that idol meat will lead them away from Christ, and others who

believe that their knowledge and faith are strong enough to with-
stand the idols. However, Paul's response is nearly as complex as
the problem. Here I shall outline his argument.

Basic principles (1 Cor. 8:1–6)

The question is not whether someone's faith and knowledge are
strong, but whether they are acting out of *love*. This is, first of all,
love for God. And it is not their knowledge of God that matters,
but his knowledge of them: it is *God's* judgment of their actions
that they should be thinking about. This brings us to one of the
New Testament's most important statements about God in an
interfaith context: 'for us there is but one God, the Father, from
whom all things came and for whom we live; and there is but one
Lord, Jesus Christ, through whom all things came and through
whom we live' (v. 6).

This clearly refers to the great statement of monotheism in
Deuteronomy 6:4. There, too, it is linked with the call to love God
with all our being. As in the Old Testament, the basic principle for
thinking about other faiths is the fact that there is only one God,
and that he demands total loyalty. Here in 1 Corinthians Paul is
making one of the clearest statements about the divinity of
Christ. He is the 'Lord' of Deuteronomy 6:4.

What about other gods? Paul first agrees with those who say
that, since there is only one God, the others simply do not exist.
This would have been understood differently by Jewish Christians
thinking of Isaiah 46, and by Gentile Christians who saw *eidōla* as
unreal. But the principle is the same: the images are nothing in
themselves. Similarly, food has no spiritual power in itself – it is
simply part of God's creation and provision for us.

So what is the problem? (1 Cor. 8:7)

The problem is that there are, in fact, many so-called 'gods' and
'lords' in the world, and that they have real power in people's lives.
This means that eating food associated with these gods can seriously affect their relationship with the one true God. Some

individuals – the 'strong' – may be able to eat idol-meat without danger. Others – the 'weak' cannot.

What is the answer? (1 Cor. 8:9 – 9:23; 10:31 – 11:1)

Christ. As in the rest of 1 Corinthians, the answer is in Christ and his cross. The real problem is not a disagreement over eating idol-meat, but danger to a sister or brother for whom Christ died.

Paul knew that there were many complicated arguments about exactly where to draw the line between what was permitted and what was not, but he does not even acknowledge these distinctions at this stage. Much more important than the question of what is right for me is the question of what is right for my brother or sister. If I sin against my brother or sister, I actually sin against Christ, because I am destroying someone who was saved by his cross.

Rights? From 8:13 the argument becomes personal. It seems that some of the 'strong' Christians were more interested in their 'rights' than in what was right. The word that the New International Version translates 'rights' (9:4, 5, 12, 15) is *exousia*, which means 'authority'. It could refer to the high status of the 'strong' Christians, which gave them the right to attend special feasts.

Paul states his own rights – he is an apostle of Christ and a free Roman citizen, so he could have a high status at Corinth if he wanted it. But the Corinthians themselves have seen how he forgoes his rights. His own principle for all action is the same principle that he is calling the Corinthians to follow: Christ is at the centre of everything. This is not only a personal loyalty, but so that the gospel may go forward (9:12). That is, he is concerned for the people for whom Christ died. There is no personal right that he is unwilling to lay down for their sake, following the example of Christ (11:1).

What is the danger? (1 Cor. 9:24 – 10:22)

So far, Paul has been speaking about the welfare of the whole church. Now he turns to individuals. Both the picture of the race in 9:24–27 and the reminder of Israel's history in 10:1–10 warn the

Corinthians that some may fall away from Christ. When Israel turned from God, it was to the sort of idolatry, feasts and sexual immorality that were associated with the gods of Egypt. When Israel tested God and grumbled, it was about food. These are the dangers Paul sees in idol-meat.

Verses 14–22 express the heart of Paul's concern: that the 'strong' will fall into real idolatry and find themselves joined to demons and not to Christ. Again, the argument is centred on the cross: the feast that shares the body and blood of Christ joins believers with Christ crucified. Idols and idol-meat are nothing in themselves, but there are spiritual powers other than God that can be associated with the idols, and participation in 'the table of demons' will cut believers off from Christ. This is real idolatry, which every Christian must flee.

Putting it into practice (1 Cor. 10:23 – 11:1)

The problem for us is that Paul does not specify what constitutes participating in 'the table of demons'. Perhaps this is deliberate. Perhaps it means different things in different circumstances. Perhaps, for the 'weak' it means eating inside the temple. Perhaps, for the 'strong' it means eating the part of the meat that has been offered on the *eidōlon*'s table. For everyone it includes being involved in the actual sacrifice. Beyond this, verses 23ff. lay down some clear, practical guidelines:

First, as has been stressed so often, the Corinthians should think about what is good for others, and not about how far they can go as individuals without falling into real idolatry. Second, they should not worry about meat sold in the market. They are not to be like strict Jews, who want to make sure that their food is kosher. They can see the meat as part of God's good creation, even if it has also been part of a sacrifice.

Third, they should accept invitations to meals. This is more difficult to interpret. It clearly involves invitations to meals in people's homes, but what about meals at the games or even in the outer parts of temples? For Paul, the place is not important. The people are important. If someone points out that the meat has been offered in sacrifice, then, for his sake, the believer should not eat it. It is important here that the word for 'offered in sacrifice' is not *eidōlothyton* – the general word for food associated with idols in 8:1. It is *hierothyton* – meat that has actually been sacrificed. Paul's practical conclusion is that, as he said in 5:9–10, the Corinthians should associate freely and eat with people who worship idols, but, for the sake of their hosts, they should make a point of distancing themselves from any sort of idol worship. A practical way of doing this was to decline food if told it was part of a sacrifice.

Paul ends this section by summarizing the whole basis of his argument: *every action, and not only eating and drinking, should be done to God's glory and for the good of others, following the example of Christ.* That brings us to the end of the discussion about *eidōlothyton*, but not to the end of the discussion about food. Chapter 11 is also about food: the special Christian meal of the Lord's Supper. Chapters 11–14 mirror chapters 8–10. Paul has looked at the question of Christians getting involved in pagan feasts. He now looks at the problem of pagan ideas affecting Christian worship. He has to explain how the Christian feast is different from the pagan feasts: it has no room for status, or for overeating or drunkenness; and it goes with moral purity.

He explains the difference between the Holy Spirit and other spirits: there is only one Holy Spirit, and he will only inspire words that bring honour to Jesus. In a very mixed, unequal society he explains the importance of every different person as an equal in the body of Christ. And he explains what kind of love should characterize all Christian worship and relationships. It is only then that he deals with the Corinthians' particular questions about their worship meetings.

There were two big questions for the Corinthians as they tried to live for Christ in their multi-faith society: How far could they be involved in the society? How should their fellowship be different from the society? How does your church deal with these questions? How can 1 Corinthians help your church to be more faithful to Christ?

1 Corinthians starts with the cross: it finishes with the resurrection. In a society full of competition for status, chapters 1–14 have constantly pointed to weakness of the cross as the pattern for Christian discipleship. Chapter 15 moves on to the resurrection. Without the resurrection, the Corinthians' faith is nothing. It is the truth of the resurrection that assures them of the truth of their faith. It is the resurrection that affirms the status of Christ. It is the resurrection that makes all their struggles worthwhile, and gives them victory over sin and death. Why? Because this is the heart of the gospel, and the gospel is where they stand (v. 1). That is where they find their true status.[7] Christ and his cross and resurrection are at the centre of what it means to be God's people in a world of different faiths.

13

The questions we want to ask

Our New Testament study so far has given us many insights into how Jesus and the first Christians related to different kinds of religion. But I am sure that it has left the reader with the questions that people often ask about other faiths. In this chapter we shall try to explore these questions; but we shall not always find clear answers. There are times when we can only go as far as the Bible takes us, and leave the questions open. In what follows I have used personal language to suggest my own tentative answers to some questions: I do not think that they are the only conclusions that seek to be faithful to the biblical text.

Is Jesus the only way of salvation?
In chapter 3 we saw that many Christians answer this question by quoting John 14:6 and Acts 4:12, but that inclusivists, exclusivists and pluralists can interpret these verses in different ways. Perhaps this is because we *want* to interpret them in different ways. Many theologians would agree that God has redeemed us in Christ, that he is God's supreme revelation, and that he is for all people. But, they would ask, why should God not have given more than one

way? Just because God has given us Christ, why should he not have given other ways to other peoples? If there are people on other planets, he may have come to them too, so why not to different peoples on the earth?

The Bible is clear that God does indeed speak to all sorts of people in all sorts of ways. Romans 1:19–20 tells us that everyone can know something about God and, as we have seen throughout the Old Testament, 'God spoke to our forefathers through the prophets at many times and in various ways' (Heb. 1:1). But the point of Hebrews 1 is that all this is completed in Christ: he is the peak of God's revelation.

We can say that all peoples can and do know about God at least in part. But is it possible to be saved from sin in part, or to go to heaven in part? Certainly, the New Testament sees salvation as a process as well as an event; but, in the end, either we are saved or we are not. Either we are forgiven or we are not. Either we go to heaven or we do not. The question is not whether God might have spoken in different ways, but whether there is any other way to salvation, to forgiveness of sin, to new life, to heaven.

To answer this question, we need to read verses like John 14:6 in the context of the whole teaching not only of John's Gospel but also of the New Testament. It seems to me that the New Testament's greatest witness to the necessity of Christ is its whole focus and subject: the Lord Jesus himself. Creation is through and for Christ, God has acted in Christ, everything is fulfilled in Christ, everything necessary has been done in Christ, and all of history will be drawn together in Christ. The New Testament simply does not leave room for any other Saviour.

The New Testament is very clear that *the cross is the only way.* Jesus of Nazareth is not some arbitrary incarnation at a particular time and place. He came to die, on the cross, outside Jerusalem, in the first century. The way to salvation for all is the way to deal with the sins of all. God has dealt with sin on the cross, and has no need to do so again.

The most powerful argument for this is not in any 'doctrinal' passage, but in the gospel tellings of the life of Jesus. All four Gospels show that the only way for him was the cross. From the time of temptation in the wilderness he was again and again tempted to avoid it. Even his closest friends wanted to spare him, but he saw in this the same, satanic temptation. The climax is seen in Gethsemane, where he prays in agony, 'Father, if you are willing, take this cup from me' (Luke 22:42). Three times the only Son prays to the Father. Surely here, if any other way were possible, God would have provided it. Surely he would have heeded the Son's tears and blood. But he who spared Abraham the sacrifice of his son would not spare Jesus the cross. There was no other way.

So all four Gospels are structured to focus on the cross, and John, so different from the Synoptics in other ways, is no exception. For John, the cross as the way does not *exclude* people. Quite the opposite! As we saw at the beginning of our New Testament study, it was the coming of the Greeks in John 12 that showed Jesus that the time for the cross had come. The cross was necessary to *include* non-Jews into God's chosen people.

John does not specifically mention non-Jews very much. Instead, he tells us, over and over again, that through Jesus God is working in *the world* (*kosmos*), and that what he offers is for *all*. 'God so loved *the world* . . . that *whoever* believes . . .' (3:16; my emphasis) is just one instance of this.[1] It is important to notice that John is not only saying that all people can be blessed through Jesus: there is another side. In 3:16 whoever believes will have eternal life, but this implies that there is also a possibility of eternal death. As 3:17–21 goes on to explain, the light needed to come into the world because the world was full of darkness. People who do not accept the light will stay in darkness and 'perish'.

These inclusive, universal themes are very evident in John 1:1–18.[2] Many commentators have pointed out that this prologue is the key to the whole Gospel. One area for scholarly discussion is where the prologue's ideas of light and life, fulness and word come from. Are they Jewish or Greek? Are they Gnostic or biblical? Are they mystical or rabbinic? The answer is, of course, that they are all of these. John has deliberately chosen language that speaks into all the cultures of his time and place.

For example, the word *logos* was used by Jews who believed in a creator God who spoke, and by Greeks who believed in a universal principle. It meant different things to different people, but all would agree that the *logos* was at the heart of reality. When he writes, 'in the beginning was the *logos*', John immediately catches the attention of readers of all sorts. He is talking about something that really matters to them.

The ideas in John 1:3–4 also echo the ideas of many religions. The *logos*, which is the absolute fact of being, is what produced all that exists. It is the source of physical and spiritual life. It is also the source of light – of all that is good and true. All religions and philosophies would also agree that there is darkness – that human beings have problems, and that, even when light shines, many do not accept it or understand it.

For religious people, the idea that God should send someone to speak about the *logos* is no surprise. Nor is it surprising that the light should shine in the world, and that some should receive it and some reject it. The shock comes in verse 14 – the *logos* became *flesh*. If we read back through verses 1–13, we realize that this is just what John was leading up to – little by little, he was telling us that this *logos* was not a principle or an impersonal power or a world soul or a set of words, but a Person. He was not coming into the world as a cosmic force or a mystical influence or a universal spirit, but as one particular human being in one particular place and at one particular time in history. What is more, says John, people have actually seen him, and the glory of God in him.

Can the light be seen anywhere else? Verse 9 says that the *logos* gives light to all people. Grammatically, the phrase 'coming into the world' could refer to the 'true light', so that the verse would mean that the *logos* gives light by coming into the world. But it could also refer to 'every man', so that it would mean that the *logos* gives light to every person who comes into the world. It is possible that John has given this double meaning deliberately: the *logos* has always been a source of light for all, but the light comes in a differ-ent way when he becomes flesh.[3] This is not surprising. We found that Abraham knew something about God through his knowledge of the high god El. We have read about Melchizedek and Jethro who worshipped the true God, and about many Gentiles who came to Israel and to Christ. We have seen from Romans 1 that something about God can be known from his creation.

Even if we do not read verse 9 in this way, verse 4 tells us that the life of the *logos* is the light of humanity, and verse 5 that the light shines in the darkness, and this appears to be before the incar-nation. If the *logos* was always with God and even was God, his light must have been shining in all these situations. We need not be surprised that God heard Cornelius' prayers, or that the Athenians acknowledged an unknown god. The God whom John is writing about is the God of the whole *kosmos*, and all the light and truth in the *kosmos* come from him. We would not expect him to leave his creatures in complete darkness. Some of the early church theologians would have said that John the Baptist was not the only witness to the light: they could also find pointers to it in the Greek philosophers.

But the *logos* has also come into the *kosmos*. It is here that God has dealt with the problem of rejection of the light. It is here that people who accept him can become children of God. John's message is very clear: whoever you are, whatever your understand-ing of the *logos*, whatever your hopes for truth and light, whatever your temptations to hide in the darkness, your answer is *here* – in the flesh. Saint Augustine, explaining how he came to Christ, says that he could find all the ideas in John 1:1–10 in the Greek philoso-phers: what he could not find was that the *logos* had *come*.[4]

C. S. Lewis made a similar discovery. He was familiar with the literature of many faiths and the myths of many peoples. He even-tually came to realize that the greatest question was not 'Where has religion reached its full maturity?' But 'Where, if anywhere, have all the hints of Paganism been fulfilled?' Then he read the Gospels again. They had all the ideas of the greatest myths, but

THE QUESTIONS WE WANT TO ASK

they were not myths: they were true. His conclusion is identical
to that of John: 'Here, and here only in all time the myth must
have become fact: the Word, flesh, God, Man. This is not "a religion" or "a philosophy". It is the summing up and actuality of
them all.'[5]

Readings of John's prologue often finish at verse 14: it is the rest
of the prologue as well as the rest of the Gospel that makes it so
clear that this is the unique incarnation of the universal Word.
John the Baptist testified, 'This is he . . .' (v. 15). This is not just a
sudden appearance, but grace following on from what has gone
before in the particular work of God through Moses (vv. 16–17). It
is in verse 17 that we find out where the *logos* was made flesh: in
Jesus Christ. Verse 14 tells us that people have seen the glory of the
logos: verse 18 affirms that the only begotten Son (Authorized
Version), the one and only (New International Version) is Jesus,
and that such a thing has never happened before.

It is in this context that we should read John 14:6. All of the rest
of the Gospel tells us that it is here, in Jesus of Nazareth, that the
logos has entered the *kosmos*. It is here that he has gone to the
cross and been raised from the dead for all people. It is to him that
all are invited. It is here that we have the way, because it is here
that we have the truth and the light. He is, as the Samaritans realized, 'The Saviour of the *kosmos*' (4:42). 'No-one comes to the
Father except through me' is only the other side of this: if this is
the Saviour for everyone, there need be no other. If the cross was
necessary to deal with the sins of the world, there can be no
other.

The Tao of Taoism is very near to the logos *idea. Hindus have Om, the
eternal sound. Muslims believe in the Qur'an as the eternal, uncreated
Word of God. Much modern philosophy focuses on the use of language.
'Postmodern' thinking asks about the nature of meaning. John's Gospel
still starts from what many people see as the heart of reality. Where do
you start when you want to explain the gospel clearly to different people
today?*

What about the other gods?

In the New Testament the Jews were obviously worshipping the one true God, even when they had wrong ideas about what he wanted, and rejected his Messiah. Samaritans and God-fearers like Cornelius were also worshipping him. But what of the other gods? The New Testament has surprisingly little to say about them.

In 1 Corinthians 8 – 10 we saw that the idols in themselves are nothing but pieces of wood or stone, but that, in worshipping them, people can actually be worshipping 'demons'. The Greek word *daimōn* does not necessarily refer to an evil spirit. It could mean an angel or other spiritual being. However, it does tell us that some people of other faiths are likely to be in contact with spiritual powers other than God.

In Acts 17 we saw that Paul was distressed when he saw the idols. He told the Athenians that they were quite wrong in thinking that the true God could be represented by idols. On the other hand, he saw that they were, somehow, looking for the true God in their worship of an 'unknown god'. This affirms the Old Testament view that it is wrong to worship anything except the true God, and that trying to make images of him is wrong. It also affirms what we learnt from our study of Abraham: that people who have many gods are likely to have one among them who is something like the true God, and who can be a starting point for coming to know him.

In all these religions – Jewish, Samaritan and Gentile – we saw that some people practised magic. It is possible for people to be in contact with occult powers whether they worship the one true God or not.

I doubt we can get any further on this question without going beyond what the New Testament actually says. Clearly, as in the Old Testament, the only right worship is exclusive worship of the one True God: all other worship is disloyal to him and dangerous for his people. The New Testament difference is that the one true God is now seen to be Father, Son and Holy Spirit.

Can people of other faiths go to heaven?

If Jesus is the only way, and worshipping other gods is wrong, does that mean that all non-Christians, including those who have never heard of Jesus, are going to hell? Some people would say that logic says 'Yes!' Others would say that this would mean that God is unjust. We know that God *is* just, so their logic says that the answer is 'No!' Is there anything in the New Testament that tells us which logic is right?

Some point to the parable of the sheep and the goats here (Matt. 25:31–46), suggesting that people will not be judged by their religion but by their actions. The righteous people did not know that they were serving Christ, and there may be people in different faiths who are serving Christ without knowing him. The main purpose of the parable in its context is to warn those who were hearing about Jesus to be prepared for their own judgment, and to let them know that they might be surprised at who was to be saved and who was not. This has important lessons for us if we are tempted to judge people of other faiths, but it does not directly address our question.

A more relevant passage is Romans 2:12–16, which is about God's judgment of the Gentiles. The argument goes something like this:

- *Romans 1:18–25*: All peoples can know about God and what he wants because they are God's creatures and live in God's creation. However, they distort that knowledge because of sin. This leads to false religion, in the worship of something that is not God.
- *Romans 1:26–32*: God's judgment can already be seen where he has allowed people to go their own way, and they have become so wicked that they say that wrong things are right.
- *Romans 2:1–10*: God will judge all peoples, with no partiality.
- *Romans 2:12–16*: However, he will not judge people on the same legal basis: the criterion for judgment is not what they

know, but how they respond to what they know. The Jews
will not escape judgment because they know the law: they
will have to keep it. Similarly, the Gentiles will not be judged
because they do not know the law: they will be judged
because they do not follow what they know.

In the Old Testament there are clear criteria for the judgment
of those who have the law, and in the New Testament there are
clear criteria for those who have heard the gospel. They are judged
for their sins, but also for their response to God and to Christ. The
Old Testament tells of judgment of the Gentile peoples because of
their crimes and barbarities and their treatment of Israel, but not
because of their religion. Similarly, Romans does not tell us *how*
God will judge those who are 'outside the law', but only that he
will do so appropriately.

There are difficulties in applying this passage to the salvation of
non-Christians. First, it is not easy to say who those 'outside the
law' are. In the context of Romans they are clearly Gentiles, but
how we can then apply this to people of twenty-first century non-
Christian faiths is not always clear. Second, Paul's argument is
leading to the conclusion in 3:9 that every person is a sinner: no-one
has kept even the laws that he or she knows. Third, this passage is
not about people who have never heard of Jesus, but about people
who do not have God's laws. So it is not about whether they can be
saved without knowing about the Saviour, but about how they will
be judged if they have not been told what is right and what is
wrong.

What can we conclude? My conclusion is that God is just,
and that I can trust him to judge everyone justly. I also conclude
that everyone deserves to be condemned and needs a Saviour,
and that the Saviour is Jesus. I should therefore do everything
that I can to make sure that everyone hears about him. This
may seem like avoiding the question, but I simply do not think
that the New Testament gives us enough information to decide
whether the 'Yes' logic or the 'No' logic is correct. However, I

do believe that it gives us all the information we need in order to please God.

A friend reading this chapter commented, 'What about Abraham? He was "non-Christian" and had never heard the name "Jesus". It seems to me that we can't know (and are not meant to know) exactly how all these principles work out, or the ways in which God makes himself known through Jesus to all different peoples.' Do you agree?

What about the Jews?
Most of today's faiths cannot be found in the Bible. It is obvious that there is some hard work to be done when we move from the world of the biblical authors to our present-day world. In other words, we can tell the difference between what we see through the text as a window, what we see in the text as a painting, and what we see of our own world in the text as a mirror.

Judaism is different, because the Jews are different. When we look through the text, we see the Jewish people and their history. When we look at the text we see Jewish writings about Jewish people. It is not surprising if we are tempted to identify present-day Jews with biblical Jews. Deciding how we should see today's Jews in the biblical mirror is not easy.

Deciding how we should see today's state of Israel is even harder. Some Christians believe passionately that current Middle Eastern politics are the direct fulfilment of God's promises of restoration for Israel. Others, equally passionately, believe that these promises are fulfilled in Christ and in the new Israel of the church. Questions have to do with both the people and the land: What are God's purposes for the Jewish people, and how are they linked with the Promised Land?

These are not just theoretical questions. From them grow attitudes that affect not only mission but also world politics and economics and wars. On the one hand, some who see the state of Israel as the fulfilment of prophecy conclude that they should fight for Israel and against her enemies – after all, the nations of

Old Testament times were severely judged when they mistreated the Jews. On the other hand, some who see the church as replacing Israel have persecuted the Jews – after all, Jesus himself had harsh words for the religious people who rejected him.

We cannot explore this in detail here, but there are some guidelines that can be drawn out from our studies. After all, I have been doing this study as a Jewish Christian called by God to reach out to Muslims – the very people whom many Christians see as enemies of the Jews. My family has direct experience of the negative results of one sort of theology. Some of my Muslim friends have direct experience of the negative results of the other. So I offer the following as a framework for Christian thinking about the Jews.

Jews are human beings

The Jewish people developed out of just one of the many groups descended from Noah's sons in Genesis 10. They are made in the image of God and fallen, just like everyone else. We have seen how, as a people, they have always had the characteristics of other peoples. They were a nation like the other nations: the only difference was that their God was not like the other nations' gods.

This means that we can find in the Jews the same variety of human characteristics we find in anyone else. As in the time of Jesus, we can still find people who focus on law, people who look for political solutions, people who want to cooperate with the powerful nations, people who turn to violence, people who want to withdraw and be holy, and lots of ordinary people who just want to get on with their lives.

All these Jews are just as much in need of the Messiah as were the Jews of Jesus' time. They, too, need Jesus' interpretation of the law and the prophets. They too need to hear and respond to the gospel. This is not only that sins are dealt with and that Israel is restored in the cross and resurrection. It is also that God's kingdom is not the same thing as a Jewish state. Jesus was simply not interested in restoring a political kingdom to Israel. And, what is even more significant, the land of Israel does not seem to matter to the New Testament writers.

As the New Testament uses the ideas associated with kingship in new ways, it uses some of the ideas associated with land in new ways.

- There is the idea of inheritance, but it is in heaven (1 Pet. 1:4). It is the meek, rather than the Jews, who will inherit land (Matt. 5:5).
- There is a focus on Jerusalem, but it is as the place of Jesus' crucifixion and the persecution of his disciples and the near-murder of Paul. As Jesus' entry to Jerusalem on the donkey shows, God's reign from his holy city is in the crucified, risen and ascended Messiah who will come again.
- The writer to the Hebrews speaks of the Israelites in the wilderness unable to enter not the Promised *Land* but the promised *rest* (Heb. 3:18). God's promise still stands, but it is reinterpreted as the rest that we enter when we believe in Jesus Christ (4:3).
- In Revelation, which gives a glimpse of God's final plan, there is a new Jerusalem; but it comes down from heaven to a new earth. There are people from all nations and languages both around God's throne and under God's judgment, echoing the refrain of Genesis 10:4, 20 and 31; but the Revelation peoples have no territory (Rev. 5:9; 7:9; 10:11; 11:9; 13:7; 14:6).

The gospel of the kingdom of God for Jewish people, as for everyone else, continues to challenge the links between religion, ethnic group, territory and power as well as to call individuals to repentance and new life.

God has not finished with the Jews
If Jesus fulfils all God's purposes in calling Israel, and if there is no difference between Jew and Gentile in the kingdom of God,

what does that mean for the Jewish people? Will they simply cease to exist?

They have not ceased to exist. In fact, the continued existence of the Jewish people, scattered among other nations, with no homeland and no political power, is one of the most remarkable facts of history. Every attempt to destroy them, including Hitler's 'final solution' of the gas chambers, has failed.

This should not surprise readers of the New Testament. As Romans tells us, God has not yet finished with the Jews. This epistle is concerned with the relationship between Jews and Gentiles. The first chapters establish that Jews and Gentiles are all sinners under God's judgment, and the next chapters explain how God's covenant with Abraham is fulfilled through the blessing that comes to all peoples through faith in Jesus Christ. Chapters 9–11 then ask whether God has rejected the Jews.[6]

Paul's answer is that God has not finished with them. To be sure, many Jews are unbelievers, and therefore do not inherit the promises to Abraham, but that is nothing new. There have always been children of Abraham who have been outside these promises. It has never been blood relationships that guarantee our place in God's kingdom. All of God's promises are moving towards Jesus Christ, and it is he who is the whole aim of the law and the covenants (10:4).

However, Christ being, as the New International Version translates it, 'the end of the law', does not therefore mean that he brings an end to the Jews. God is the Lord of all peoples, but the Messiah is physically descended from the Jews, and that makes them special. They also have the privilege of having been the people through whom God chose to work (9:1–5). Now comes the sobering part: God's work among the nations is not only through the faithful, but also through the unfaithful. Even Pharaoh, the archetypal opponent of God and his people, was raised up 'that I might display my power in you and that my name might be proclaimed in all the earth' (Rom. 9:17).

Israel has been hardened in her unbelief, says Paul, just as

Pharaoh was hardened in his. We cannot escape the conclusion that it is through God's judgments on unfaithful Israel as much as through his blessing on faithful Israel that he will fulfil his plans to bless the nations through her. And that is just, Paul explains, what he is doing.

But this is not the end of the story. All the results of Israel's unfaithfulness as well as everyone else's have been carried by her Messiah on the cross. Not only will there continue to be faithful Jews: God continues to have plans for Israel. As the Jews were to be God's means of drawing Gentiles to himself, so the Gentiles will now be the means of drawing Jews to himself (11:11ff.).

God's purposes for the Jews remain

A key verse in these chapters of Romans is 11:29, 'God's gifts and his call are irrevocable'. I want to suggest that this twofold understanding of God's *irrevocable gifts* and *irrevocable call* is the essential basis for any Christian thinking about Israel today.

- As the context shows, *God's irrevocable gifts* means that he continues to love his Jewish people.
- *God's irrevocable call* means that his purpose continues to be to bring blessing to the nations through them.

This means that, whatever their interpretation of the current state of Israel, Christians have no basis either for treating the Jews as people whom God hates or for treating Israel's enemies as people whom God hates. *Any theology that leads either to hatred of Jews or to hatred of Muslims must either be wrong in itself or have been wrongly applied.*

At the same time, the context of Roman 11:29 reminds us that both God's love for the Jews and his blessings for the nations through them are likely to continue to be in the context of Jewish sin. God's love for them does not preclude his judgment: quite the opposite. We remember Amos's clear declaration of God's special love for Israel – 'you only have I chosen of all the families of the

earth' – leads to the most sobering declaration of responsibility
and judgment – 'therefore I will punish you for all your sins'
(Amos 3:2).

The context of Israel's call is also the sin of the peoples of the
world. It was sin that led to the fall and the flood and to Babel, and
it was because of sin that the nations needed a means of blessing.
We expect to see sin in the other nations' responses to Israel as
well as in Israel herself. This too is under God's judgment.

And that brings us back to the purpose of Israel seen, above all,
in her Messiah. According to Jesus, the whole history of Israel
points to and is gathered up in one place: his death and resurrection (Luke 24:26–27). He gathered and suffered for Israel's sin and
everyone else's sin. As priest and king and nation, he stands for us
at the centre of our history. I want to suggest that it is not only
that the Old Testament history of the Jewish people points
forward to the cross. In some way, the whole history of the Jewish
people since the time of Jesus must also be understood through
the cross.

Here, thoughts and feelings appall me. How do I understand
the centuries of exile and persecution? How do I understand the
destruction of the Holocaust? How do I understand the triumph
of return to the land? How do I understand ongoing conflict and
terrible injustice? Where are the Jewish people under God's judgment? Where are we a sign to the nations of the dreadfulness of
human sin? In what ways is God showing himself through us?
How can the present situation work for the salvation of Jew and
Gentile, Israeli and Arab? In what way can I see Christ crucified in
Jewish suffering? Or should I be asking how I can see Jewish suffering in our crucified Messiah?

I can only say with certainty that God is still committed to his
Jewish people, that the pattern of his love for us is the pattern of
his righteousness and justice and mercy on the cross, and that his
whole purpose is that we are here, in the midst of the nations,
whether scattered or in Jerusalem, to demonstrate his power and
his name and to open his blessing to *all*.

PART 4

SEEING OURSELVES

14

THE BIBLE AS A MIRROR

In 1999 I attended an international conference on Muslim–Christian relations held in Nigeria.[1] One of the Bible studies was on Joshua, and participants were asked, 'Is the example of the conquest of direct relevance to Muslim–Christian relations today?' Most replied, 'No. This was a unique time.' But some said, 'Yes. We can expect God to fight for us in the same way now as then.'

How would you have answered the question? It is not always easy to decide how to use the Bible in today's world.

We have completed our survey of the Bible and other faiths using the text both as a window on the world of Bible times and a picture that tells us about God's interaction with his peoples. The next step is to ask what all this means for us, now. That is, we want to use the Bible as a mirror, and ask, 'What does this tell us about ourselves and the peoples we meet?'

This is not as easy as it might seem, mainly because it is not always easy to know where we should see ourselves and the peoples we meet in the Bible. This is, perhaps, where we can make the greatest mistakes in our theology and therefore in our actions: we can make false assumptions about people of other faiths by jumping to conclusions about where we see them, and, at the same time, we can miss what God is saying to us.

This chapter will not attempt to cover the whole Bible or all peoples of all different faiths: instead, it will aim to open up some ways in which readers can apply the Bible's resources to their own situations. One key is that the Bible shows us human beings, and both Christians and people of other faiths are also human beings. Thus biblical insights into people, as individuals and in families and societies, are also insights into us and into today's world.

For example, we have seen how people of biblical times tended to link their gods with kings, places and peoples, and how both Old and New Testaments radically challenge this idea. Western Christians sometimes think that Islam is strange because it links politics and religion, or that Sikhism is strange because it is almost entirely for the Punjabis. Our study should show them that it is Christianity that is strange, because it challenges the political link and embraces all peoples. It should make us ask how we take account of the faith–people–power links in our mission, our churches and our social and political relations.

We have also seen that both Israel and the church have the characteristics of other human communities, so that there is a tension between living under God's rule and organizing ourselves under human rule. Non-Western Christians sometimes dream of a Christian state, and criticize Westerners for separating 'sacred' and 'secular'. Our study should show them that wanting to link state and faith is natural, but can be dangerous. It should make us ask to what extent the separation of church and state reflects a wrong separation of faith and the rest of life, and to what extent it is a unique and liberating Christian idea.[2]

Seeing the other faiths

We have seen something of how the Bible views idolatry, but this does not tell us which of today's faiths we should view as idolatrous. The Bible contains critiques of religion that makes law and tradition primary, of religion that seeks mystical experience at the expense of moral action, and of politicized religion that focuses on preserving a particular culture or fighting for a particular ethnic group. But none of this tells us which of today's faiths falls into which category of religion.

Further, it is difficult to fit a whole faith into a particular category. The fact is that any faith is believed and practised in different ways by different people. Just as the Canaanite religions changed with time, today's religions are changing. Just as popular wisdom in Egypt was closer to that of Israel than might be expected from the differences in ideas of gods, Muslim, Hindu and Sikh people's day-to-day concerns may be much closer to those of Christians than might be expected from the differences between their respective faiths.

I want to suggest that it is impossible to find any one place in the Bible that shows us any particular faith as a whole, let alone one place that shows us how to regard all non-Christian peoples. It is also impossible to say that any one group of biblical times represents any one group today. The first example below asks how we can move from the Bible to other faiths today, and the next two examples ask how we can see today's faiths in the Bible.

Example 1: Seeing Canaanite religion in today's world

Chapter 4 introduced the gods of ancient Canaan. It suggested that you think about where these were similar to religions in your area. African readers may have thought about African traditional religion, which usually has many different gods or spirits, with one high creator God. It also has altars, sacrifices and rituals, and each tribe or group of tribes has its own gods. Indian readers may have thought of popular forms of Hinduism, with their many deities, their rituals, and the link of these with families. On the other hand, readers from secularized countries may have thought of their economic systems, with their shopping malls (temples?), role models (priests?) and grand economic theories (high gods?). In

Edinburgh, where I live at the moment, a local store advertised its decision to open on Sundays with the slogan 'Come worship at XXX'!

In my home town in England it is football that bears all the characteristics of the gods:

- *The link with particular people and places*: people in Newcastle are expected to support Newcastle United. People in the next town, Sunderland, are expected to support Sunderland United. There is rivalry between these two towns.
- *The temple*: I have heard people call the football ground 'the shrine'.
- *The sacrifices*: even people who are unemployed and have little money will save up to buy tickets for the matches.
- *The religious figures*: the players are celebrities. They earn enormous salaries, every aspect of their lives is reported in the media, and people often choose one as their own favourite and role model.
- *Rituals*: going to the grounds or the pub to watch the match. People go in groups, they shout the same slogans, and sing the same songs as the game proceeds.
- *Affecting the rest of life*: people wear club shirts, decorate their houses with club colours, and read football magazines. Football is talked about as frequently as is the weather!

This is not a flippant comparison: it is serious. Vast sums of money are spent on football, and many people find in it their main source of identity. The whole atmosphere of a town, and even its suicide rate, may depend on how the local team is faring.

Example 2: Seeing Hindus and Hinduism in the Bible

Some would look at the statues of Hindu gods and say that Hinduism is idolatry; but this is not the whole story. There are many kinds of Hinduism, and many different understandings of the different gods. Sometimes, Hinduism is parallel to the idolatry of Egypt or Ephesus, sometimes it is parallel to the philosophy of Athens, and sometimes it leads people into the horoscopes and astrology condemned in Deuteronomy. As our study of 1 Corinthians showed, a religion full of images can be very complicated.

We can also see something of Hinduism reflected in Israel's religious practices. People who come to Christ from Hinduism are often fascinated by Leviticus. They too have temples, sacrifices and purity rules. One such friend told me how comfortable he had felt in an orthodox Jewish home: the kosher rules reminded him of his own family and upbringing. This means that Hinduism can have some of the problems of legal religion that Jesus dealt with in the Gospels. There can be an emphasis on rules and traditions that excuses people from holy living. There is the idea that uncleanness makes people unfit for worship. There is also the caste system, which treats people of a lower caste as 'unclean'. The straightforward teaching of Mark's Gospel may come as a challenge and as wonderful good news. Jesus' teaching on 'clean and unclean' in Mark 7:1–23, or the story of the bleeding woman of Mark 5:25–29, can speak directly. A Hindu doctor reading the latter was amazed: 'I have women coming to me, asking me to help them because they are bleeding and cannot go to the temple. Jesus allowed this woman to touch him! This is really good news.'[3]

Old Testament situations, too, can speak directly into Hindu situations today. Here is Pradip's story:

> I am one of ten children from a Hindu background in East Africa. I became a follower of Jesus Christ over thirty years ago. I had great difficulties when I first became a Christian as I was deeply misunderstood, but I tried to retain my family links as far as it was possible. Things started to get better when I got married and especially when our two children were dedicated.
>
> My mother died from cancer in 2000 and I was surprised to find that my wife and I had been asked to be the executors of her will. This was a big responsibility. When it came to practical issues, we had no problem.

But, when it came to spiritual issues, we had many dilemmas, because I would have to be involved in her funeral ceremony. My mother was a Hindu; I am a Christian. How can I be engaged in a ritual which I did not go along with? Am I compromising my faith?

I used to cry myself to sleep because I loved my mother and I love God too! With a heavy heart, my brother and I took her ashes to our ancestral home in India and the next day I would have to do all that was required of me. I was praying and crying out to God to guide me. He did this by reminding me of the story of Naaman the Syrian (2 Kgs 5:1–27). I read and reread this. I noted that Naaman too had a problem and he asked God to forgive him when he bowed to other gods. I was most amazed to note that the monotheistic prophet of Israel, Elisha, simply says, 'Go in peace'. When the realization dawned on me as to what God was saying to me, I was overwhelmed with his love and care for me – the weight had been lifted.

In this story Pradip saw his own situation in the Bible. This is an example of very direct use of the Bible as a mirror. However, Pradip did not simply go to the story of Naaman and say, 'This means that I can go and worship the Hindu deities at my mother's funeral.' He knew from the rest of the Bible and from his own experience of Hinduism that there was a tension here between his allegiance to Christ and his family responsibilities. It is also interesting to notice what Pradip learnt from the story: this was not primarily a lesson about how he should act at the funeral, but a reassurance that God knew the tensions and cared for him. That this practical problem is in the Bible shows God's concern about our actual situations and not just about abstract rules.

What were Pradip's priorities in his situation? What do you think God was saying to him through the story of Naaman?

Example 3: Seeing Muslims and Islam in the Bible
Some would look at shariʿah, the Islamic law, and say that Islam is legalistic, and that we can therefore see Muslims in the Pharisees of

the Gospels. Others would look at militant Muslim groups, and say that Islam is political, so that we can see Islam in the Assyrian and Babylonian conquests. But this is not the whole story. There are Muslims who sincerely seek God – they pray, fast, give to the poor, and are ready to obey God at any time. We might see them in the Gentile Cornelius, whose prayers God heard and to whom he sent Peter.

There are also Muslims who keep the outward requirements of their law, but who tell lies and cheat and beat their wives – like the hypocrites of the Gospels or the Jews condemned in Isaiah 1 – 10. There are Muslims who use magic to try to persuade God to help them – like the magicians of Acts. There are Muslims who, like the zealots of Jesus' time, see themselves as freedom fighters. And there are millions of Muslims who are poor and oppressed, like the poor of the Gospels, and the widows and orphans so often mentioned in the Old Testament. In other words, we can see a spectrum of human beings among Muslims, just as we can among Hindus or Christians or people who say they have no religion.

Three places where Christians have often seen Muslims are Cornelius and his family, the woman at the well and the disciples on the road to Emmaus.

Cornelius (Acts 10) was a believer in the one God, but he had not become a member of the covenant community. Like a pious Muslim, he prayed regularly and gave alms. We find that God accepted his prayers and his alms-giving (v. 4); but that was only the beginning of the story. God's response to Cornelius' prayers was to send him the message of the gospel. We might infer that there are pious Muslims whose prayers are accepted by God, and to whom God wants to send the gospel message.

The interesting thing is that the resistance was not from Cornelius but from Peter. Peter's understanding of holiness meant that he did not want to visit Cornelius' house (v. 28); and he was very surprised that God should want to give the Holy Spirit to non-Jews (v. 45). It is easy to see parallels here: there are many places where Christians are reluctant to visit Muslims, and there

are many Christians who doubt that Muslims can come to faith in
Jesus Christ.

The woman at the well (John 4) had a faith similar to that of the
Jews, but with different ideas about worship and had a long
history of enmity with the Jewish people. Similarly, Islam has
many similarities with Christianity, and has a long history of conflict with Christians. Jesus' interactions with Samaritans have
sometimes been taken as a model for Christian–Muslim relations,
especially in situations where Muslims are in the minority and are
a different ethnic group from most of the Christians.[4] Jesus' cross-
ing of the barriers of prejudice and personal treatment of the
outcast woman in John 4 have been a model for many Christian
women relating to Muslim women.

The disciples on the road to Emmaus (Luke 24:13–35) could not
understand Jesus' death until he had explained to them the whole
plan of God. Some Christians have taken this as a model of
Muslims who deny the crucifixion. They have therefore introduced interested Muslims to the whole Old Testament story, and
have found some accepting the gospel in response.[5]

All these parallels are helpful for relating to particular Muslim
people, but what about Islam? Can the Bible help us to understand
it as a *system*? People often ask me, 'Is Islam from God, or from the
devil, or from human beings?' This is not so easy: the Bible is interested in human beings and their relationships with God rather
than in systems. We might even say that the very idea of 'systems'
is a modern Western one, because it is an attempt to describe
groups of people in terms of particular ideas and characteristics.
However, there are some places in which people have 'seen' Islam
in the Bible.

Muslims themselves see Islam in the religion of Abraham. The
Qur'an points out that Abraham lived before Judaism or
Christianity came into being, and presents him as a prophet who
brought the same essential message as Muhammad. It also tells of
his building the Ka'abah at Mecca, and of Hagar's journey to
Mecca with Ishmael, who is believed to be the forebear of the

Arabs. Most of the rituals during the Hajj pilgrimage relate to these stories.

Muslims also see Islam in the other biblical prophets, from Adam to Jesus.[6] All these, they say, preached Islam, and the Bible predicts the coming of Muhammad as the final prophet in, for example, Deuteronomy18:18 and John 14:26 and 16:13.

Some Christians see Islam in the antichrist of 1 John or the beast of Revelation. The antichrist denies that Jesus is the Son of God (1 John 2:25), and so does Islam. However, the antichrist also denies that Jesus is the Messiah (1 John 2:24), whereas 'Messiah' is the main title for Jesus in the Qur'an. John also says that there will be many antichrists (v. 18). Islam certainly denies the divinity of Christ, but it is only one of many world views that does so.

As we have seen (pp. 159–160), the beast of Revelation pictures a violent religious system; and it seems to be the link with economics, politics and tyrannical power that makes the religion so beastly. There have been, and are, some Islamic governments like this; but there have also been, and are, other governments that are just as 'beastly', as well as Islamic governments that are not 'beastly'.

So the antichrist and the beast can give us some insight into some aspects of Islam, and remind us of the spiritual battle we are all involved in as we seek to lift up the Lord Jesus Christ. However, such insights also apply to other systems that deny the gospel. I want to suggest that we be careful in the way we talk about this, since a focus on these pictures can make us forget the things Muslims and Christians have in common, so that we see Muslims as enemies rather than as fellow human beings. There are many different 'powers and authorities', but Christ is over them all and it is our job to fight spiritual battles with spiritual weapons (Eph. 6:12–18).

Perhaps the closest thing to Islam in the Bible is the Jewish religion of Jesus' time. This is not surprising, as Islam grew out of Jewish and Christian roots. We can see in Islam the following:

- *Close links between religious law and culture.* Islamic law affects so many of the details of life that people often find it difficult to distinguish between what the religion requires and what are optional local customs.

- *Strict monotheism*, which makes the incarnation seem like blasphemy, together with an expectation that God will honour his Messiah, and which cannot understand the cross.
- *Strong ideas of what is and is not permitted.* The Islamic concept of *halal* and *haram* can be close to the idea of clean and unclean.
- *Links between religion, peoples and politics.* Islam, like first-century Judaism, is linked to communities. Muslims' expectations, like those of the first-century Jews, are often of God showing his power by giving them political freedom and power.
- *Variety.* Like first-century Judaism, Islam varies in its attitude to other communities of other cultures and faiths. It has religious leaders like the Pharisees, who emphasize purity and exact keeping of the details of the law, and others like the Sadducees who cooperate with the ruling powers. It has political activists like the Zealots, who fight for their religion and nation; and it has millions of ordinary people who, like the ordinary people of Jesus' time, just want to live their lives in health and in peace.

This suggests a model for Christian response to Muslims: the model of Jesus' life and teaching among Jews while he was on earth.

Seeing our sociopolitical situation

For many Christians worldwide, the most urgent question about people of other faiths is whether we can live in peace. The New Testament tells us that politics should not come first – Jesus breaks down the link between kings, peoples and gods, and his kingdom is not of this world. But we are in this world, and we live in human communities. Just as Israel had to be 'like the nations' because she was a nation, so we have to be part of a nation. In Christ there are no ethnic barriers – 'no Greek or Jew' (Col. 3:11) – but we all belong to ethnic groups.

More than this: when Christianity becomes rooted in a place over several generations, we find whole groups and even nations who see themselves as Christian. Some individuals are not personal Christians, but Christianity is still part of their identity. Such groups – and they include most of us – need to ask how they should relate to other groups, who have other faiths as part of their identities. This is not only for the sake of peace but also for the sake of witness. Jesus may have broken the people–king–god link, but people of other faiths (and many Christians) have generally kept it in one form or another. This means that they see the Americans and the Filipinos and the Zambians as Christians, just as they see the Indians as Hindus, the Thais as Buddhists and the Turks as Muslims. They will judge our faith and our Lord by our social and political actions as well as by our personal living and preaching. They may also see Christian minorities as foreign agents, evangelism as a political threat, and converts as traitors.

It is not enough, then, to say that we belong to the kingdom of heaven. We also have to live in some kingdom on earth. How can the Bible help us here? It gives no rules for politics, and our situations are so varied that we cannot expect to find one political model that we can apply everywhere. However, we can look at all the different sociopolitical situations the Bible tells of, and find something of our own situation reflected there.

There were times when God's people were under pressure. They were an oppressed minority in Egypt in Exodus 1 – 15, and in Persia in the book of Esther. They were in exile at the time of Daniel. They were under a colonial power during the life of Jesus. They were facing persecution when Peter wrote his letters. Revelation 13 describes a totalitarian regime.

There were times when God's people were secure, and even in power. Joshua and Judges show us a group of tribes finding land and identity. Deuteronomy 17 and 1 Samuel 8 tell us about the beginning of the monarchy. Many of the prophets tell us of God's sociopolitical expectations of peoples (e.g Amos 1 – 3). The books of Kings and Chronicles show us good and bad regimes. Leviticus 19,

Deuteronomy 10 and Ruth speak of the treatment of minorities. Acts 25 and Romans 13 show the possibility of security under a non-Christian government.

These passages recount much that God's people did wrong as well as some things that they did right, and we need much discernment about which might mirror our particular situations. However, they offer insight into how human beings react in different situations, and into what God wants of us and how he will act for us. They can therefore help us to discern how to act in a way that will please him.

Reread the section on 'The kingdom of God and the kingdom of Caesar' on pp. 154ff. Which parts of the Bible are helpful 'mirrors' of the political situation in your country?

Seeing our mission

We saw in 1 Peter 2:9 that the followers of Christ are to be a holy nation and a royal priesthood: they are so to live that 'the pagans' will see their good lives and give glory to God (v. 12). Chapter 15 will consider the whole spectrum of right living that is our mission in the world. Here, we look at the more specific call to evangelism. The New Testament makes it clear that Christians are to share the good news of Jesus Christ with every person whom God has made, and that includes people of all faiths and none.

But what are we to do, and how are we to do it? Here are some places where we can look for answers:

We can see our mission in the apostles' mission (see pp. 164–177)

As Peter was called to preach the gospel to Jews, so some of us are called to preach to people who already know some of the Bible story. As Paul was called to preach the gospel to the Gentiles, so some of us are called to preach to people from different faiths. Here are some suggestions of how the Acts accounts of Paul's mission might help us to think about our own mission.

In Jerusalem Peter preached a very effective sermon following a healing (Acts 3). He carefully reminded his hearers of what they knew already, and so led them to the expected Messiah.

Today we often speak to people who know something of the Bible story.

What did Peter's hearers already know about God and about Jesus? Think about the last time you shared the gospel with someone. What did you assume that they already knew?

In Lystra Paul and Barnabas were mistaken for gods, following a healing, and had to preach a different message.

Today God often works among people of other faiths by healings in the name of Jesus.

What were the main differences in the responses to the healings in Jerusalem and in Lystra? What are the main differences between Paul's and Peter's sermons? How might you explain a healing to (a) a Muslim, (b) an atheist, (c) someone who practices a traditional religion?

In Athens Paul seems to have been better prepared. He spent time looking and listening, and he had studied enough to be able to quote Greek writers. His sermon is still different from Peter's in Acts 3, but this time he is able to start from what his hearers already know, to correct them, and to tell them enough about Jesus for some to repent.

Today there are many opportunities for Christians to discuss their faith with well-informed people of other faiths.

How might Paul's example help you to start from common ground and move on to share the gospel in your context? What might you have to learn in order to do this?

In Ephesus Paul chose a strategic place where he spent three years discussing and preaching, and many came to Christ. This implied competition first with spiritual powers and then with economic interests.

Today we need strategic thinking; we need to spend much time in particular places and we can expect opposition to the gospel.

Where should your church be investing its time in mission? Are you ready to face the opposition that will accompany growth?

We can see our mission in Jesus' mission to his Jewish people

The Lord Jesus Christ himself is surely our model missionary. As we consider mission to people of different faiths, we can remember that his mission was in a religious context. Among his own Jewish people Jesus faced nationalistic religion, legalistic religion and self-righteous religion as well as genuine seeking after God. The Gospels show us how he dealt with all sorts of people, from needy individuals to hostile leaders. They therefore offer us a wonderful resource for our own mission in places where we see similar aspects of religion.

We can see our mission in God's mission to Abraham and his family

In chapter 5 we saw that God's mission to Abraham was the beginning of his mission to a fallen world of many gods. In order to reach this multi-religious world, God spoke directly to one individual, and, from him, built a family and then a people to be his witnesses.

God's overall method here suggests a *strategy* for mission: first, finding a key person and nurturing him or her in the faith of Christ; next, building up families who will live the Christian life, and then growing communities that can show others what God is really like. This makes good sense when we remember what we have learnt about the necessary links between faith and human communities.

We have seen how the early church struggled with seeing what God might require of non-Jews who followed Christ, and how Paul affirmed Abraham's pattern of faith in his letter to the Galatians. God's specific dealing with Abraham's family suggests a pattern for calling people to Christ from other faiths. It was a direct call and promise that required a response of faith and obedience, but allowed Abraham to choose his own way of worship. Mission is not finished when people come to faith in Christ. There is also the job of incorporating them into the church; and that means that the church as well as the new disciples will have to change.

Reread the material on Abraham in chapter 5. How can this help your church in its mission to people of other faiths today?

Reluctant missionaries?

We can make the mistake of becoming too close to another religion, so that we mix our faith with the other faith. However, we can also make the mistake of separating ourselves completely from another religion, and so not caring about its adherents. Through most of its history, Israel seems to have been reluctant to bring blessing to the nations. The first Christians, too, needed persecution and persuasion to get them to move beyond their own people. Jonah and Peter can act as a mirror for Christians who are reluctant to obey God for different reasons.

Jonah resisted God's call because he was *angry* (Jon. 1 – 4). To put it bluntly, God wanted to save the Ninevites, and Jonah didn't want them to be saved. He hated them because they were Israel's enemies, and he wanted them to be judged for their sins.

Peter resisted God's call because he was *afraid* (Acts 10). To put it bluntly, he thought that visiting a Gentile would pollute him. He did not want contact with someone like Cornelius, and he did not expect that God would want contact with him either.

Jonah and Peter learnt well. Peter learnt fast, and was glad when he saw God's universal generosity. Jonah learnt slowly. He obeyed only when he knew that he would otherwise be destroyed, and even at the end of the story he is sour at Ninevah's escape.

Can you see yourself or your church in Peter's fears or Jonah's anger? How can you and your church learn to be glad about God's universal love?

Seeing current issues

So far in this chapter we have tried to get a general picture of how
we can see ourselves and our world of different religions in the
Bible. However, questions of how we relate to other faiths often
arise over particular issues that are not obviously dealt with in the
Bible. Sometimes even the most conservative Bible-believing
Christians take opposite sides.

The example we shall consider in this section is, *Should Hindus
be allowed to build temples in Britain?* Some say, 'Yes! The Bible says
that we are to love resident aliens and to treat others as we would
like to be treated. These are people who live in Britain. They
should have freedom to practise their religion, even if it is not
true. We would want freedom to build churches in India.' Others
say, 'No! The Israelites were severely punished for allowing the
worship of other gods in their land. Look at the story of Elijah and
the prophets of Baal! Hindu worship is idol worship, and we
should not encourage false worship in a Christian country.' The
debate can be even fiercer over Muslims building mosques.

Another hotly debated question is where Christians should
cooperate with people of different faiths in social and political
concerns. Some say that we are all human beings fighting for
similar values in a secular society. Others say that we should not
be 'unequally yoked' with unbelievers, but rather focus on honor-
ing Christ. Then there is the question of praying together. Some
say that on, for example, civic occasions, leaders from the different
faiths can all make contributions because they are all equal citizens. Others say that Christians cannot cooperate with people of
other faiths in any form of worship because this would suggest
that they are worshipping other gods.

Such issues can cause serious divisions between Christians –
not just locally, but worldwide. The questions arise in different
forms in different contexts, but I have deliberately chosen a British
example for discussion, because I often find Christians from Africa
and Asia deeply critical of their Western brethren (and, of course,
vice versa). 'Why do you allow Islam to grow in a Christian

country?' is a typical question. This may be because their information comes mainly from the media; or it may be because they have heard some Muslims predicting the conversion of the West to Islam. It may also be that Western Christians are being unfaithful to the gospel. But I think it is largely because it is difficult to perceive all the different factors in someone else's context.

All the issues mentioned above raise the same tension: it is between relating to people of other faiths as human beings just like us, and serving the one and only God. We do not have to look far into the biblical mirror to find this tension: it is there throughout the Old Testament, as Israel had to learn to be a nation like the other nations, belonging to a God unlike their gods. One key for her, as for us, was that she was called for the sake of the other nations.

Perhaps the most helpful New Testament mirror is the Corinthian question about idol-meat. How can this help us with the issue of *Hindus building temples in Britain*? As in Corinth, the underlying question is how to relate to the people of the other faith without being disloyal to Christ. As in Corinth, the issues are more complicated than it might first appear, and are complicated still more by the sinfulness of human beings both inside and outside the church.

Understanding the issues. The first answer above focuses on Hindus as fellow human beings, and the need to treat all people as equal before God. It might be the answer of the 'strong' Corinthians, who stressed their call to share with unbelievers. The second answer focuses on Hinduism as a different religion, and the need for Christians to be pure in worship. This might be the answer of the 'weak' Corinthians, who needed to separate themselves from their former faith. Paul's discussion of idol-meat suggests that both answers might miss the most important question: 'What about witness?' What will we be saying about Christianity and about Christ to Hindus if we let them build temples? And if we do not? What will be saying to our fellow Christians? And to people of other religions and of none?

There are other important questions that are not directly dealt with in the Corinthian discussion, but that are equally important.

Just as idol-meat could be linked to civic gatherings and to the emperor cult, so religious questions today have social and political dimensions. Here are some relevant questions:

- What is the position of these Hindus in the UK? Are they tourists or immigrants? Are they refugees or Hindu missionaries to Britain? Are they British citizens? If they are full members of British society, should they be treated any differently from any other members of society who wish to build a place of worship?
- What is the intention of the Hindus in building this temple? Do they simply want to be able to practise their faith? Do they want to use it for aggressive propagation of Hinduism? Do they want to build a prestigious building that will, for them, symbolize the superiority of the Hindu gods over Christ?

If the Hindus are British citizens who want the freedom to practise their faith, the key biblical principle might be the just treatment of minorities. At the other extreme, if the Hindus are foreign missionaries bringing foreign funding to build a prestigious temple to declare the superiority of the Hindu gods, the key biblical principle might be witness to the Lordship of Christ. Unfortunately, situations are seldom so simple, and we need much discernment to decide what is best.

However, there is another question, that is, in practice, more important than all the others.

What kind of society is Britain?

It is not a predominantly pagan situation like Corinth, since it has, at least nominally, a Christian majority. But it cannot be a 'Christian country' in the same way that Israel was God's people. The New Testament's understanding of the kingdom of God tells us that there can never be a Christian society that combines national, social, political and religious identity as did Israel.[7] So it is not easy to decide what a 'Christian country' might be and how it should treat non-Christians living in it.

Anyway, in practice, most people are not interested in even trying to be a Christian country, and, since we are a 'democracy', the Christian voice is only one among many. So the British planning authorities are not likely to give great weight to Bible teaching in their decisions about building places of worship. Practical questions about car parking facilities and the appropriateness of the architecture are more likely to predominate. The fact is that practising Christians are a minority in Britain, as they were in the Roman Empire in New Testament times. As there were many people practising different religions then, there are many people practising different religions in Britain. They are citizens, and they have the right to practise, provided that they do so within the laws of the country.

As the Jews of Jesus' time would have liked their society to be pure and Jewish, we may want our society to be pure and Christian. But Jesus challenged the identification of religion and society. In particular, he refused to take the political power that alone would have enabled him to meet those expectations. Perhaps, like the early church, British Christians need to focus on living holy lives and sharing the gospel with people of all faiths, rather than on how those faiths might be permitted to express themselves.

What practical issues relating to people of other faiths are Christians discussing in your context? Where can you see the tension between treating people as human beings and faithfulness to the only God in these discussions? What are the other factors to be considered? What might be the best witness to the gospel? What advice would you give to British Christians about the building of mosques and temples in Britain?

15

WHAT DOES THE LORD REQUIRE
OF US?

I asked these questions in chapter 1: 'Is Christ the only way? Is there any truth in religions? Where does it come from? Can people of other religions get to heaven? Are they worshipping God or the devil? Should we try to convert them? How can we convert them?'

These are the sorts of questions people ask about other faiths. As we saw in chapter 2, theologians often try to organize their answers through the ideas of 'exclusivism', 'inclusivism' and 'pluralism'.

We have now come to the end of our studies. Do you think the Bible is exclusivist, inclusivist or pluralist?

Perhaps you expect me to answer this question for you, but I am not going to do that. The categories 'exclusivism', 'inclusivism', 'pluralism' and even 'religion' can help us to organize our ideas, but they do not begin to encompass all that the Bible shows us of human beings and their attempts to find their way back to God.

The Bible's focus is not on our attempts to reach God, but on his gracious coming to us. It tells of his universal sovereignty and of his commitment to all his creatures. It shows that all human beings are equal both as made in the image of God and as fallen into sin. In this it echoes 'pluralism'. However, it tells the story of God's work through a particular people and then through a particular person, and insists that this is his chosen way of coming to and saving all peoples. In this it echoes 'exclusivism'.

What we see of religions in the Bible is part of its story, as it relates God's dealings with human beings of all sorts. As 'pluralists' might expect, it shows us that religions are part of human life, and that all religious practice is limited in its cultural and temporal relevance. As 'exclusivists' would expect, it shows us that peoples of all religions are under the judgment of the one and only true God, and that it is the absolute of Christ that makes religious practice relative.

What I have tried to do in this book has been to explore the whole Bible story with the question of other faiths in mind, and to show how many resources it offers for understanding, for relationships, for mission and for building the church. As far as theology is concerned, I am content to leave the reader with the challenge of continuing to look for people of other faiths in the pages of Scripture, and of seeing God's plan for them.

But I am not content to stop writing there. This book takes its subtitle from Micah 6:8: *What does the Lord require of us?* We can be so busy asking what God thinks of others that we forget to look for ourselves in the mirror of the Bible. We cannot always expect God to tell us what he thinks of others, but we can always expect him to tell us what he wants of us.

This was the great question for the religious Jews of Jesus' time: What were God's requirements? What did you have to do to be truly one of God's people? One of the experts came to ask Jesus, 'Teacher, what must I do to inherit eternal life?' (Luke 10:25) Jesus responded with the two Great Commandments: '"Love the Lord your God with all your heart and with all your soul and with all your strength and with all your mind"; and, "Love your neighbour as yourself"' (Luke 10:27).

This led to the parable of the good Samaritan, which is one of the Bible's greatest challenges to our response to people of other faiths. Jesus knew that the original 'love your neighbour as yourself' occurs in Leviticus 19 – twice. The first time is about loving your fellow Jew (v. 18) and the second about loving the resident alien (v. 34). Perhaps that is why he went straight to an interfaith situation to explain it. He told a story that challenges us to see good in others and asks us whether our own religion really pleases God, or whether it keeps us from seeing the human beings to whom he has called us.

In this last chapter we shall follow his example: we shall explore what God requires of us in relation to people of other faiths through the great commandments, using the Ten Commandments, and Jesus' own explanation of them in the Sermon on the Mount. As Jesus warns us, the most urgent question is about what we should do and be, and not about what others should do and be. There is no way that we can correct someone else's faith unless we first pay attention to our own responsibilities (Matt. 7:1–5). It is not others, but ourselves, who stop us from doing what God requires.

Loving God

Commandment 1: I am the LORD your God, who brought you out of Egypt, out of the land of slavery. You shall have no other gods before me (Exod. 20:2–3)
Israel's biggest temptation was to add other gods to Yahweh. In New Testament times there were temptations to Gnostic ideas of god. Jesus pointed out that, for example, riches or family can take the rightful place of God. Our first challenge in our multi-faith world is total loyalty to the one God.

But this is not just any monotheism. This is not a Hindu or philosophical idea of one reality behind the universe. This is not a Buddhist or New Age idea of the oneness of being. This is more even than the Muslim idea of the one all-powerful creator god who sent prophets. *This is the God who brought Israel out of slavery in*

Egypt. As Paul implies in 1 Corinthians 8 (see pp. 181–182), this is also the Lord who came in Christ and brought us out of slavery to sin through the cross.

This god is to be *our* God: we are called to covenant relationship with him. Without that relationship, we have no basis for our faith. Sometimes, we ask what we should *do* in relation to people of other faiths. The final sections of the Sermon on the Mount warn us that this is not the most important question. We are told to make sure that we have entered God's kingdom (Matt. 7:13–14), and that right actions grow out of right being (vv. 15–21). Perhaps the best test of this is our prayer life: do we begin with knowing God as our Father and longing for his will and his kingdom (Matt. 6:9–10)?

Commandment 2: You shall not make for yourself an idol in the form of anything in heaven above or on the earth beneath or in the waters below (Exod. 20:4)

Israel's second temptation was to worship Yahweh as if he were like the other gods. We have seen how this was probably behind the golden calves made by Aaron and Jeroboam. In the Gospels Jesus did not have to tell either the ordinary people or the religious leaders which god to believe in, but he did have to teach them what their god was like, and therefore how they should worship him. For the early church, there were temptations to add bits of other religions to faith in Christ. 1 Corinthians discusses worship at temples; Colossians discusses holy days and fasts; the letters to the churches in Revelation mention various sects.

It is easy for us to look back at Bible times and to see the mistakes God's people made. It was not so easy for them, because they were immersed in societies that took different ideas of god for granted. The same is true for us today. We need wisdom and discernment to see where we are treating God as if he were like other gods. Studying the different temptations faced in the Bible will help us to see parallels in our own situations. I would also like to suggest that interacting with Christians from different cultures and with different religious backgrounds is essential. Just as it is easier for us to distinguish what went wrong when looking back to New Testament times, it may be easier for someone looking at us from outside to see where we have absorbed ideas from our surroundings.

However, it is also possible for people from outside to misunderstand our cultures. Even with respect to actual images of other gods, it is not always easy to distinguish between cultural sensitivity and disloyalty to God, as Paul's discussion in 1 Corinthians 8 – 10 and Pradip's story (pp. 206–207) show. Perhaps the key to faithful worship is in Pradip's twofold love – for God and for his family. This follows Paul's conclusion in 1 Corinthians 10:31–33: that we should do all for the glory of God, with concern that we do not make anyone stumble, and work for the salvation of all. That is, we make our decisions out of love for God and love for our neighbours.

This is the second challenge for us in a multi-religious world: that our total faithfulness to God is expressed in our worship. Jesus' teaching in Matthew 6 gives a straightforward basis for this: we should worship God as the heavenly Father that he is, and everything else will follow.

Commandment 3: You shall not misuse the name of the LORD your God (Exod. 20:7)

This is an awesome commandment. I have met Muslims who would not speak about God – not because they were fearful of speaking with a Christian, but because they felt ignorant and feared judgment if they said something wrong. This commandment calls us not only to pure language, but to making sure that we speak and live the truth about God. It also warns of the seriousness of breaking it: 'the LORD will not hold anyone guiltless who misuses his name' (v. 7).

- It calls us to careful Bible study to find out what the truth about God is, so that we do not confuse it with our local customs and concerns. This study is not only for church

leaders and theologians. In nearly every conference I attend
on Muslim–Christian relations, we are told that there is an
urgent need for Christians to understand the gospel and see
where it is different from and where the same as Islam. All
Christian people need to learn what the name of the Lord
means if they are to use it rightly.

- It calls us to careful study of other faiths and cultures so that
  we can communicate accurately. We have seen how even
  Paul and Barnabas were misunderstood in Lystra (Acts
  14:8–18). They had not spoken anything wrong about God –
  they had not spoken at all – but people treated them like
  gods, and they had to find ways of explaining. Today, we may
  think that we are speaking the truth about God, and then find
  that our hearers have understood something quite different.
  Do we use God's name rightly when we tell a Muslim that
  Jesus is the Son of God, and he might misunderstand us to
  mean that God and Mary had sexual relations? Do we use
  God's name rightly when we tell a Hindu that she must
  be born again to know God, when Hinduism teaches
  reincarnation – being born again and again and again?
- It calls us to careful living. People are likely to judge our
  religion by our lives. What do our lives say about our God?
  This question may have different answers depending on who is
  seeing our lives. For example, if I wear a skirt to go to church
  in Scotland, it still tells some people that I worship a god who
  is to be respected. If I wear a skirt at all, some Muslims might
  think I am saying that God allows sexual permissiveness.
- It calls us to check our motivations. How often do we justify
  our actions by saying that God allows them, that God will
  forgive them, or even that God has told us to do them?
- It calls us to humility. In discussions with people of other
  faiths, it is tempting to want to answer all their questions and
  to show them where we are right and they are wrong. As
  human beings, we are always limited in how much we can
  know about God. We know only what he has shown us. I find

this commandment very comforting here: it encourages me
to speak with confidence what I know from the Bible and
from my own experience, but also to be equally confident in
saying that God is so much greater than me that there is
much that I do not and perhaps cannot know.

The Old Testament prophets often taught that God's dealings
with his people were because they were 'called by his name', and
the nations were watching them. Christians are called by the name
of Christ. This commandment calls us so to live among people of
other faiths that they will understand what that name means: we
can be the answer to our own prayer 'Hallowed be your name'
(Matt. 6:9).

Commandment 4: Remember the Sabbath day by keeping it holy (Exod. 20:8)

This is the only one of the Ten Commandments that is not
obvious. The first three follow logically from belief in one God.
The last six can be found in some form in almost any religious or
ethical teaching. The one commandment that we could not guess
without being told it is this one, that calls us to worship in the
context of communities with a right rhythm of work and rest. It is
not primarily a rule about how many days to work, but a call to
live according to our nature. Human beings are made in the image
of God, and this Sabbath commandment reflects the pattern of
God's own work and rest.

Different faiths have different ideas of the nature of the universe and of how their deities work. This is reflected in the
ordering of their communities. For example, Muslim communities are ordered by the five daily prayers and the yearly fast of
Ramadan. Western communities are more likely to be ordered by
the seven-day shopping opportunities required by the 'gods' of
consumerism. Christians, like Jews, are called to live according to a
different pattern. If Christian households live this commandment
in places where they are surrounded by people of other faiths, it

will not only give them the spiritual, mental and physical strength to be faithful disciples. It will also be a powerful witness to the nature of the Lord they serve.

Jesus' life gives us a pattern, showing that the Sabbath is not so much a rule to be followed as the way that God has ordered our lives for our benefit (e.g. Mark 2:27). This means that, for example, we do not need to insist on taking the Jewish Saturday or even the Christian Sunday for our Sabbath. In an Islamic context, where Friday may be the weekly holiday, that might be the best day to choose. For a pastor, who has to work in leading worship, a Monday or Tuesday might be better.

Jesus' life also makes us ask what 'keeping the day holy' might mean (e.g. Luke 13:10–17). It is interesting that neither Exodus 20 nor Deuteronomy 5 describes the Sabbath as a day of worship: it is primarily a day of *rest*. Human beings need patterns of worship, and God certainly gave them to Israel. But these patterns were fulfilled in Christ, and our expressions of our faith must now vary according to our culture. Jesus in Matthew 6 points us to the essence of worship – being in the presence of our heavenly Father. This is our clue for our Sabbaths, and it distinguishes our worship from that of faiths that require particular forms of worship.

This is not only an individual matter. Our first job as humans has to do with building communities – with 'filling the earth' – so it is unsurprising that verse 10 underlines the importance of the whole household being rightly ordered. It explicitly includes all the lower-status members: the children, the servants and the resident aliens. This is even more clear in Deuteronomy 5:12–15, which adds the emphasis 'so that your manservant and your maidservant may rest as you do', and reminds the Israelites of their slavery in Egypt. It is striking that the central commandment about how the basic unit of Christian community should function is not about family prayers but about work and *rest*. This is something that even unbelievers living in the household can observe.

Love your neighbour as yourself

Commandment 5: Honour your father and your mother, so that you may live long in the land the LORD your God is giving you (Exod. 20:12)

Families are important. When he wanted a new start for the world after the flood, God chose the whole family of Noah. For his plan of blessing the nations, he chose Abraham and promised him a family. The Passover is a family feast, during which the story of God's salvation is passed on to the next generation (Exod. 12:26; 13:8; 13:14; Deut. 6:20). God's covenant to David is to his descendants; and the New Testament begins by placing Jesus within this whole family history.

We have seen throughout this book the links between religions and peoples. Families are the basic units of peoples, because God made us that way. It is therefore unsurprising that, in almost any context, religion goes with family: people are born into the religion of their parents. In our context of interfaith relations, the fifth commandment has much more to say than 'Do what your parents say.' We have the parents we have, and we are part of the family into which we were born, and it is our responsibility not only to accept this family as God-given but also to give due respect to it.

In its immediate context, the commandment addresses the families whom God was forming into a holy people. It was essential that these families were united, and that the next generation accepted the family history, identity and traditions. Even at a purely social level, they would not last long in the land they were going to without strong families. This was so important that defying parents was a capital crime (Exod. 21:15, 17). In our situations, too, family respect is essential to building God's holy people. Further, our family still places us in our ethnic context. Honouring our parents means acknowledging that we are part of their people, culture, language and history. It means being who we are.

But this is not the whole story. We have seen how the New Testament challenges links between religions and peoples at ethnic and political levels. It also challenges those links at family levels. Jesus warns us that the gospel will disrupt families (Matt. 10:34–36), and calls us, in the strongest possible language, to put him before our families (Luke 14:26). He apparently insults his own mother to make the point that the kingdom of God gives us a new family that supersedes our natural families (Matt. 12:46–50).

All this is very relevant to interfaith contexts. People whose families follow a different faith may experience strong opposition when they follow Christ. For them, Matthew 5:10–12 may be the part of the Sermon on the Mount most relevant to their relationships with their parents. They need reassurance that, in this matter of joining God's kingdom, they should go against their parents' wishes.

Does this mean that the fifth commandment no longer applies? The New Testament answer is definitely 'No!' Jesus' direct teaching on 'honour your father and mother' rebukes those who make God an excuse for dishonouring parents (Matt. 15:3–9). He provided for his own mother even from the cross (John 19:26–27). Paul, too, affirms existing family relationships, when he tells new Christians not to break their marriages with unbelievers (1 Cor. 7:12–14). Other epistles have commandments for parents and children (Eph. 6:1–4; Col. 3:20–21).

There are tensions here, and many practical questions. How can a person honour his or her parents when the parents reject their faith? How should Christian parents react when one of their children converts to another faith? How should a Christian family organize itself? How can the church become 'family' to those who have to leave their own families to follow Christ?[1] But the commandment remains: we are to acknowledge our parents, and therefore our families and our people, and to give due honour to them.

Commandment 6: You shall not murder (Exod. 20:13)

As violence between people of different faiths continues, this commandment speaks to our world. It is sad that we keep on needing to hear it. We know that we cannot and must not propagate our faith through violence. We know that we cannot even defend it through violence. We know that Jesus tells us that we are not even to speak against people, or to nurse anger against them (Matt. 5:21–22).

But the fact is that human beings, including Christians, continue to kill each other. There may be times when war is forced upon us, but history tells us of unnecessary violence: of inquisition and crusade, and, in our own time, of Christians killing other Christians in Rwanda, Northern Ireland and the Balkans. The fact that Hindus, Sikhs, Muslims, Buddhists and Jews also kill innocent people does not excuse us. Followers of Jesus – who said, 'Do not resist an evil person' (Matt. 5:39) and obeyed this even to the cross – have less excuse than others.

We should be grieved that Christians should act in such ways, but we need not be surprised. Warning against murder is first found after the flood in God's restatement of the creation blessings in the post-flood world (Gen. 9:5–6). This restatement comes after God's recognition that human beings will continue to be wicked (Gen. 8:21). As before the flood, one of the most serious aspects of that wickedness is that people will kill each other. The murder of Abel by Cain was about which religious act God accepted, and was one of the first results of the fall. Christians can fall into murder as they can into any other sin – and that includes you and me.

Jesus' summary of the law at the end of Matthew 5:45 reminds us of God's commitment to all human beings in Genesis 8:22 – he sends his sun and his rain to all of us. However much we disagree with people of another faith, this commandment reminds us that they, like us, are God's creatures made in his image. The lives of Iraqi children are as important as the lives of American businessmen; and the lives of American businessmen are as important as the lives of Iraqi children. Deciding how to obey this commandment in our situation is not easy, but the commandment is clear.

Commandment 7: You shall not commit adultery (Exod. 20:14)
In the Old Testament some of the strongest words about sexual morality are in the context of other faiths (Lev. 18). The New

Testament epistles, including the letters in Revelation 2 – 3, often call believers to right sexual relations, especially when they are surrounded by religions that include sexuality in worship. Jesus, in the Sermon on the Mount, shows us that right sexuality is a matter of eyes and heart, and not just of body (Matt. 5:27–28).

Today's religions continue to stress sexuality.[2] This is not only true of New Age harnessing of sexual energies and of popular Hindu concerns about human fertility, but also of Islam with its permission of divorce and polygamy and strict prohibitions on extramarital sex. In the West it sometimes seems as if sex is almost a religion in itself!

As the Sabbath reflects the Bible's picture of God and his universe, so the Bible's teaching about sexuality and marriage is based on its picture of humanity: the image of God is, first and foremost, male and female (Gen. 1:27). The seventh commandment calls us not only to a sexual purity that might be different from that of other faiths, but also to faithful marriage relationships as the basis of families and communities. Paul says that marriage as it ought to be is an image of Christ and the church (Eph. 5:32). Keeping this commandment will not only give Christians a secure foundation in the midst of pressure and temptation, but also be a powerful witness to the Lord Jesus Christ.

I doubt that there is one of my readers who is unfamiliar with the contradictions between what religions teach in this area and what people actually do. Christians may be no better. People of other faiths often point to overt sexual practices in the West as proof of Christianity's poor moral values. Apparently Christian societies in Africa may not be so open about sexual behaviour, but may be no more faithful to biblical standards than the West. At the same time, models of marriage vary from culture to culture: like other biblical principles, Christian marriage can mirror Christ differently in different places. This is not new. Paul's most stringent church discipline was over an act of sexual immorality, which he described as being worse than anything that happened among the followers of pagan religion (1 Cor. 5). 1 Corinthians also deals with questions about marriage in the particular situation in Corinth (1 Cor. 7).

In the Bible, even some of the most godly people followed patterns of marriage that reflected the surrounding nations, including polygamy and divorce. Jesus makes it clear that these patterns are not God's ideal: they are not the patterns of his kingdom. They were allowed only because of 'hardness of heart', and there were laws to limit the harm done when things went wrong because of sin (Matt. 5:31–2; 19:1–9). In present-day interfaith situations, there are also many challenges to and variations from what might appear to be a biblical ideal. What happens when one partner in the marriage becomes a Christian and the other remains Muslim, Sikh, Jew or atheist? What should a Christian do if his or her spouse turns to another faith? What happens when a polygamist turns to Christ? What about the many pressures towards mixed-faith marriages? There is no space here to explore these crucial issues, but there are many resources in the Bible that can help us think through different situations: Abraham, Jacob, Joseph, Moses, Ruth, David, Solomon, Ahab, Esther, Nehemiah and 1 Corinthians 7 are some of the most relevant.

Commandment 8: You shall not steal (Exod. 20:15)

This is a commandment with an obvious meaning: our relationships with people of other faiths, as all our other relationships, should be entirely legal and honest. Yet there are challenges here. The commandment not only means that we should not steal items that belong to others: it also means that we should not deprive them of anything that is rightfully theirs. We have seen how the Old Testament prophets announced God's judgment for exploitation and injustice on both Jew and Gentile. This brings challenges for our daily interaction with people of different faiths, and also for national and international relations.

In our daily interactions it may seem natural to give preference to our own people. But this commandment forbids, for example, charging a Hindu customer more than we might charge a

Christian. And a Christian administrating an aid project or a local government department should be completely fair in allocating resources to people of all backgrounds.

At national and international levels this commandment speaks to our divided world of 'haves' and 'have-nots'. In many regions and countries rich and poor are largely divided along ethnic or religious lines. In the world as a whole the rich countries are often seen as Christian or Muslim. This commandment asks us whether the 'rich' are rich because they rob the 'poor'; but it does not allow the 'poor' therefore to rob the 'rich'. It raises issues about the responsibility of rich Christians to poor Christians, of rich Christians to poor non-Christians, and of how poor Christians should relate to richer people around them.

Jesus does not deal with this commandment directly in the Sermon on the Mount, but both there and elsewhere in the Gospels he has plenty to say about wealth. The basic principle is in Matthew 6:19–24: it is not wealth that is to take priority in our lives, but God. 'You cannot serve both God and Money' (v. 24). The rather shocking parable of the shrewd manager in Luke 16:1–8 tells us what to do with money: we should use it to make friends. Of course, the 'shrewd manager' did this dishonestly, and the following verses are about the importance of being trust-worthy in the use of wealth (Luke 16:10–13). But the point is clear: wealth is to be used to build relationships here on earth and to store treasure for ourselves in heaven.

Negatively, then, we are not to steal from people of other faiths any more than we are to steal from Christians. But what should we do positively? How can we use our money to make friends for the sake of Christ? Paul gives former thieves instructions: they are to work hard, so that they may have something to share with other people (Eph. 4:28). Perhaps this is the clue: the opposites to stealing are hard work and generosity; and there is much about generosity in the Sermon on the Mount.

We are to give freely, and to pray even for people who harm us (5:42–44). Even when someone wants to take from us, we are not to demand repayment but to give. We are to be generous because our heavenly Father is generous, and we are called to be perfect like him (5:45–49; 7:9–11). It is better to be robbed than to rob.

My friend Benita lives in multi-faith Sri Lanka. She has little money, but always gives generously to people who ask, and often omits the customary 'bargaining' for low prices. 'Why?' I ask. 'I've known what it is to be poor, and to rely on the Lord to provide the next meal for my children,' she replies. 'I'd rather risk being robbed ten times than hurting someone in real need once.'

It was from Benita that I learnt another lesson about theft. Quite a large sum of money disappeared from my purse while a man was doing some repairs in her house. The man disappeared too. His friend, with whom we were dealing, said that he denied having seen it. I wanted to go to the police. 'You don't know what the police might do to him,' Benita said. 'And you don't know what his need might be. He's a Buddhist. Maybe he needs to learn something about God's mercy and forgiveness.' I prayed hard and struggled with my British sense of justice, and eventually told the friend, 'Please explain to your colleague that I really believe he took the money, but that I will not go to the police. I do not want to risk him being mistreated. If his family really needs that money, then I am happy to give it to them. If not, he can settle the matter with God.' And, of course, Benita and I prayed for both men.

Of course, this is a very personal response to theft. The New Testament as well as the Old recognizes the responsibility of government to punish crime (e.g. Rom. 13:1–5; 1 Pet. 4:15). The Sermon on the Mount is not a programme for criminal law, but a challenge to Christian discipleship.

Commandment 9: You shall not give false testimony against your neighbour (Exod. 20:16)

This commandment is, for me, the basis for all my attempts to talk about other faiths. It has been the driving force for my study of Islam. I want to speak the truth about God in my theology and in my mission, and I want to speak the truth about my neighbour in my teaching. This is no easy task: it involves careful study to find out what their faith teaches, careful attention to find out who my neighbour is and what he or she believes and feels and does, and recognition that the faith includes a great variety of people in a great variety of situations who have different attitudes and ways of living.

I get quite angry when I read some of the things that people of other faiths say about Christianity and about Christians. So often they seem to be half-truths, or distortions, or to compare the best of the theory of the faith with the worst of Christian practice. Then I hear Christians talking about Hindus or about Muslims or about Jews. Some are so positive that they don't seem to see the problems in the other faith and the sins of its adherents. Others can see only the negatives, and the activity of the Devil.

Human beings like to simplify: to think of the other people as a whole group, and to understand them by making simple general statements: 'Hindus worship idols,' 'Jews are legalistic,' 'Muslims believe in holy war,' 'Traditional religions worship evil spirits.' This leads us to think in terms of stereotypes. But people of other faiths are, like us, human beings. They are *both* made in the image of God *and* fallen, and they are all different. The faiths themselves represent human attempts to understand and to live in God's world. They can all include magic and lead to bondage to Satan, but they can also include genuine seekers for God. We can see good things and bad things, truth and falsehood, in them all. And, if we are honest, we shall see the same mixture among those who are called Christians. Christ is the truth, but we do not always honour him.

Commandment 10: *You shall not covet . . . anything that belongs to your neighbour (Exod. 20:17)*
This is the commandment that showed Paul his sinful nature (Rom 7:7), and it can show us ours. It reminds us that God is not only interested in what we do, but in how we think about other people. To put it briefly, what do we want for ourselves? And what do we want for them?

Recently there were some very good programmes about the

hajj on British TV. *I wish they had such good programmes about Christianity*, I thought. What's wrong with that? Perhaps nothing. There is a right jealousy for the gospel, and a Christian should long for Christ to be honoured in the media. Yet even this small incident warns me that I can be tempted to envy: to wanting what someone else has. As Hindu and Buddhist nationalism grow in some countries, and as oil money funds Islamic missions, it is easy for Christians to covet the status or wealth of people of other faiths.

This may be a bigger temptation for those who have grown up in a society where Christianity has been linked with power and wealth. In Britain many still feel that Christianity *ought* to be in control, and resent the freedoms given to other faiths. In parts of Africa where education and health care was originally established through missionaries and colonial authorities, many Christians are now horrified at the amount of foreign money being put into Muslim schools and hospitals.

We have seen again and again that we are called to see and to treat people of all faiths and none as human beings, made in the image of God and fallen. They are our neighbours, whom God loves and for whom Christ died. But we can very easily fall into seeing them as competitors, and wanting our people and our faith to win.

There is a sense in which this is true: other gods and wrong ways of worship have always competed with the one true God for human attention. There is falsehood as well as truth, and darkness as well as light. We should long that the truth is told and that light shines and that falsehood and darkness be exposed. The challenge of this commandment is different: do we want the good things that others have for ourselves?

In the Sermon on the Mount, Jesus does not directly address this commandment, but he does make us think about what we want for ourselves, and about what we want for others. *For ourselves*, we are to ask for our daily necessities, for forgiveness of sin, for protection from temptation and evil and for God's will to be done in our lives (Matt. 6:9–13). We are not to worry about even our basic needs, but to seek and work for God's kingdom (vv.

2–33). *For others*, we are to want what we want for ourselves (7:12), and to forgive them if they sin against us. The former summarizes the whole of the law, and the latter is so important that our own forgiveness depends on it (6:14–15). It is, surely, an outworking of the commandment to love even our enemies.

How can we do this? Jesus gives us a way forward: we are to pray for people (5:44). This is the most fundamental thing we should do in relating to friends and enemies alike, and, I would suggest, the single most important thing that Christians should do in relating to people of other faiths. Even if people curse us, we should bless them, and even if people hate us, we should do good to them. What we should seek for others, whether in our prayers or by our actions, is the good, the blessing, that we want for ourselves.

This is what we should covet: not the belongings or the status of our neighbour, whether he or she is a fellow Christian or follows another faith, but the blessings of God's kingdom. These are announced to the poor in spirit, the mourners, the meek and the persecuted. They are for people whose greatest desire is for righteousness, and who reflect their heavenly Father by being merciful and making peace. The commandment against covetousness calls us to the purity of heart that goes with seeing God; and that is surely what we want for ourselves and for people of other faiths. It is the most difficult of the commandments. It calls us towards the perfection of our heavenly Father (5:48), and makes us realize again our need for his transforming grace and power.

Epilogue
There are many more things I could say about what the Lord requires of us. There are many more passages that tell us explicitly what love is, and the whole Bible tells of God's love for us and our responses to him. I want to end with just one passage, which we have studied before – 1 Peter 2:9–25 (pp. 152–154).

How we live depends on who we think we are. Peter tells us that, as followers of Christ, we follow Israel in being God's holy people and royal priesthood. It is our very purpose to live holy lives, to teach others about him, and to show them how to come near to God, to have their sins forgiven, and to share fellowship with us and with him. This is not only for our benefit and for the benefit of the people we serve, but to the glory of God: 'that you may declare the praises of him who called you out of darkness into his wonderful light' (1 Pet. 2:9). It is for this reason that Peter urges his readers to abstain from sin, and to live good lives. As we have seen, this is explicitly to be done 'among the pagans' – among people of other faiths.

Peter, like the other biblical writers, has no doubt that this one true God is the god of all peoples, and that Christians are called to witness to him and to what he has done in Christ among all peoples. We have explored, through the Ten Commandments, what this might mean, and Peter too gives a number of explicit instructions about living. But he goes on to point us to the great example of Christ. For living holy lives is not easy. It is not only that, as sinful beings, we struggle to be holy. It is also that the world we live in is a fallen world, and that people's response to us is as likely to be persecution as acceptance.

And this, of course, is what happened to Christ. He lived a holy life, not only among the 'pagans' but primarily among the Jews. Even there, few of the religious people accepted him. Rather, they sent him to the cross. It is by that cross that we should live, following Christ in accepting hardship and laying down our lives for the sake of others.

So we finish at the centre of our faith. Even those who have God's revelation are sinners. What God has done for us is Christ's coming and death and resurrection. We are called to accept him, to follow him, and to live and speak his cross among all peoples – be they Jew or Gentile, atheist or Buddhist, Muslim, Hindu, Sikh, Confucianist, traditional religionist, football supporter, materialist, agnostic or Christian. We may think that this is too hard, and say, with Christ, 'if it is possible, may this cup be taken from me' (Matt. 26:39), but we shall find, as he did, that there is no other way. And that way leads to salvation and to resurrection.

NOTES

1. PEOPLE AND PLACES

1 *Guardian*, 15 September 2001, p. 20.

2 The Muslim creed in Arabic, *la ilaha illallah, muhammad arrasul ullah*, 'There is no god but God, and Muhammad is the prophet of God.'

3 The concentration camp in which millions of people died at the hands of the Nazis during the Second World War.

4 Using the vocabulary of M. Polanyi, *Personal Knowledge* (Routledge & Kegan Paul, 1958), all theologizing arises from the passion and commitments of the theologians. An account of how Polanyi has influenced my thinking on this matter, and how this has led to my approach to contextualized Bible reading, can be found in my unpublished PhD thesis, 'An Experiment in Contextualized Comparative Hermeneutics', University of Durham, 1995, ch. 1.

5 In section 17 of his *Church Dogmatics*. The relevant passages are included in R. J. Plantinga's selection of readings, *Christianity and Plurality* (Blackwell, 1999), pp. 223ff.

2. THE ACADEMIC SCENE

1 Well-known examples include Samuel Zwemer, Henry Martyn and Kenneth Cragg.

2 D. A. Hughes, *Has God Many Names? An Introduction to Religious Studies* (Apollos, 1996). Another helpful introduction to religious studies, not from an overtly Christian perspective, is J. Waardenburg's *Classical Approaches to the Study of Religion. Vol 1. Introduction and Anthology* (Mouton, 1973). The introduction gives an overview of the development of religious studies, and the rest of the book gives extracts from the writings of influential thinkers.

3 Quoted by Hughes, *Has God Many Names?* p. 26. The context makes it clear that Kant does not only mean different Christian churches here: he would include all religions.

4 Comte himself wanted to start a new religion that put humanity instead of God at its centre. He was unsuccessful.

5 D. L. Pals, *Seven Theories of Religion* (Oxford University Press, 1996), explains and discusses some of these theories.

6 See, for example, P. B. Clarke and P. Byrne, *Religion Defined and Explained* (St. Martin's Press, 1993).

7 See Hughes, *Has God Many Names?* ch. 10.

8 Quoted in ibid., p. 45.

9 SCM, 1987.

10 Ibid., p. vii.

11 For example, from Sri Lanka, Vinoth Ramachandra argues against the pluralism of Samartha and Pannikar in *The Recovery of Mission* (Paternoster, 1996).

12 See ch. 1, n. 5.

3. READING THE BIBLE

1 The Greek word *thrēskeia*, used in Acts 26:5 and James 1:26–27, refers to religious practice. The more common word *eusebeia* refers to right service of God. It is sometimes translated 'religion', but more often 'piety' or 'godliness'.

2 For example, Hendrik Kraemer, one of the best-known exclusivist writers of the mid-twentieth century, uses these verses in his *The Christian Message in a Non-Christian World* (Edinburgh House, 1938), p. 106.

3 The Doctrine Commission of the Church of England, *The Mystery of Salvation* (Church House, 1995), p. 168.
4 In *The Bible and People of Other Faiths* (World Council of Churches, 1985), pp. 125–126.
5 See Ariarajah, *Bible and People of Other Faiths*.
6 The section 'Religion and judgment' in ch. 8 is relevant here.
7 Trinity Press International, 1999.
8 We could, he admits, look directly at the material about idolatry; but, he says, this would be to start in a very negative way, and might choose 'too narrow a context' (ibid., p. 62). That is, we might assume that 'idolatry' is the only way to think about other faiths, and therefore both misunderstand them and miss much relevant biblical material.
9 Many of the ideas in this section come from Chris Wright's 1998 Henry Martyn Lecture on *Interpreting the Bible among the World's Religions*, available from Global Connections, London.

4. Peoples surrounding Israel, and their gods

1 I have not footnoted this chapter, as the information it contains can be found under the relevant headings in most good Bible dictionaries and Old Testament introductions.

5. Beginnings: Genesis

1 This excludes Nimrod, who was an individual rather than the father of a people.
2 For many of these stories we have only fragments, and scholars are still discussing how to translate parts of them.
3 See R. J. Clifford, *Creation Accounts in the Ancient Near East and in the Bible*, Catholic Biblical Quarterly Monograph Series 26, 1994.
4 See D. Winton Thomas (ed.), *Documents from Old Testament Times* (Thomas Nelson, 1958), pp. 3–16. This and the following account are my own summaries of the stories.
5 It uses the word 'El' for God; that is, it uses the name of the high creator god of some of the surrounding peoples, which

comes to mean any 'god' in Hebrew. See the section 'Abraham among the nations' below for the names of God in Genesis.

6 It is possible that the 'sons of God' of Gen. 6:2 are heavenly beings, although they may also be powerful human leaders. If they are heavenly beings, then their attempt to mate with human women marks a violation of the boundaries between heaven and earth – a threat to the created order, which has to be removed.

7 For some of this analysis I am indebted to Dan Beeby.

8 'The Religion of the Patriarchs', in A. R. Millard and D. J. Wiseman (eds.), *Essays on the Patriarchal Narratives* (IVP, 1980), pp. 157–188. See also Wenham's commentary *Genesis 16–50* (Word, 1994), pp. xxx–xxxv.

9 This is an area in which there has been much speculation. Scholars write long books on 'the religion of the patriarchs', trying to work out which of their practices related to the local religions and which to later Jewish religion.

10 See, for example, the article 'Covenant, Alliance' in *The Illustrated Bible Dictionary* (IVP, 1980), vol. 1, pp. 326–331.

11 See Wenham, *Genesis 16–50*, p. 273, for references.

12 Ibid., pp. 323ff.

13 Gen. 34 – 35 also raises two other issues relevant to interfaith relations: mixed marriages, and the impossibility of the Israelites merging totally with another group.

6. DEVELOPMENT: THE CALLING OF A PEOPLE

1 J. B. Pritchard (ed.), *Ancient Near Eastern Texts Relating to the Old Testament* (Princeton University Press, 1950) [hereafter *ANET*], pp. 173–176. *ANET* includes selections of other similar laws from different parts of Mesopotamia. 'Seignior' translates a word that can indicate (1) a nobleman, (2) a free man of any class or, occasionally, (3) a man of any class, depending on the legal context.

2 Ibid., p. 344. The ellipsis indicates that the text is incomplete.

3 Ibid., p. 346.

4 Ibid., pp. 421ff. See also *The Instructions of Ani*, ibid., p. 420.

5 W. Beyerlin, *Near Eastern Texts Relating to the Old Testament* (SCM, 1978), p. 34.

6 Ibid., p. 40.

7 Ibid., pp. 110–111.

8 Ibid., p. 222.

9 A. R. Petersen, *The Royal God: Enthronement Festivals in Ancient Israel and Ugarit?* (Journal for the Study of the Old Testament, Supplement Series [hereafter cited as JSOTSup], 259; Sheffield Academic Press, 1998); V. H. Matthews, B. M. Levinson and T. Frymer-Kensky (eds.), *Gender and Law in the Hebrew Bible and the Ancient Near East* (JSOTSup, 262; Sheffield Academic Press, 1998); J. Day (ed.), *King and Messiah in Israel and the Ancient Near East* (JSOTSup, 270; Sheffield Academic Press, 1998).

10 See V. Hurowitz, *I Have Built You an Exalted House: Temple Building in the Bible in the Light of Mesopotamian and Northwest Semitic writings* (JSOTSup, 115; Sheffield Academic Press, 1992).

11 Ibid., pp. 297–298.

12 The Egyptian god Apis took the form of a calf (see picture in J. D. Douglas and N. Hillyer [eds.], *New Bible Dictionary*, 2nd ed. [IVP, 1982], p. 225), and the Canaanite god Baal was also sometimes symbolized by a calf.

13 This was also the recurring problem of the northern kingdom of Israel from the time of Jeroboam, who made golden calves as an alternative to temple worship. See ch. 7 below.

14 In 'The Religion of the Patriarchs', in A. R. Millard and D. J. Wiseman (eds.), *Essays on the Patriarchal Narratives* (IVP, 1980), pp. 157–188.

15 I am indebted to Dick Seed for this analysis.

16 His hymn to Atun has some passages very similar to Ps. 104. See *ANET*, p. 370.

17 It is interesting that the Canaanite Baal stories include an account of Baal challenging El's authority and taking over as ruler of the gods. Some scholars think that the story reflects this historical development.

18 It is such sexual practices that are the context of the strong
prohibition of the practices of Egypt and Canaan of Lev. 18:3.

19 Exodus uses the word '*am*, a people, very frequently. In the
accounts of the first plagues, there seems to be a deliberate
contrast between God's people and Pharaoh's people (chs.
7–9).

20 See also Gen. 18:18–19; Deut. 4:5–8.

21 This is from the English Standard Version. Its translation '*for
all the earth is mine*' is more relevant here than the '*although
the whole earth is mine*' of the New International Version.
The Hebrew word is *kî*, which could even be translated
'because'.

22 This is also evident from the way the achievements of
Hammurabi that introduce his code parallel the account of the
acts of God in Exodus.

23 The laws of Hammurabi (see *ANET*, pp. 164–180) are almost
entirely concerned with property. Even those about crimes,
slaves and marriages focus on payments and on reparations in
terms of property. The slaves themselves are treated as property, and it is arguable that wives are also treated in this way.

24 God is 'jealous', and will not allow the worship of any other
god. This is not because the other gods are in competition
with him: quite the opposite! He does not want people to be
led astray into worshipping non-gods.

25 This is the thrust of the 'fellowship' or 'peace' offerings
(Hebrew *šĕlāmîm* – things of *šālôm*) of Leviticus 3. See also Lev.
7:11–18. The eating that goes with some sacrifices is a potent
sign of fellowship.

26 There are details of the gods' daily requirements, as well as of
how they were to be woken and dressed in the morning and to
be put to bed at night. See *ANET*, p. 325, on Egyptian daily
rituals, pp. 343–345, on Akkadian daily rituals.

27 See, for example, the purification rites included in the instructions for the worship of Marduk, *ANET*, pp. 331ff.

28 An Akkadian ritual, *ANET*, p. 337. Some of the ritual meals

given to the gods had to include a bowl of water for hand washing.

7. GOD'S NATION AMONG THE NATIONS

1 There will be references to Joshua and the land in ch. 10 of the New Testament study below. When you get to the end of the section 'A dangerous triangle', you might like to think about the following: (1) 'You shall call his name Joshua, for he shall save his people from their sins' (Matt. 1:21, my translation); (2) The first Joshua gave Israel her inheritance by conquering the Canaanites, and Israel and the land had 'rest' (Josh. 1:13, 15; 11:23; 14:15; 22:44; 23:1). Read Joshua, and then read Hebrews 3 – 5. How is the second Joshua like the first Joshua, and how is He different? How are we like the people of Israel, and how are we like the Canaanites? What do these chapters teach about holiness? (3) Why do you think the Messiah was called 'Joshua', and not, say, 'Moses' or 'David'?

2 It might be argued that God would have given wider conquest had Israel been more obedient, but it seems to me that the emphasis on God's sovereign giving of the land (e.g. 10:30, 32, 42) implies that God did what he wanted to do.

3 See the section in ch. 6 'Holy people and resident aliens'.

4 This is the inscription of Mesha, king of Moab. The Bible describes the incident rather differently in 2 Kgs 3. See W. Beyerlin, *Near Eastern Texts Relating to the Old Testament* (SCM, 1978), p. 239.

5 Ibid., pp. 194–195.

6 In 1 Sam. 4 the Israelites make the same mistake as the Philistines. They think that they need to bring Yahweh into the battle: the Philistines think that it is possible to bring a god into the camp. Neither seems to realize that the ark is but a symbol of Yahweh's presence: he is the real God, who is present whether they like it or not. Capture of the ark is not a capture of Yahweh, and neither is a defeat of Yahweh's people a defeat of Yahweh himself. What happens next makes this plain. Israel

cannot control Yahweh by carrying the ark into battle. He is the real, living, holy God. After their lesson, they repent and get rid of other gods (1 Sam. 7:1–4). Next time the Philistines attack, God himself fights for Israel by thundering from heaven (v. 10). This happens not by a king leading them into battle, but while Samuel is offering sacrifice. The message is clear: they do not need a king like the other nations. They need to repent and keep covenant with their holy God.

7 An interesting paper that looks for promises of a king in the Pentateuch is T. D. Alexander, 'Royal Expectations in Genesis to Kings', *Tyndale Bulletin* 49.2 (1998), pp. 191–212.

8 See the discussion on this in, for example, J. Baldwin, *1 and 2 Samuel* (IVP, 1988), pp. 82–84.

9 See J. Niehaus, 'The Warrior and his God: The Covenant Foundation of History and Historiography', in A. R. Millard, J. K. Hoffmeier and D. W. Baker (eds.), *Faith, Tradition, and History* (Eisenbrauns, 1994), pp. 299–312, for a study of similarities between Assyrian and Israelite ideas of kingship and war.

10 J. B. Pritchard (ed.), *Ancient Near Eastern Texts Relating to the Old Testament* (Princeton University Press, 1950), p. 288.

11 See 2 Kgs 23 and 2 Chron. 33 – 35. Josiah made extensive reforms, but the very next king (Josiah's son) 'did what was evil in the sight of the LORD' (2 Kgs 23:32, 37) and, in his time, Judah was conquered by the Egyptians and then the Babylonians.

8. GOD, GODS AND NATIONS

1 Note that Israel did not fight only other nations – there was plenty of fighting within Israel, and between its northern and southern kingdoms (e.g. 2 Chron. 12:15; 13:2; 25:17; 28:5).

2 There are also some very close parallels in the Psalms: see ch. 6 in this book.

3 SCM, 1978, pp. 133–142.

4 We can compare this to Luke's careful research into the life of Jesus (Luke 1:1–4).

5 Interested readers might reread ch. 2 here, and think again

about the relationship between the human and divine dimensions of religion and its study.

6   C. J. H. Wright and J. E. Goldingay, 'Yahweh our God, Yahweh One': The Old Testament and Religious Pluralism', in A. F. D. Clarke and B. W. Winter (eds.), *One God One Lord in a World of Religious Pluralism* (Tyndale House, 1991), p. 34.

7   For example, the Egyptian Wisdom Teaching of Merikare tells of the god giving magic as a weapon to ward off disaster (Beyerlin, *Near Eastern Texts Relating to the Old Testament*, p. 46). This idea is omitted from the biblical wisdom literature and is rejected elsewhere in the Bible (e.g. Exod. 22:18; Deut. 18:9ff.).

8   *The Contemplative Face of Old Testament Religion in the Context of World Religions* (SCM/Trinity Press International, 1989).

9   See also 6:2, which tells Israel that she is no better than other nations.

10 See also above, pp. 108–109.

11 For example, Jer. 46. See also Jer. 10 and Hab. 2:18–19.

12 In addition, Zech. 9:7 mentions blood and unclean food being snatched from the Philistines' mouths. This could be a reference to food consumed during their worship.

13 It is clear that this woman was not a worshipper of Yahweh, since she speaks to Elijah of Yahweh as 'Your god' (1 Kgs 17:12).

14 His honesty contrasts sharply with the dishonesty of Gehazi, Elisha's servant (1 Kgs 5:21ff.).

9. SETTING THE SCENE: THE WORLD BEHIND THE TEXT

1   Information about the Stoics and the Epicureans, the best known of these schools, can be found in any New Testament introduction or commentary on Acts 17.

2   Much of the information in this chapter and more details about the period can be found in J. Holder, *The Intertestamental Period*, Indian Society for Promoting Christian Knowledge Study Guide 31 (ISPCK, 1994).

3   The Jews under John Hyrcanus had conquered the Idumaeans

in about 130 BC and forced them to convert to Judaism if they wished to remain in their country (see p. 145).

4 An excellent discussion of Jewish thinking in New Testament times can be found in N. T. Wright, *The New Testament and the People of God* (SPCK, 1992).

5 Job 19:25–27 and Dan. 12:2–13 have hints on life after death, Deut. 32:17 mentions demons and Job 1 and Zech. 3, 'Satan'. Apart from Michael (Dan. 12:1), even the angels are not named, and we learn little about them.

6 In, for example, the *Sibylline Oracles* and the books of *Enoch*. See Holder, *Intertestamental Period*, pp. 61ff.

7 Holder, *Intertestamental Period*, pp. 68–71.

8 *1 Enoch* is not really one book, but five, so strictly speaking this is a variation within the Enoch tradition rather than in one book.

9 Isa. 26:19 also speaks of the dead rising, but some scholars see this as referring to the earthly restoration of Israel, like the resurrection of the 'dead bones' of Ezek. 37.

10 See Holder, *Intertestamental Period*, pp. 81–82.

11 See n. 4 in ch. 12.

12 See P. Borgen, *Early Christianity and Hellenic Judaism* (T. & T. Clark, 1996), ch. 2.

10. A NEW PEOPLE

1 These can be found in all religions. Martin Goldsmith shows how relevant the parables of Jesus are in the specific context of Islam in *Islam and Christian Witness* (Hodder & Stoughton, 1982), pp. 127–132. Colin Chapman explains the parable of the prodigal son in this context in *Cross and Crescent* (IVP, 1995), ch. 33.

2 John 21:11. People interpret the number 153 in different ways. There are various ways of explaining it as a number of completeness (e.g. 100 stands for the Gentiles, 50 for the Jews and 3 for the Trinity). Perhaps the most common suggestion is that the people of the time believed that there were 153

different kinds of fish in the world. Either way, or even if 153 is simply a large number without any special significance, the miraculous catch indicates the complete gathering of peoples into God's kingdom.

3 The circumcision of Timothy (Acts 16) is interesting here. It shows both that Jews could keep their Jewish culture, provided it did not spoil their relationships with Gentile Christians, and that a different circumstance can make a different practice appropriate.

4 Of course, the principles for living on which the laws were built were still important: Paul as well as Jesus taught that these were to be kept at a greater depth than most Jews had imagined.

5 For example, his treatment of family relationships in 1 Corinthians, Ephesians, Colossians and the pastoral epistles follows closely the patterns of Roman households, but alters the personal relationships and power balances radically.

6 Of course, this happened later. Under Constantine, and for centuries to follow, Christianity became linked to the state, which sought to conquer in the name of Christ. Other examples can be found in forms of Islam that claim to be both universal and political, and that have sometimes conquered territory to spread the rule of God as they understand it.

7 N. T. Wright, *Following Jesus: Biblical Reflections on Discipleship* (SPCK, 1994), p. 22.

8 See C. Chapman, *Whose Promised Land?* 2nd ed. (Lion, 2002), p. 174.

9 This is comparable to the proportion of the Gospels given to Jesus' confrontations with Jewish and Roman authorities.

10 See Rom. 13:1–7.

11 Exceptions are Acts 22:25–28 and 25:11, when he uses his citizenship rights.

11. FACING SAMARITAN RELIGION

1 Most scholars therefore think that the identification of the Samaritans with the Samarians of 2 Kgs 17 and Ezra is wrong.

It has even been suggested that Samaritan religion began with a group of Jews who moved away from Jerusalem because they wanted to keep their faith pure! For a helpful summary of scholarship on the Samaritans, see the article by H. G. M. Williamson, 'Samaritans', in *The Illustrated Bible Dictionary* (IVP, 1980), vol. 3, pp. 1378–1381.

12. FACING THE GENTILE RELIGIONS

1 See, for example, A. Fernando, *Jesus and the World Religions* (MARC, 1987). There are some who suggest that this Athenian mission was a failure, because not many people believed. After this, they say, Paul went back to his old style of preaching, which was much more effective. 1 Cor. 1 – 2, they say, shows how he rejected the use of wisdom and therefore of philosophy. However, we do not have any records of his other sermons to Gentiles, so this conclusion seems to me to be wrong.

2 Most scholars see Ephesians as being addressed not only to the church at Ephesus, but to a number of churches. However, we can be sure that the Ephesians were among those it was written for, and that other churches also had to face occult powers. This fits with the epistle's obvious awareness of the spiritual powers, and its call to fight against the forces of darkness. See C. E. Arnold, *Ephesians: Power and Magic* (Baker, 1992) for an extended discussion of magic practices in the world behind the text of Ephesians.

3 1 John is also interesting in this context.

4 At one time, scholars saw Gnosticism behind many of the New Testament texts. As they learnt more about it and about other thinking in the New Testament world, their ideas changed; and they are still changing. For example, in 1977, James Dunn, discussing the false teaching at Colossae, wrote, 'it looks very much as if we have to do with a syncretistic teaching which drew together elements of mystery cults, Christianity and probably also more specifically gnostic ideas' (*Unity and*

Diversity in the New Testament [SCM, 1997], p. 281); but his 1996 commentary on Colossians (Paternoster), pp. 23–25, argues that it can be understood entirely in Jewish terms. Clinton Arnold's study of the world behind Colossians, C. E. Arnold, *The Colossian Syncretism* (Baker, 1996), is helpful here.

5 I have relied on A. Thiselton, *The First Epistle to the Corinthians* (Eerdmans / Paternoster, 2000), and B. W. Winter, *After Paul Left Corinth: The Influence of Secular Ethics and Social Change* (Eerdmans, 2001), for details of first-century Corinth. Derek Newton's PhD thesis, 'Food Offered to Idols in 1 Corinthians 8–10' (University of Sheffield, 1995), has helped me to think about 1 Corinthians' treatment of Gentile faiths.

6 Thiselton, *First Epistle to the Corinthians*, p. 10.

7 'Status' means 'standing'.

13. THE QUESTIONS WE WANT TO ASK

1 Others can be found in, for example, John 1:29; 3:15; 4:13; 4:42; 5:22–29; 6:35–40; 6:51; 8:12; 9:39; and 10:9.

2 Many of these ideas on John's prologue come from Philip Seddon's contribution to the course 'Reading the Bible in its own Inter-faith Context' at Selly Oak.

3 See, for example, G. R. Beasley-Murray, *John* (Word, 1999), p. 12.

4 Quoted in ibid., p. 6.

5 *Surprised by Joy* (Fontana, 1959), p. 188.

6 I have been much influenced by Tom Wright's reading of these chapters in his *The Climax of the Covenant* (T. & T. Clark, 1991), ch. 13.

14. THE BIBLE AS A MIRROR

1 The proceedings of this conference can be found in *Transformation* 17.1 (2000).

2 See Lamin Sanneh's argument in L. Newbigin, L. Sanneh and J. Taylor, *Faith and Power: Christianity and Islam in Secular Britain* (SPCK, 1998), pp. 45–47.

3 This paragraph is based on the experience of Suneel Shivdasani. See also the stories in S. J. Sutcliffe (ed.), *Good News for Asians in Britain* (Grove, 1998).

4 See ch. 11 above, and my 'Scripture and Mission in Inner City UK', in J. R. W. Stott et al., *The Anglican Communion and Scripture* (Regnum, 1996), pp. 161–170.

5 J. D. Woodberry (ed.), *Muslims and Christians on the Emmaus Road* (MARC, 1989), takes this story as its starting point.

6 Qur'anic prophets include, for example, Adam, Noah, Isaac, Jacob and Job, who are not really prophets in the Bible.

7 There have, of course, been many attempts to establish Christian kingdoms.

15. WHAT DOES THE LORD REQUIRE OF US?

1 I have discussed some of these issues in 'Family and Faith', *Transformation* 19.1 (2002), pp. 23–33.

2 They raise many issues, including homosexuality and transsexuality, in such widely different contexts as India and the USA, which are extremely important but for which there is no space here. I have discussed questions of gender in relation to Islam in I. Glaser and N. John, *Partners or Prisoners? Christians Thinking about Women and Islam* (Paternoster, 1998).

John Stott Ministries

The vision of John Stott Ministries (JSM) is to see Majority World churches served by conscientious pastors who sincerely believe, diligently study, relevantly apply and faithfully expound the Word of God.

For over thirty years JSM's Langham programs have helped burgeoning non-Western churches to balance *growth* with *depth*. Three key programs help Majority World church leaders disciple their congregations toward greater spiritual maturity.

JSM-Langham Scholarships have enabled more than 120 Majority World church leaders to study theology at the postgraduate level in the West. Upon completion of their degrees, these church leaders have returned home to train the next generation of pastors in their countries.

JSM-Langham Preaching Seminars gather pastors for instruction in biblical preaching and teaching. These seminars provide intensive training for pastors largely unschooled in Bible exposition, bringing greater skill and clarity to their preaching.

JSM-Langham Literature works with seminaries and Bible colleges in over seventy countries to give needed books to tens of thousands of pastors, many of whom before had nearly empty bookshelves.

You can participate in the global church. Find out more by visiting JSM at <www.johnstott.org> or contacting JSM at <info@johnstott.org>.